# Good Slut

# Good Slut

*How Money, Sex and Power Set Women Free*

Zoe Strimpel

CONSTABLE

CONSTABLE

First published in Great Britain in 2026 by Constable

1 3 5 7 9 10 8 6 4 2

Copyright © Zoe Strimpel, 2026

The moral right of the author has been asserted.

All rights reserved.
No part of this publication may be reproduced, stored in a retrieval system, or transmitted, in any form or by any means, without the prior permission in writing of the publisher, nor be otherwise circulated in any form of binding or cover other than that in which it is published and without a similar condition including this condition being imposed on the subsequent publisher.

A CIP catalogue record for this book is available from the British Library.

ISBN: 978-1-40872-097-4

Typeset in Adobe Garamond by Hewer Text UK Ltd, Edinburgh
Printed and bound in Great Britain by Clays Ltd, Elcograf S.p.A

Papers used by Constable are from well-managed
forests and other responsible sources.

Constable
An imprint of
Little, Brown Book Group
Carmelite House
50 Victoria Embankment
London EC4Y 0DZ

The authorised representative
in the EEA is
Hachette Ireland
8 Castlecourt Centre
Dublin 15, D15 XTP3, Ireland
(email: info@hbgi.ie)

An Hachette UK Company
www.hachette.co.uk

www.littlebrown.co.uk

'The proper sphere for all human beings is the largest and highest which they are able to attain to.'

Harriet Taylor Mill, *Enfranchisement of Women*, 1851

# Contents

Introduction     1

Part 1: The Betrayal
1. Bonfire of the Actual Liberals     17
2. Let's be Careerist, Bitches!     31
3. 'But the Science Says!'     51

Part 2: The Business of Bodies
4. Trad Femmes and the Menstrual Left     73
5. Why Money and Capitalism are Good for Women     89
6. The Politics of Pain     103

Part 3: Good Slut
7. In Defence of Promiscuity     139
8. Choice: Free and Miserable vs . . . Unfree and Miserable     161
9. The Tenacity of the Romantic Ideal     179

| | |
|---|---:|
| 10  In Praise of Single Motherhood | 193 |
| 11  Motherhood Unshackled and the Fertility 'Crisis' | 205 |
| | |
| Outro | 223 |
| | |
| Acknowledgements | 227 |
| Endnotes | 229 |

# Introduction

It's February 14, 2023, and the most surreal Valentine's Day of my life. I am standing before a room full of self-styled hipsters and intellectuals in their twenties, the men sporting well-sculpted beards, arguing something that a decade ago, at least in Central London, would have been pretty unlikely to be an argument at all, and an unpopular one at that, for a crowd like this one. Yet here I am, in the dim lights of the UnHerd Club in Westminster, standing at a lectern and arguing passionately in favour of the 'sexual revolution' and its legacy: sexual freedom for women; their right to be promiscuous, and why the things so many women – and some men – fought tooth and nail for over the past century are essential victories, not to be dismissed.

Facing the charming and beautiful Louise Perry, a star of the new 'feminist' right wing, I am pleading not just the case of universal contraception and safe abortion but the clear progress entailed in levelling the consequences of casual (or non-casual) sex, so that women don't risk illness, death or unwanted pregnancy (which has always led to some illness and death) for an impulsive, cheeky or even unwanted shag. Or a 'serious' one. I do this, I tell the crowd, as a former anti-hookup culture evangelist. In my early twenties, as a fledgling journalist, I wrote quite a few articles about how women compromised their souls and true desires by pretending to want nothing more than what men wanted. I still think that does happen, I admitted, and I am sure that some of hookup culture is facilitated by women's eagerness to please men and experience sexual validation, rather than rejection. But this is the collateral consequences of a much bigger, seismic transformation for the good that has to be defended. And never more so than now, when that good is under threat – and so soon after being won!

I'm enjoying myself as the crowd is a friendly one and the material is rich. But the weirdness of the situation suffuses the air like incense and I think again of the meta-view: of me, a secular Jew on that February evening of love arguing before intellectual London millennials *against* an essentially religious worldview of sexuality and *for* a liberal attitude towards what people do with their private parts and the manner in which they deal with the consequences of that liberty. It felt a deeply strange thing to have to defend a quarter of the way through the twenty-first century in *opposition* to a best-selling 'feminist'.

In the end, I lost the debate. The anti-promiscuity bunch – at least among a growing number of well-coiffed people who either don't know what things used to be like, or who are drawn to the hottest of takes – is winning in new circles, including in the heartlands of progressivism. Perry's book, *The Case Against the Sexual Revolution*, was positively reviewed in the *Guardian* and gave many old lefties, as well as new righties, a tempting reason to think about 'the system' as a damaging delivery mechanism for sexism and sexist capitalism.

Perhaps this isn't surprising. Reactionaries have new youthful appeal, fired by the aesthetics and louche sexual coding of social media. In Britain and the US, edgy young women now styling themselves as conservative feminists are arguing for marriage, motherhood and monogamy through confident polemics full of cherry-picked evidence topped off with saucy or winsome photoshoots. Many are using the highly curated world of their perfect kitchens and cute kids to show how women could and should enjoy the rewards of family life and sexiness that their confused single or unmarried careerist sisters are deprived of. Trad wives are banking millions of followers and millions of bucks for their banal yet politically charged footage of domesticity.

The many, many millions swimming with this tide want things, with different degrees of intensity and awareness, to return to the way they were when religion determined what you could do with your body. It's no coincidence that many of the new guard of anti-promiscuity warriors are discovering or rediscovering religion. While the right-wingers flock to Catholicism, and the left starts to re-pitch their idea of empowerment and liberty around the sartorial modesty of the headscarf and hijab (anything to spite the 'capitalist', allegedly pro-Israel West), I find myself thinking more often than I'd like: why has everyone gone mad?

## *The Aliens Test*

Perhaps it's me who is mad. After all, it has become a habit of mine to conjure two aliens landing in one of our planet's socially liberal societies and imagine what they would conclude about the state of women today. But bear with me.

One alien is a time traveller from pretty much any era before about 1982. The other is an alien with no knowledge of history but decent language skills. It's a pleasurably simple game: the first would be dazzled by the extent of women's freedoms: physical, social, sartorial, professional, emotional, verbal. Our right to freedom *from* things too: open misogyny at work, unequal pay, sexual harassment, abuse, bad marriages. Our relative physical safety would be remarkable: safe childbirth, safe abortion, the erasure of the social *norm* of domestic violence and the illegality of rape in marriage.

The second visitor would rapidly conclude that things were awful for women, indeed have never been worse. They would read about unequal pay, especially after children are born. They would read the headlines about grooming gangs, the murder of innocent young women like Sarah Everard by a member of the UK's finest police force, the dozens still killed every year by their intimate partners past or present, predation on girls and women by men ranging from the rich and famous to those who hang round the streets, the widely-reported vogue, derived from porn, for choking women during sex, and the internalised pressures that lead to women participating in such acts.

Their eyes would pop at the reams and reams of testimony about female physical hardships, ranging from endometriosis, adenomyosis to menstruation and menopause, and cruel and seemingly widespread blows like infertility. To be a woman, this alien would be forced to conclude, is to be everywhere in the chains of society and nature; undervalued, objectified, seen as prey, constantly in danger of being assaulted, harassed and frequently handicapped by poorly understood bodily pain and disease – not to mention mystified and traumatised by the pressure to become pregnant when the body won't cooperate.

My reverie continues: which visitor's impression is correct?

The first one!

While the events described in the headlines are true, they aren't the whole story, nor I would venture, the real story. They occlude the much bigger context in which women now have opportunity and autonomy, not just on a par with, but, thanks to reproductive possibilities, greater than those of men.

Our bodies, our pain – our oppression. But this *is* the best time in history to be a woman in the West. After all of human history, where the opposite was true, being a woman now comes with enormous choice, and we should relish the opportunities that are now available to us in a wide range of fields.

I cannot get over how fervently and often women, especially young ones, are encouraged to express our 'truth' about our physical misery just at the moment when medical care for women in our society is so greatly improved. The medical profession is finally seeing decent numbers of female consultants and bosses. Best practice, medical knowledge and technology within obstetrics, gynaecology and beyond are finally catching up to other areas of medicine, albeit with a lag.

Outside medicine, we are also at our most aggrieved, yet social evolution has seen formal sexist barriers fall away in all fields, even – inexcusably late – in armed combat. It's not that everything is rosy for women, but relatively speaking, it's pretty rosy nonetheless, and it shouldn't feel like a crime of naivety to say so – especially at a time when study after study shows us how poorly men are doing.[1]

The crudest and most devastating measure of this is the suicide-rate gap, which is three to four times higher among men than among women. And a significant achievement gap is apparent in education.[2] 'Women are much more likely to go to university than men and have been for many years,' according to the House of Commons library website.[3] They are also more likely to complete their studies and gain a first or upper second-class degree. Hard to be more plain-spoken than that.

Women also generally seem to have more sense of purpose and ambition than men. In 'All the Ladies', her still-influential 2011 cover story for *The Atlantic*, the suave New York writer Kate Bolick made the following announcement: 'As women have climbed ever higher, men have been falling behind. We've arrived at the top of the staircase, finally ready to start our lives, only to discover a cavernous room at the tail end of a party, most of the men gone already, some having never shown up – and those who remain are leering by the cheese table, or are, you know, the ones you don't want to go out with.'[4]

She was writing in a moment: the same one that animated Hanna Rosin's 2012 book *The End of Men*, which explored the implications for society when women, for the first time, outnumbered men in the US workforce.

That moment has passed, though it was seismic; a flashpoint for the flipping of many (though not all) long-established gendered patterns of success and self-definition. From the vantage of today, barely a decade later, this feels like it belongs to another universe.

Using our freedoms to highlight sex-based injustices, pain and danger is important, but when this becomes an addiction – the dominant impulse, occluding the good things – girls and women suffer.

For instance: we know from numerous studies that rumination – the response to stressful life events, which can include negative pieces of news or narrative – causes and intensifies anxiety and depression. Across the board, higher levels of rumination are reported among women.[5] It's a cycle: the more ruminating we do, the more susceptible we are to negative narratives, which in turn fuel more rumination and reduce our resilience.

Bombarding girls with well-meaning material about how vulnerable they are and how widespread their suffering is, is both a sign of victory in the war against shame and an unintended way of making them feel weaker, sadder, angrier and more cursed than is necessary – by a long way. No wonder so many women make their ailments the foundation of their politics.[6] Even women interested in leading the free world, like Lina Hidalgo, a rising star in the Democratic Party of the US, has turned her mental health condition into a political identity, according to the *New York Times*. There is plenty of evidence showing that the embrace between identity and pathology can be a toxic one: in her outstanding treatise on the ills of ubiquitous juvenile therapy culture, the LA-based journalist Abigail Shrier shows that the more children are therapeutised around the idea that there is something wrong with them, the more something ends up being wrong.[7]

There is no doubt that attitudes to, and understandings of, women's health have improved (although they are still patchy) to an extent that would have made even our mothers in the 1970s drool. Definitely mine, who faced harsh discipline in a patriarchal home, a mother who discouraged her from pursuing science and who told her she was too stupid to go to university but also too bossy to attract a husband, and a grandmother who warned her that she was at risk of becoming an 'old maid' as a still unmarried at twenty-five-year-old, albeit one going out with my father. She also encountered teachers who hammered home the 'science-is-not-for-girls' message and reinforced the 'you're not good enough' narrative, nastily and explicitly. At huge cost and against many odds, my mother was one of the lucky ones. She made it to Bristol University, studied microbiology, then went on to do a PhD at Oxford, followed by a job in a laboratory researching the herpes virus (you have to start somewhere). Later, she became a patent lawyer for a company that supplied Moderna with the stuff it needed for its Covid vaccine and was the breadwinner for our family.

## *Freedom Froms*

It's not just what we are free to do, it is what we are free *from*. Enshrined in the law, 'freedom froms' are all-important. Whenever I talk about something good, like rights, being 'enshrined in the law', I get a lot of scoffing and ridicule and accusations of naivete. But I persist, because the law sets limits that can be used to enforce justice and which give all women recourse – however flawed the system and difficult the path. This translates into the *possibility* of escape from shackles, abuse, violence, poverty, joblessness, lack of education. For the first time, by right even the poorest woman, of any religion or ethnicity, can carve out the future she wants and force it into existence. This process is cluttered by miscarriages of justice, complicated statutes and laws and a furious discourse driven by hyperbole and anger, generalisations and inaccuracies: but the fact remains. This is Western women's birthright now.

So why do we insist on acting like the whole horizon for women is one nuclear cloud of radioactive misery? The gloomy cherry-picking of the legacy of the sexual revolution has enshrined the narrative of women being mis-sold, lied to, exploited, endangered, made miserable and used. With that idea of badness and danger firmly in place, the tendrils of negativity multiply daily. Why are we told that we are everywhere threatened, on the back foot, our power stolen or attacked, our prospects curtailed along with our bodily wellbeing? That because challenges and outrages remain, a hostile 'system' warps everything against us? That – even though we patently do not – we somehow still live in a world governed, delimited and lorded over by men and their evil ways?

Misogynistic shit happens. It happens a lot. It's a pattern, and it's not sad coincidence that it's committed by men. Some of it is the raw terror of violence – physical and verbal. Among educated men, misogyny's most brazen expressions are often replaced with more subtle but no less ardent regimes of condescension, manipulation and gaslighting, sometimes laced with coercive or controlling sexual behaviour.

But still. The reason the first alien visitor is right and not the second is that the fundamental point about today in the liberal democratic corners of the world is that although shit happens, often devastating shit that should be rooted out, it is not institutionally sanctioned shit. The conspiracy of old among everyone – from male law-makers to church leaders, to wife-beating men and their mates down the pub – to hold women in contempt, to treat them as chattel, if they so desired, has collapsed. There is no conspiracy now. Actual patriarchy does not exist in countries like Britain (of which more in Chapter Four). Which means, I repeat, that women from all walks of life, in all circumstances living in the West, at least have the chance, in law and supported by cultural and social norms, to be free (of abusive men), independent (through the right to education, vocational training and work) and even rich and powerful (through careerism and entrepreneurialism). Having children always makes all this harder, but women – all women – have control over when and if they have children and access to some support once they do.

The truth is we have more than the technical possibility of escaping hell and oppression, more than the improved options facing women in the lowest income brackets and most difficult life circumstances. There is something much more optimistic afoot, and, curiously, something way more controversial to say out loud: this is a great time to be a woman.

Of course, if you don't like birth control; wealthy, successful women; sexual freedom for women; women dressing immodestly and whorishly at their whim, then you probably won't think there's been much progress. But what I – naive, old-school, dated old me – mean by progress still revolves around your basics of reproductive control, education, professional opportunity and the ability to make money, lots of it. To me, the degree to which women can lay claim to these is a marker of how good things are for us. And because these things are associated with personal advancement, greater autonomy, agency, intellectual development and the emotional freedoms that go with these, they are, in fact, not just good but great, life-giving things.

There is countless evidence that demonstrates that horizons are finally free and open for women across the board. Teen pregnancies are massively down. The old reality in which women laboured away under male-made structures is simply ceasing to apply as widely as it did. Apart from significantly outnumbering men in higher education, as they have for years, women dominate in careers from Whitehall and Westminster to life sciences and publishing, in which they were outliers just twenty years ago.[8] All this hasn't happened just by chance, of its own accord. And it has happened not tangentially to the sexual revolution but because of it.

But what is the 'sexual revolution', exactly? Like 'neoliberalism' and 'patriarchy' it's a term that's been chucked around so much it's lost its meaning, especially for those who didn't live through it.

The sexual revolution refers to the cultural upheaval that took place in the West in the 1960s and 1970s, around a raft of progressive (or, one might say, simply overdue) legislation that enshrined universal access to abortion (1967) and the pill (1968), decriminalised homosexuality (1967), introduced no-fault divorce (1969) and made sex discrimination at work illegal (1975). Hence the 'swinging' sexual revolution isn't a fixed thing. It can be questioned, stretched and analysed. For instance, in the historian Hera Cook's brilliant book, *The Long Sexual Revolution*, which charts the growing use of fertility control from the eighteenth century onwards. (Surprise! They used birth control methods in the 1700s).[9] Or in Jeffrey Weeks's work on sexuality and the history of homosexuality, where he claims that from the late 1960s to the 1990s, there was actually 'little progress in achieving basic citizenship rights for LGBT people'.[10]

But generally, caveats notwithstanding, and even just boiled down to the pill and the divorce and abortion acts of the 1960s – with the feminism of the 1970s set aside – the sexual revolution unleashed a new world order of possibility for women. This was the taste of a new kind of freedom, bittersweet perhaps, but there all the same. It set us on the path to, well, everything.

So why doesn't it feel like that? Why are you, why am I, why are we constantly being invited to feel afraid and angry, to see only the negatives in being a woman in the West today? Why does the discourse surrounding us suggest that the whole story is the continued presence of the old problems still facing women? That men are still as powerful and scary as they once were? That patriarchy still exists?

No wonder the alien number two, with no knowledge of our history, would conclude from its stop-off in Britain in 2026 that women are, by and large, predated, objectified, diminished, conspired against, endangered and relentlessly made to suffer the indignities of female embodiment.

But it doesn't have to be like that. You don't have to feel angry and scared in order to be an honest woman, a feminist woman, a realistic and empowered woman. You can be angry about certain moments, or things, or pockets of regressiveness, and you can be scared of men (as we all are) from time to time, even though we shouldn't have to be.

You can also grab life by the ovaries. You can take advantage of the fact that you can do what you want, when you want, within the law, encouraged by countless schemes and charities and educational opportunities. You can make money however you like within the law, you can keep and invest it. You can own stuff. You can buy stuff and try stuff. You can travel far and wide, take one hundred or zero lovers. For most women, this sense of an open plain gets more complicated when you become a mother, but it is important to remember that the decision to take this leap is more optional now than ever before. And that, despite all the frenzied panic over fertility rates (of which more in Chapter Eleven), is a good thing.

This book emerged out of a particular moment, in this case the counter-intuitive boom in negative discourse, and the resulting conclusions, increasingly influential, that the only way forward is to roll back, especially, sexual freedoms. And financial freedoms. And political ones.

Louise Perry's book is one of the more lucid manifestations of a global reactionary movement from the left and the right that, keen to upend the idea that women enjoy wildly improved and overall worth-it freedoms emerging over the past half-century, contains worrying implications for perceptions of freedom, history and sexual morality. Perry's recommendations, shaped by her commitment to ending rape, sexual abuse, misery and emotional numbness, especially where sex is concerned, make some sense, particularly if you accept her somewhat totalising view of men's criminal urges and female sexual backfootedness. But they also, and I would say more importantly, describe a set-up with uncomfortable, unmistakable similarities to the situation in some parts of the world, or the crueller aspects of Victorian-era law, whereby young women should essentially be vigilant, withhold their sexual availability, and take responsibility for controlling the flow and play of vice.

Perry advises that women should not sleep with men before a commitment has been made and should not allow themselves to be alone with men, and certainly not when alcohol is present. Elsewhere, she has written that 'the sexual revolution shackled my generation'.[11] But as I hope this book will make clear, this is like reducing modern air travel – safe, fast, pleasant, cheap, opening up the world, for the world, like never before – to the risk of a plane crash.

The sexual revolution did not shackle us; it bequeathed us, and it is up to us how we use that bequest.

If this all sounds weirdly, naively positive, then let me say that I've been around the block. I've had nasty experiences, felt scared, diminished and been subjected to vomit-inducing unwanted attention. And yet. To me it is clear that the gap between discourse and reality – the discourse of doom versus the reality of opportunity, general fairness and even encouragement – is a problem. I am

## INTRODUCTION

anxious about the missed opportunity for pleasure, growth, excitement and contentment as we instead stir the pot of discontent. Let's step away from this particular spoon and this particular pot; see what else is cooking. Let's see if we can't work towards a new normal in which we can be tough and confident, no more hampered by fear and frowns than is strictly necessary.

To begin to see things differently, we need to get back to some untrendy basics and unpick some unhelpful, widespread assumptions about money, power and sex. It has become voguish to argue that these are masculinist entities, part of a patriarchal umbrella under which women still labour. I disagree. Sex, money, capitalism and hard power are not just for men. They are for women, and part of the structure that helps us realise our infinite human potential. That it is has become inflammatory, provocative and downright taboo to say this is why it should be said.

In my gender history research over the past decade I have come across something I called 'emotional lag'. Women's social status was transformed in the post-1960s period, and yet in the 1980s 'liberated women' and feminism still enraged many, who claimed they and it were ruining romance, society, sex, civility. A suite of gender norms and practices – occupational, educational, social, sexual – had long since changed but many men and women, especially men, clutched on to the old feelings associated with those norms. These feelings lagged about twenty years behind the reality.

I see emotional lag at play now, in the success of the reactionary movement in sexual politics, the endless wheel-spinning over the old terrain of whether women are really just labouring victims under patriarchy, and whether casual sex is a nerve-level insult to nature, and to women, that is destroying society. We know things have changed. We know things are way better; the hundreds of improvements in daily life are taken for granted right through our daily lives. We know we'd hate to return to any strictures controlling our bodies and our dress. And yet an emotional residue, a suite of feelings belonging to a former time, keeps rearing its head, keeps demanding the rolling back of good things to cure us of the bad.

In *Man's Search for Meaning*, the psychologist Viktor Frankl's totemic reflection on what he learned from surviving Auschwitz, he outlines the theory of 'logotherapy'. Logotherapy is about finding meaning in life. Frankl identifies three main sources of meaning: creating and achieving (at its most basic, the completion of tasks); experience and encounter (loving or caring for someone else and appreciating beauty); and choosing how one responds to unavoidable suffering.

I keep Frankl's nuggets of wisdom to hand as a useful guide to being a human being. With their existential reach, they apply here too. Boiled down, Frankl's insight is: 'you be you', not through ever-more baroque forms of self-care and complaint, but through leap-frogging over the self into the world beyond – loved ones, tasks, accomplishments. Crucially, his own devastating experience taught him that while we can't always control events, we can choose how we respond to them. We can also choose to see our cup as half full or half empty. For women, today, in the West, the cup is full to overflowing – we just have to allow ourselves to see it.

# PART ONE

## *The Betrayal*

## Chapter One

## Bonfire of the Actual Liberals

I grew up assuming that 'liberal' was where most normal people wanted to be, and where most normal people one came across were; these were the Bill Clinton and later the Tony Blair days. A mood board of the era would include fun, live-and-let-live within limits, and relatively new and confidently defended freedoms for women and minorities but also for markets and business and America. These were freedoms that my intuitive, admittedly partial, youthful perception clocked as key to that good-sounding word: 'liberal'. Then, as now, I liked liberal helpings of dessert, and I liked a liberal attitude to doing and having the things I – and others – were keen on.

That was my starting point. As a boys-and-horses-focused teenager growing up in coastal New England I knew little of the distinctions between classical liberalism, progressivism and the 'neoliberalism' that was, as people insist, already underway. But still, I knew that that subtle mixture of lenient and firm, morally robust but not authoritarian, encouraging of most appetites but not without curbs, messy but forward-moving was what made America the end of the rainbow for the whole world and was what 'liberal' basically meant.

And I was into that. So I found that while I was not a bleeding-heart liberal (I had managed to pick up what that meant, too, from certain Boomer friends of my parents), I was a liberal: no hypocrisy required. And then I didn't think much more of it for quite a few years.

That kind of trajectory is no longer possible. We live in too-weird times. 'Polarised' and 'fragmented' are the usual words commentators use to describe them. But 'weird' is just as effective. When Kamala Harris's would-be Veep, Tim Walz, called the Trumpers 'weird' in September 2024 he hit a nerve, perhaps the only one of the doomed Democratic campaign – not just because the new right in America are weird, but because the whole caboodle, including the left, has gone weird, everywhere. Campaign spats about animal-eating in Springfield, Ohio, or Elon Musk threatening not to send someone to Mars if Kamala became president (phew, eh?), marked a new departure in weirdness – a weirdness that has gone so deep so fast that Donald Trump's second presidency feels almost . . . normal.

Meanwhile, in the UK, as the US gallops off into its new big-weird era, weirdness rules too. Keir Starmer's government, which may well have fallen by the time this book is published, is disconcertingly odd, sporting a daily dissonance and incompetence that plays like it's part of a bigger plan, except that it isn't. Nobody would want me to spend time here on the excessively well chronicled U-turns and the droning, stunningly boring tones of Starmer (again, one always wondered: a joke? But no). But I do think the insane fiddling with trivia while sinister collusion, conscious or not, fuels the greatest return of murderous anti-Semitism in Britain since Jewish expulsion in 1290 deserves a mention. It's the nature of things these days, which are riven with contradictions that are not interesting, just off. Under the influence of catchy bad ideas, we keep trying to reverse all the most valuable improvements in our culture.

As for popular politics, these lurch ever further from party lines, and both left and right, born of the disruptive, anti-globalist dynamics that produced both Trump and his fanboys and the burnished, thrusting pro-Palestine movement on the left, sees the sexual revolution and its legacies as a 'liberal lie'.

The focus of this chapter is the right. And, unlike their forbears in the late twentieth century, AIDS is no longer the compelling evidence for the bad things that happen when people have too much sex. No – this is about a deeper, wider confusion, whose harms are hard to pinpoint, but exist in a hazy space of confusion and untethering. Party lines are not irrelevant: even in the sexually liberal UK, a cadre of ambitious politicians are defining themselves around the push to encourage a rose-tinted view of the traditional family: incentives to marry and breed, parents who stay together forever and, above all, mothers who give up careers to look after children full-time in their early years, which often means irreparable damage to their professional ambitions.

Miriam Cates, who lost her parliamentary seat and is now a broadcaster for GB News, is horrified at what she sees as 'the idea that the role of a parent, the role of a mother is to get back to work and contribute to GDP, and that you can somehow outsource that unbreakable bond to institutional childcare', adding: 'As brilliant as those care workers may be, no one can replace Mum.'[1] Cates, along with Danny Kruger, the thoughtful MP for East Wiltshire run a project called the New Social Covenant Unit (the biblical ring to 'covenant' is not a coincidence) whose goal is to 'strengthen families, communities and the nation'. As Kruger remarked dolefully to me, the surging Reform Party has now taken up the New Social Covenant Unit's slogan: Family, Community, Nation (only substituting Country for Nation). Not long after this conversation, in September 2025, Kruger left the Tories to join Reform.

This is a heavy load for families half a century after Betty Friedan showed that it is just such a vision that, when successfully embedded, ends up breaking people, marriages and, specifically, women because, in practice, this model is not joyous and nurturing, but rather – unless borne of real desire – oppressive, often abusive, limiting and boring. What child, at least some of the time, doesn't ache to break free of the iron-clad, mystifying, often upsetting and frightening dynamics of the family home and into the world?

A swatch of other international groups are also advancing these ideas. Louise Perry is now director of a new think tank called the Other Half, dedicated to advancing arguments for more full-time motherhood. 'Our government's single-minded push to maximise the working hours of mothers has left today's mums with no choice, no "balance" and no village: just work,' the Other Half claims upfront, saying that 'polling' mums in the course of twenty-three interviews showed that mums regard more childcare provision negatively.[2] Other areas of research include the evils of egg freezing (depicted as a form of pressure on young women to delay having babies) and of porn.

Reactionary hearth-and-home-promoting think tanks are mushrooming. One big hitter is the Alliance for Responsible Citizenship (ARC), of which Jordan Peterson is one of the founders, which is overseen by a board of advisors including the Christian hedge-fund mogul and budding publishing tycoon Paul Marshall; Louise Perry; and a glossy stable of other heavy hitters in the free-speech, breedery, pro-family world, from Baroness Philippa Stroud, leader of several conservative think tanks, to public academics like Niall Fergusson and more explicitly Christian figures, such as royal courtier and faith-leader Nims Obunge. Its 'research' publications include essays such as: 'Migration, Stagnation, or Procreation' and the dubious-sounding 'Them Before Us: Putting Children First'. The thesis here is that 'stable nuclear families are the pillar of society', bolstered by studies 'showing' that children whose parents aren't married, even if they cohabit, suffer terrifying psychological problems. Then there is: 'Playing Alone? Why the Best Gift You Could Give Your Child is a Brother or Sister'; 'Who Cares? The Real Cost of Childcare' (again, by Louise Perry); 'Being There: Raising Resilient Children'; and, reminding us of the Christian spokes holding up this intellectual umbrella, 'Identity: Individual and the State versus the Subsidiary Hierarchy of Heaven' (as you can guess, the latter is favoured).[3]

The ARC's annual conference has been held in London. Another organisation dedicated to promoting conservative values, the US-based National Conservatism Conference (NCC) run by the Edmund Burke Foundation, had its inaugural shindig in 2023. The foundation is headed by Yoram Hazony, a Princeton-educated Israeli who now lives in Jerusalem with his wife and nine children; he is credited with getting the 'national conservatism' ball rolling. The NCC would make the subtle Burke cringe: conference agendas tend to be crudely regressive, sometimes conspiratorial, glorifying mater-run hearth and home, and demoting women's capabilities, interests and wishes for opportunities in paid work as so much liberal warfare on nature, to say nothing of the widespread belief among NCCers that Covid vaccines and lockdowns in the West were primarily a nefarious plan to rob people of liberty and shore up deep-state super-control – rather than to control the pandemic's burden on the health service or save lives.

It's fair enough to suggest that societies work best when individuals feel connected to a larger entity, like a nation, or a community or family. But in practice, national conservatism ends up sounding like the totalising armchair hypothesis of a few about what's best for everyone else, lending it an authoritarian strain that undermines its free-speech tilt. But it's a big moving feast with a large haul of speakers, attendees and media attention. If the pro-family/

women-can't-be-mothers-and-careerists blob were an onion, it would be growing layers so fast that soon it would be one of those freakish state fair onions. The conferences, think tanks, movements, covenants, associations and lobbies: they just keep on a-coming.

## *The Wolf Comes in Influencer's Clothing*

The think tanks in the US have a not-so-secret weapon: the magical world of Instagram and TikTok stars, where food is all luscious and home-made, children are healthy and well-behaved, mums tired but happy and beautiful. We have those in the UK, to be sure, but like most things, our trad wife scene is child's play compared to the US. In her first book *Consuming the Romantic Utopia*, the Israeli sociologist of intimacy Eva Illouz offered a history of desire influenced by advertising.[4] Marketing and the consumerist motifs in films and glossy magazine spreads have entrenched the symbiosis between romance and the things you have to buy to really feel it: dinners, candles, mini-breaks, wine.

In a similar vein, we are now at a point where young women who could have it all are mesmerised by a carefully-filmed, curated, orchestrated mirage of chucking 'it' all away to focus on the Betty Friedan nightmare dressed up in high-spec shots of fruit-studded muffins, table-settings and flowing white linen. Then they try to make everyone else do it too. In other words: women are consuming, even binging, on the regressive, illiberal domesticity utopia. I know because I watch that stuff, too, especially the cooking stuff. If the kitchen, the food and the complexion looks like that, then sure, it is tempting to 'return' to the basics of hearth and home. A fair few of my female friends with children, facing a professional impasse, have chosen to be full-time mothers, supported by their husband's work, and they're some of the more progressive.

I don't watch the explicitly Trumpy content, but thanks to my addiction to ironic New York-based magazines about the phenomenon, I know that a new brigade of beautiful young Trump-supporting influencers who intermix shrewd political hot takes with Taliban-style bon mots is growing more powerful, the fizzy allure of influencers solidifying into actual influence. To quote seductive blonde American Isabella Maria DeLuca, who often posts pictures of herself in scrappy tops eating large pieces of red meat and who was one of those pardoned by Donald Trump for her involvement in the Capitol riots of January 6, 2021: 'I'm not a marriage counsellor but have you tried being quiet and cooking your husband a steak?' To which Elon Musk responded: 'That would work pretty much every time fwiw [for what it's worth]'.[5]

I find this utterly gross, but hard to look away from. After all, the DeLucas of the world are a quintessentially American tribe that has fine-tuned its formula for virality in tandem with the roaring success of 'trad wife' (read: sex doll) material.[6] These ladies are at the brisker end of normal, but in Trump's America, they hover closer to the flame of presidential power than they do elsewhere, embraced by the regime whose sterner stars include the horrifically assassinated Turning Point USA Charlie Kirk's wife Erika Kirk, Maga wellness influencer Alex Clark, and former spokesperson for the National Rifle Association Dana Loesch. In the UK these women are not yet the norm in policy and intellectual discussions or milieu. But that doesn't necessarily mean their ideas are peripheral.

The feminist Marilyn French, author of *The Women's Room*, one of the most wrenching, beautiful novels of the late twentieth century, was a shrewd analyst of gender. She reminds us in another of her books, *The War Against Women*, published in 1992, that what tends to happen in spheres like politics and think-tankery, where sexism isn't meant to happen overtly, is that women's interests begin to be eroded through the use of code words like 'protection of the family'.[7] We see that in the UK, in a movement that dresses up its agenda in terms like 'responsible citizenship', 'what mums want', 'human flourishing'. The same dynamic, of course, is also true of influencers and trad wives: the cutesy look and stars 'n' stripes cheerleader vibes are furiously peddling the same decidedly un-cute ideas, though on social media, where sexism is most certainly allowed to happen, they need hardly speak in code, and plenty don't.

## *Flush, Flourishing and Fabulous: Feminism and the Free Market*

Meanwhile, the bit of the right that wants less state interference in the lawful business of moneymaking is hardly making a name for itself as an evangelist for the protection of women's rightful freedom to be careerist (and literal) sluts. Some of this cohort call themselves Thatcherites but they're not doing a very good job of honouring her legacy. Thatcher, of course, isn't known for her promotion of promiscuity. On the contrary, consider her many anti-feminist remarks or the famous speech delivered by her cabinet minister Keith Joseph on how the rash of single motherhood was symptomatic of a sexually and morally decaying society bolstered by excessively indulgent welfare provision. But apart from (rightly) riling feminists, this speech went nowhere.

By contrast, today, conservatives in Britain (powerless, for now), Europe and the US have joined with the left in placing the domains of sexuality and sexual values – and the corrupting force of the greedy, marketised economy – in the foreground. Ironically, swathes of the sexually illiberal right have coalesced around what began as a fight for free speech. But, in reality, freedom, as imagined by the likes of John Stuart Mill, doesn't figure. What began as a free-speech movement has become a campaign run by people who, exploiting the fight against cancellation, have dug in as sexual reactionaries.

To me, the properly Thatcherite view includes a liberal way of looking at female promiscuity: namely that the freedoms that extend across markets and into personal life tend to make for richer and happier people and nations. If your policy is to allow people to make money and, indeed, encourage them to do so, a goodly number of those will be women, who will thereby be buying themselves a very real form of power, independence, freedom and safety. Sometimes this includes selling sex, however unpleasant this may seem to the well-insulated outsider. Mostly, it doesn't. Regardless – and at the risk of sounding like a GCSE politics student enumerating what they've learned for a mock exam – I find that like Thatcher and the economists who informed her thinking, Friedrich Hayek and Milton Friedman, I too prefer freer markets. The possibility of getting stinking rich through hard work or the lottery or whatever – and then being able to hang on to most of that money for whatever legal purpose is desired, palatable or not – is not some right-wing stitch-up. At the risk of sounding grandiose it is the very cornerstone of individual liberty.

When women finally have individual liberty in its entirety, they may accrue money, power, freedom, all good things. They will prioritise comfort or sex appeal or both, and either way they will probably be immodest.

It's not just that freedom to make money might apply to sexual appetites in ways that concern the new Perryite chastity belters: it goes the other way too. Women who feel free to shag their way around the place are likely to export that sense of freedom to other areas, like careerism, moneymaking and other domains of ambition. Unboundedness is catching. Perhaps this is why women who have become extremely rich through their own creativity and artistry – like pop star Lily Allen and singer Kate Nash – both have OnlyFans accounts. Allen sells access to pictures of her feet, while Nash sports her bottom to fund her music.

'I think it's bit of a punk protest as a woman to take control of my body and sell it to be able to fund my passion project, which is actually my 18-year career,' Nash explained. How felicitous she can do this, as punk protest, savvy business plan or just because she feels like it. Allen, a lefty by posture, should by rights find OnlyFans exploitative and anti-feminist, but oops! She too finds it empowering, amusing and lucrative. Her handle is LilyAllenFTSE500, and she regularly announces 'drops' of feet pics, including of her feet playing the guitar. Like Nash, this side hustle earns her more than her music career, and she is a very, very successful pop star.

Of course, doctrines of individual freedom have long been in tension with what is thought of as a more 'social democratic' – virtuous – interest in curbing the potential and winnings of some for the sake of 'all'. The rich often like these views as much as union leaders: the motto of Bedales, the independent school I attended (albeit one founded and sustained by good-hearted idealists), is 'the work of each for the weal of all'. This is on school merch, some of which – especially the mugs – washes up in common rooms provided as part of a school experience that costs tens of thousands a year.

But virtue is invariably sidetracked when it focuses on the evils of 'individualism'. Complaints about 'individualism' are always accusations of 'selfishness'. By imposing rules and caps and heavy taxes and restrictions on those who have done well, we try to curb 'selfishness'. Which, as Thatcher knew, is just a fast track to reducing the whole pie so that there is less overall to give to 'all' as well as for 'each' to have and enjoy, and an incentive for even more bad, dishonest and dishonourable behaviour.[8]

And it is the same with women and their alleged selfishness in choosing careers over early motherhood, or to have abortions, or in becoming hapless single mothers, or in getting pregnant in the first place, or appearing to pursue hedonism over family. The past fifty years have shown that when women are allowed to be autonomous and to suit themselves, there will be costs. But also, and more important: in being allowed to act on their desires, needs and curiosity – 'individualistic' or not, 'selfish' or not, 'healthy' or not, 'natural' or not, culturally produced by capitalistic greed and so-called vested interests or not – women have real space in which to be full human beings; they are motivated, capable, ambitious and independent. This results in their having more to give – materially and emotionally – than a system of compulsory motherhood, or modesty, would allow.

And if I sound like a selfish, greedy capitalist, I hope that I am not just that, and that this argument for women's freedom – understood and imagined within the systems we already have in place, not within utopian visions that have never gone anywhere for leftists or feminists – has communal benefits. Again, a thought for John Stuart Mill, who, right as usual, argued that individuality, like truth, was as essential to the collective whole as to individual persons: nothing short of 'one of the principal ingredients of human happiness, and quite the chief ingredient of individual and social progress'.[9] Sadly, politicians and journalists make little effort to build the bridge between the concepts of self-interest and individual freedom, and the collective good (enlightened self-interest, as it used to be called).

## *The Circularity of Women's Problems*

Certainly, there is no escaping what Marilyn French, called 'the circularity of women's problems'. With their 'collective solution' to men's allegedly out-of-control sexual liberties and women's attempts to fit in with them, the new feminist reactionaries are also echoing a post-1970s 'feminist' conservative backlash about how things have gone too far and it might be good if there were more social constraints after all. Elizabeth Fox-Genovese, an American historian of women who was raised by secular intellectuals only to find Roman Catholicism in middle-age, provides a template for what we are seeing now: 'Although the sexual revolution has 'liberated' young women from many of the older constraints of propriety, it has also deprived them of the attendant protections,' she wrote. '[They] have cause to worry that when they choose not to have sexual relations with a particular man, their "no" may not be respected.'[10] Likewise, the feminism of journalist Robin Warshaw led her to write in *I Never Called it Rape: The Ms. Report on Recognizing, Fighting, and Surviving Date and Acquaintance Rape* (1988) almost admiringly of the days when universities had 'curfews (often more strict for females than males), liquor bans, and stringent disciplinary punishments'.[11] Warshaw seems to praise measures that entail restrictions on general freedoms. 'In that era,' she writes nostalgically, 'students were punished for violating the three-feet-on-the-floor rules during co-ed visiting hours in dormitories or being caught with alcohol on school property. Although those restrictions did not prevent acquaintance rape,' she admits, 'they undoubtedly kept down the numbers of incidents by making women's dorms havens of no-men-allowed safety.'[12]

My frustration with the way in which concepts of women's choice and freedom are being chipped away at on the basis that they are failures of hope, naivety and neoliberal hubris after just a few decades of progress echoes similar frustrations expressed in the nineteenth century. Harriet Taylor Mill, philosopher, essayist and wife of John Stewart Mill, writing in 1851, expressed the same irritation at arguments against women's rights to an equal share of the economic pie as men. 'We deny the right of any portion of the species to decide for another portion,' she wrote in *Enfranchisement of Women*, 'what is and what is not their "proper sphere". The proper sphere for all human beings is the largest and highest which they are able to attain to. What this is, cannot be ascertained, without complete liberty of choice.'[13] Well, we have only had near-'complete liberty of choice' for a few decades and already women are deciding it's either not liberty at all, but capitalist patriarchy, or that we've had too much and all that freedom is bad for us.

Taylor Mill would have been surprised by the similarities between her time and ours. She saw around her a society steeped in unscientific, sentimental and misogynist ideas about what were properly male and properly female spheres – ideas that today, cloaked in revealing gym wear and enabled by smart phones, still underpin the 'new' reactionary feminism. Then, as now, those craving a universal essence of the 'natural', which will strip away all the badness and allow us to be reborn as we should be, are in fact the most ardent followers of trends.

Take the modern history of ideas about gender and work. In the nineteenth century, the notion of working middle-class women became abhorrent and improper; new evangelical ideas connected religious and domestic virtue and confined women's ideal status to 'angel in the house'.[14] There was nothing to be denigrated about women's role: it was as important as men's, just 'different'. Women got a 'key role in the moral regeneration of the nation through their centrality to the private sphere but absence from the public' though, as Deborah Valenze has asked, 'Why were female workers praised for their industriousness in the eighteenth century, but a century later, damned or pitied?'[15] And then there was the anti-capitalist sexism masquerading as humanitarianism, as women were lumped together with children in requiring protection from merciless and exploitative market forces. The 1842 Mines and Collieries Act, the UK's first gender-specific piece of legislation, expressed the fear that mine work was bad for women, not for the same reasons it was bad for anyone, especially children, but because it would 'destroy that purity and delicacy of character which ought ever to invest her with a hallowed atmosphere; and to lay the foundation for a life of sensual indulgence, domestic thriftlessness, dirt, dissipation and quarrels.'[16]

Those who seek to limit women's sphere of acceptable behaviour out of concern for the 'natural' and the seemly, whether in terms of what work they are fit for, or their sexual habits or choices, tend to lump together all facets of female life, shrinking it all down to something smaller, pokier, meaner and more dangerous. It's not that women's lives would be fabulous if they had the right to perform immensely dangerous, backbreaking, underpaid work in the mines; it's that the ideas of what constituted women's sphere were persistently misshapen, and therefore, on a totalising level, persistently working against women's right to self-sufficiency and independence, even if the odd dangerous workplace was banned. And so, the project of utterly reconceiving gender over the past century achieved its apotheosis in the late twentieth century. The shift was momentous. Finally, for the first time, those old ideas were unpicked – and they were just ideas, received from culture – about women's essence and proper scope. Now those ideas are being pulled back into circulation, hugged close, as if they are a brand-new proscription for a different kind of life, rather than one that, in fact, we have only recently and laboriously escaped.

## Chapter Two

# Let's Be Careerist, Bitches!

What makes today's female traditionalists so vexatious is that they have all – every single one – benefitted from the painful struggle waged over nearly two hundred years to lay the foundation, not only of absolutely basic tenets of equality – such as the vote or being able to hang on to your own wealth – but also the language, and the framework, for this equality. Some of the most vocal female advocates for 'remembering' women's biological function and 'celebrating it' come from Western countries, and particularly the Anglosphere, and were born into societies where they learned, almost with their ABCs, that the spangly plains of choice ought to lie ahead of them, with bodily autonomy defended in the legal and medical domains.

Women are equal but different, say the new vanguard, male and female. Full-time motherhood is actually more precious than the messy, laborious business of money-making – it's just undervalued. This is the core of my friend David Goodhart's argument for returning value to the domestic, 'care' sphere, which happens to be predominantly female, still, and thus remains at odds with women's professional lives. 'Official surveys repeatedly show that many women feel things have slipped out of kilter,' writes Goodhart. 'The need to prioritise paid employment outside the home, even for couples with young children, is bending them out of shape.'[1] Goodhart does not say he wants a return to the good old days where women were expected to sacrifice all hope of a career for non-stop pregnancies and thankless domestic drudgery. And yet he is concerned about the hearth and the home and offers findings from major surveys suggesting that women are concerned about not being there too.

For the vast majority of women, he says, work is a chore – according to the women – and the failure to let them be carers carries a huge cost to children and the elderly. It is true that many women would prefer to be home with their babies and young children rather than full-time in cold and demanding 9–5s. But many of those women do not want to entirely dispense with their careers or their capacity to earn an income, and find when they are ready to return to work the door has closed. A major study from University College London (UCL) found that the single biggest reason educated women wanted to delay having children was: 'I am developing my career'. Joyce Harper, the study author, was at pains to point out that: 'It's not necessarily that they want to reach the top of the ladder or are ambitious.' Heaven forfend. It's that 'many are nervous because they feel their career will suffer after returning to work after having a baby.'[2] If young women are terrified of their careers suffering with a baby, why would they experience a lobotomy-style effect after giving birth that suddenly makes them desperate to abandon that career? Women between the ages of twenty-four and fifty-four now represent more than three-quarters (77.89 per cent) of employees returning to work – this cannot be mostly out of duress.[3]

It is clear that careers for women, mothers and non-mothers, are extremely, profoundly important, in themselves as an income-stream, and as a pillar of identity, to the point that young women are choosing work over babies. As Susan Faludi showed in *Stiffed*, her iconic account of American masculinity in crisis, when work fell away, men simply folded – psychologically, as fathers, husbands.

Why should work be so much less of a big deal for women, just because we also have the amazing superpower to become mothers, too? Motherhood is not a lobotomy!

In fact, Mum Internet is full of women guiltily confessing they are excited about going back to work, for reasons directly related to being a cog in the capitalist machine. This account from *Women Aloud*, a blog, sums up a lot of what I read. 'I enjoyed my maternity leave but I was ready to get back to the rat race. I missed the routine and purpose of a working day and a working week. My brain had turned to mush; my topics of conversation with friends were too often about babies (dull!) and I missed my financial independence.'[4] The writer says after a challenging start with sleep and a new regime of chore-sharing, things settled and felt right.

For those who embrace domesticity fully or choose to give up work to skirt the high cost of external childcare, regret quite often follows, as well as the uncomfortable reality of depending on a male partner's handouts and work for spending money and to keep the household going. It is impossible to get everything right but preserving the skills and option to work for pay outside the home, ideally in a field of interest, is not some sad red herring felt by a tiny fraction of women. It's really important.

But the wheel spins. Women's sphere is at home, but it's just as vital as men's public sphere, insisted commentators in the nineteenth and twentieth centuries. Women are peaceful, chaste and caring to men's equal but different ambition, drive and sexual questing – but both serve a purpose. As late as the 1970s, a strand of women's liberation thought was known as 'difference feminism', whereby women's mothering potential and reproductive characteristics were seen not just as difference, but the final, master difference which, in extreme application, requires a different society entirely.[5]

In making women's biological difference the core of their outlook – mostly where motherhood and lesser physical strength are concerned

– the Chastity Belt Feminists return to old arguments that fail to move women, or society, or the economy, along. To move things forward for women and everyone else requires a liberal outlook, one that refuses to fall for the zero-sum games that loom everywhere (either biology is nothing or everything; feminism has destroyed or saved women; sexual liberation has been all bad or entirely brilliant). It says: women are physically different from men and can be mothers. It says: yes, that's all true, but women should embrace their desire, if they have it, to be careerists, to be professionally competitive and stimulated and motivated by accruing wealth with their own education and hard work, – or wealth and fulfilment, or pleasure, or intellectual interest or all of the above. This vogue for throwing up hands and saying welp, didn't work, you can't be a mother and a careerist or else you'll damage yourself and your kids, and then society as well, is really very wrong. Shifting the painful edifice of that zero-sum thinking, which stretches back for hundreds of years, will take time and slow change requiring big policy shifts and fine-tuned logistical thinking. To get it right will require some clear thinking, some understanding of why the end goal is worth fighting for, and not some nasty joke played on women, their bodies and their desire for familial bonds.

### *Trad Kills Women*

Not for the first time, a cross-party current in political thought has taken the ideas of money, greed and moral selfishness and lassoed them to a damnable disregard for family, hearth, home, the bonds of marriage and child-bearing. The worldview of the new sexual reactionaries is megaphoned across the internet as well as IRL festivals, given intellectual standing by 'political theorists' like Gladden Pappen, a Harvard-educated American who is now head of the Hungarian state's Institute of International Affairs; trad wife influencers; social media-savvy journalists and academics.

The resuscitation of old, old ideas about women and the primacy of motherhood in prescribing solutions to social problems should set off an alarm. When it comes to women's autonomy, physical freedoms, professional and legal equality and protections, if you give an inch, a mile or more will be taken. Yes, you can pay intelligent homage to reality – men and women have key physiological differences. Motherhood should be respected and facilitated: a complex process not nearly complete. But reopening the old, old doors behind which lurk the glorification of motherhood as a calling above and in contest with careerism, or the pursuit of wealth and sex, is not humane or more 'real' in terms of women's actual lives – but scary. When I read the words of self-styled realists like Perry and Harrington and Bridget Phetasy, I think of parallel worlds to the one they live in, apparently either forgotten or under-interpreted.

I think of testimonies like those in *Sex and Lies* (2019), the bestselling French-Moroccan novelist Leila Slimani's collection of essays and interviews with women and men in Morocco, in which 'thousands of women sent us their stories . . . humiliation at the hands of the police; backstreet abortions; mistrustful doctors refusing to treat women in emergency situations due to fear of the authorities; and the violent arrest of people in cars and hotels'.[6] In short, as Slimani makes clear with her collection of testimonies in this brave and interesting book, you give the chastity brigade an inch and a dystopian mile is taken.

Trying to make people have less sex, or the 'right' kind, just never works; in fact, it does just the opposite, making people more obsessed with sex, and drawn, or forced, into its darkest recesses. The Moroccan filmmaker Nabil Ayouch, interviewed by Slimani, triggered a dangerous furore after the release of his film *Much Loved*, about four Marrakesh prostitutes. Describing the hypocrisy of his society's attitudes towards prostitutes – who enjoy widespread custom – he observed:

> We are at an impasse. We cover ourselves in false virtue even while, by forbidding sexual relationships outside marriage, our system promotes the commercialisation of the body, and especially violence to, and exploitation of, the female body . . . We cannot ask young people to abstain from sex between puberty and whenever they marry . . . so we devise a spatio-sexual kind of DIY. We hide in cars, on staircases, on roof terraces, on beaches and in the forest.[7]

The same thing is observable in other conservative Muslim countries. After sojourns in countries including Yemen and Pakistan, the travel writer and one-time pole dancer Elisabeth Eaves – writing at a time when white women could comment on non-white cultures – remarked on how societies that punish female promiscuity and take an oppressive stance towards sex are all violently obsessed with it.[8]

One hundred years ago in Britain – a setting with something in common with the Morocco described in Slimani's book – the kinds of laws intended to secure the kinds of values and behaviours yearned for by the present crop of reactionary sexual 'realists' did not have the desired effect either. The 1912 Royal Commission on Divorce observed that the literal impossibility of divorce for the vast majority did not actually stop 'large numbers' from separating and cohabiting with others.[9] This led it to conclude that divorce reform was actually 'in the interests of morality' so that people could more easily remarry. And the danger, sometimes lethal, of sex before marriage did not stop it from happening either. In the contemporary West, America provides the starkest and in a sense the crudest example of how catastrophic the disregard for history can be for women. The overturning in 2022 of Roe v. Wade, the federal protection for abortion rights, led directly to thirteen states banning all abortion, and two banning it after six weeks, which is often before women become aware they are pregnant. Nineteen states ban abortion or restrict the procedure to earlier in pregnancy than the standard set by Roe v. Wade.

And what happens in America tends to spread. The Alliance Defending Freedom, a conservative Christian anti-abortion group instrumental in the anti-Roe campaign, doubled spending in the UK between 2020 and 2022, from £390,000 to £770,000 in 2022 – with extra support for the legal fees of anti-abortion protesters.[10] The broader anti-abortion movement, fuelled by their success with Roe v. Wade, is now establishing footholds in the UK and elsewhere in Europe. Their imported tactics are out of sync with the British consensus now, but this could change.

In America, the new abortion landscape is one in which the concept of maternity, which must surely include maternal welfare, is completely erased. There is more respect for mothers in ancient Talmudic Judaism, where imperilled maternal life is prioritised over that of the unborn child, than there is in contemporary Texas.[11]

The majority of American obstetricians say the overturn of Roe v. Wade has led to a sharp increase in maternal death – along with a dramatic rise in women seeking sterilisation.[12] In Texas, the law is called S.B. 8, and it offers an incentive for informing on anyone involved in facilitating or practicing abortion: tattletales get $10,000 from the state, and breaking the law carries a fine of $100,000 and up to life in prison. Since S.B. 8, numerous harrowing accounts have emerged of women nearly or actually dying from ectopic pregnancy complications, due both to a lack of proper provision in antenatal medicine due to the parlous underfunding that preceded S.B. 8, and to a surge in pregnancies that directly followed the abortion ban.

Day in and out, Lorie Harper, the director of maternal-foetal medicine at the University of Texas in Austin, who practices at a Catholic hospital chain called Ascension Seton, has faced the results of the ban. 'Some women just cannot take the stress of pregnancy, so they may basically die or develop a life-threatening condition. In those cases, I have to recommend an abortion in order to prevent a maternal death. And that is getting much harder.' She added,

'Physicians are having to choose between their own personal wellbeing and, at times, a patient's wellbeing.'[13]

Amanda Zurawski wanted her baby but was informed the foetus was unviable due to 'cervical insufficiency' (a condition in which the foetus cannot be held in the womb long enough) and that neither she nor the baby would survive if pregnancy continued. She was barred from having a surgical abortion and was forced to wait to miscarry despite the risk of deadly infection. 'I waited for my daughter to die so I wouldn't die,' she said, of going into septic shock a few days after being denied the abortion.[14] Her fallopian tubes and uterus have scarring and one tube is permanently blocked because of the sepsis. Kate Cox, another Texas woman, filed a lawsuit against the state for being denied an abortion – at great cost to her mental and physical health – when at twenty weeks she discovered her foetus had Trisomy 18, which is incompatible with life. In other states, too, in which this savagery is mandated, there is a growing trickle of law suits from pregnant women who have been denied abortion.[15]

Pockets of Europe are every bit as bad. Abortion has been illegal in Poland since 1993, but a 2020 ruling by Poland's Constitutional Tribunal removed one exemption – foetal abnormalities – resulting in an almost total ban. Just like in Texas, women have died after being denied terminations for unviable foetuses.[16] The cultural climate, as in Texas, is also intimidating, violent and death-obsessed under the guise of being pro-life. This is just what tends to happen when those who see women as baby-producing vectors rather than whole, including sexual, human beings – and who restrict access to contraception – are in charge. In Poland, some activists have been detained or slapped with what appear to be politically motivated criminal charges for vocal disagreement with the Constitutional Tribunal's abortion ruling. Others have received multiple bomb and death threats – but police have not pursued suspects.[17]

This may seem too dystopian and extreme for Britain, but what happens in America (if not Poland) often comes here in the end – we import their fast food and, as Black Lives Matter showed all too clearly, their social movements and grievances as well, with ludicrous, painful results.[18] In the US, arguments against abortion began as words and became fatal, agonising reality. In the UK it is still words, despite a growing number who – galvanised by the success of the anti-Roe lobby in America – want the law changed.[19]

Which is why these debates about how the world should treat women, and how women should ask to be treated, have a hard, scary edge. It's not just discourse; it's women's flesh and blood, life and death, that is on the table, from Texas to Poland to the conference centres of Budapest and London.

## *European Family Values*

The somewhat surprising triangle of US–UK–Hungary has emerged as a network pushing for these changes. Hungary is an interesting case: a key vector of natalism fuelled by Christianity and the tough-guy conservatism of Viktor Orban, but where abortion is still legal up to twelve weeks and in some cases afterwards. In Hungary, the approach has been more nativist and family-led: foreigners should be kept out, and Hungarians should reproduce. Families are good: women should be mothers, men should be fathers; men are men, women are women. Women who have four children are exempt from income tax for the rest of their lives. Rough translation: men deal with the big stuff, women with the home. There are no legal bars on women's professional ambitions, but of 197 members of parliament, only thirty are women. This is no coincidence.

The Hungarian government has a downhill glide in promoting such ideas. Across EU member states, 43 per cent of men and 44 per cent of women believe that 'the most important role of a woman is to take care of her home and family'.[20] This is depressing enough, but in

Hungary that figure is 78 per cent of people, the second highest rate in the EU, after Bulgaria, according to Eurobarometer data. Of course, given the fall in the western European birthrate, more liberal European countries may soon find themselves promoting conservative ideologies in attempts to avert more severe population decline: in January 2024, even liberal France saw Emanuel Macron proclaim a campaign to 're-arm French fertility' – he has described France's alleged infertility (averaging 1.58 children per woman) as nothing less than a 'scourge'.

The formal conservative machinery promoting this obsession with gender and reproduction is persistent, well-funded and outward looking. The Hungarian conservative youth movement celebrate no fewer than three festivals per year in quick succession: Tusványos (a pastoral romp full of wholesome, muddy sport at which Orban makes a yearly appearance, held in the Transylvanian wilds); MCC Feszt (divided between worthy panel discussions, crafts and hit Hungarian pop bands that sound excruciating to the foreign ear, held in Esztergom, home to Hungary's largest Orthodox cathedral); and Tranzit in Budapest (Orban made an appearance in 2024 with the tagline 'We want Hungary to be rich and strong!'). These festivals are attended by thousands, with panels organised by a large network of well-funded rightwing think tanks. 'Having dissenting voices shut out of these events may seem tempting to some for political reasons,' the *Hungarian Conservative* magazine noted smugly, as the Hungarian Conservative movement often does of its cancel-free, free-speech/thought-embracing atmosphere. 'But,' it added coquettishly, 'it would also lead to a much less engaging experience for the attendees.'[21]

You might say, who cares about some festival attendees? But it all fits together in that thing we call culture. In Hungary, women who want an abortion have to listen to the foetal heartbeat first – and the doctor must send paperwork testifying to that effect. But if a woman wants an abortion before six or even seven weeks, there is often no audible heartbeat (and it's not even a heartbeat, because there is no heart; it's the pulsing of cardiac tissue). But anyway she will have to wait.

Of course there is a plethora of responses to this issue, and not all of the abortion-hesitant ones are offensive, cruel and mad. But there is a whole world, a whole history, of experience that suggests that even Hungary's laws are emotionally abusive, steeped in a deep disregard for women's reasoning abilities and also their feelings.

Some of that experience belongs to me. Which is how I know that choosing an abortion can either be a mind-flipping nightmare, a dilemma that haunts for years, or a decision made intentionally and quickly, and acted upon quickly, to limit the mental upheaval. That's if you're in two minds. If you find the sudden fact of pregnancy terrifying, unwanted, or have a phobic response to it – as I did aged twenty-seven back in the mid-2000s – there is no speed too quick for returning to normal. I had a surgical termination as soon as I could under the civilised, efficient and non-judgemental aegis of the 1967 Abortion Act. Years later, a desperate scramble for a morning-after pill in Catholic Berlin – to save myself the possible palaver of a messier, life-sapping decision, as it then felt – resulted in the shock of being told that, despite its twenty-four hour night clubs and world-famous hedonism, the state of Brandenburg was more restrictive than the UK, and so I would need a prescription for it. Eventually, after wasting a whole day in stressful bureaucratic negotiations with unfriendly, non-English speaking administrators, my stress levels rising along with the chances of pregnancy (and fury at the brazen hypocrisy in a place like Berlin), I saw a doctor, who asked if I was an alcoholic or if I used the morning-after pill as a form of contraception – as if answering in the affirmative might mean he would deny me the pill.

In all cases, delay – mediated not by one's own deliberation, but a top-down decree – is insufferable. Being forced to listen to a heartbeat and then saying you still want the abortion is intended to make you feel like you are a murderer, even though you are not killing a baby. You are removing a cluster of cells, caused by a man ejaculating in you without one or both of you taking precautions (to say nothing of rape): a cluster of cells with the potential, over many months, to become a human life viable outside your body.

That is my view; others take a more spiritual or sentimental one towards an early or non-viable pregnancy. Either way, Hungary, Poland and Texas provide an insight into what happens when enough pressure is applied by those who think the bodily gains in freedom and safety for women (and men) of the last sixty years have produced worse results than if women still died due to illegal abortions or killed themselves rather than go through with unwanted pregnancies. The argument may begin in an armchair and in crudely edited but wildly popular home-made videos and podcasts – or on the podium at lively conferences – by unravelling the gains of the sexual revolution as so much exploitation. But it sooner or later becomes punitive towards women, wishing them to suffer the worst consequences of sex, with norms, and laws, to follow suit.

The trans rights cause is partly to blame for poisoning discourse around gender. Leaving aside the excesses of its own epistemology, the surge of the trans rights movement has led to the new reactionaries digging in to argue that post-1960s Western society in general has become insanely untethered from reality where all matters of gender are concerned. Women casually shagging around and transgenderism are apparently the same side of a coin. 'Once you've accepted in principle that we can upgrade normal when it comes to women's reproductive physiology,' Mary Harrington has said, 'why should we not extend that, for example, into people remodelling their bodies in line with their inner identity?'[22] Because, quite simply, they are different. The denial of biological sex isn't a failure of liberalism run amok – or an extension of the kind of thinking that allowed women to harness their reproductive capabilities. It comes from a different place entirely: identity politics, critical theory, intersectionality and the worship of the underdog, which has Marxist roots. The new feminist right – and the right in general – has made a serious error: in rebutting the idea, advanced by trans ideology, that biology isn't real or important, they have thrown the baby out with the bathwater. They think not only is biology real, which it is, but that it determines – or ought to determine – everything.

## The Myth of the Systemically Undervalued Mother

The new reactionaries – feminists and otherwise – claim that motherhood has lost currency, respect and value. They say that it is the essence of female identity and embodiment, which, in being ignored or downtrodden or undervalued (they say), means society is arrayed against, not just our happiness, but our very beings. I find this to be both a false and a highly contingent view. False because mothers' wellbeing, their physical and mental health, is monitored and bolstered by unprecedented networks of support, within and outside the NHS. It has, like almost everything else relating to women, *never been better by a country mile.*

The NHS is patchy and too many people's lives have been scorched by birth trauma or negligence resulting in death for mother or baby in maternity units for us to pretend that the protocols are settled smoothly across the health service. However, such, at times, criminal callousness is the exception: the egregious exception, but the exception. To again take a personal example: having expressed mixed feelings and anxiety in the first trimester of pregnancy, for which I was enrolled at UCL Hospital in Central London, I was given weekly psychological treatment by the hospital's antenatal unit, was promised a health visitor and ongoing psychological therapy for a year after my baby was born and, after the birth of my baby, I was regularly asked searchingly about how I was doing (whether the help on offer through NHS antenatal support if I said 'badly' would actually help was less clear). After four days on the ward after I had my baby, my head was throbbing with tiredness and I had to leave. The midwife charged with mental health care tried so hard to persuade me to stay another night to make sure I was really fine that she pulled strings to offer a private room because I was so tired. This was a kind offer, but one I felt I was in a position to decline, nonetheless.

This fits with a large-scale and earnest push to improve perinatal and maternal mental health in the UK. The aim of the NHS's Long Term Plan, drawn from its Five Year Forward View for Mental Health, is to 'transform specialist PMH [perinatal mental health] services across England', with the target date long passed for 66,000 women 'with moderate/complex to severe PMH difficulties to be able to access care and support in the community'. A £2.3 billion investment in mental health is bolstered by additional care: increasing access to specialist care for those who need it twelve to twenty-four months after birth, 'improving access to evidence-based psychological therapies for women and their partners', mental health checks for partners and help if needed. 'We will also work to make it easier to access psychological support for those who experience mental health difficulties arising from, or related to, the maternity experience through the development of Maternity Outreach Clinics.' To me, this does not sound like the health service of a country that 'systematically' degrades and exploits mothers. And the NHS fully owns up to historical weakness here: in the late 2010s, 40 per cent of the country didn't have access to specialist teams – these are now available in all parts of the country. In the new mother and baby units, new mothers with severe mental episodes are able to receive in-patient care while keeping their babies with them. There are now twenty-two of them, mostly in England.[23]

Childcare can be too expensive for some, but the dynamics leading to its high price may in part be a result of the persistence of another lazy, old-fashioned notion: that mothers really shouldn't work earnestly and committedly full-time and, if they do, they will simply pick up the slack – instead of being properly free to work. And now, because of the state scheme offering thirty free nursery hours per week for children over nine months old, nursery care has been brought into the realms of the more manageable for those who want, or need, to use it. Plenty of people argue that it's an example of exploitation to only fund nursery places, rather than paying mothers to care for their babies instead. But that seems like an indignation overreach. A lot of mothers want to get back into the workforce and can't afford to. And the workforce needs mothers, who are, after all, a significant chunk of the working age, sometimes highly trained professional citizenry.

So that's why the argument that motherhood is under fundamental threat and systematically denigrated is false. As for its contingency, well, the hand-wringing over the slide in motherhood's holy reputation can change on a dime, depending on cultural climate and political and religious vogue, and right now that vogue, on left and right, is illiberal. The historical record shows that ideas about motherhood have changed often in the modern world.[24]

More broadly, Dror Wahrman, the historian of the eighteenth century, makes a decisive case for the fundamental mutability of human gender in culture: the seventeenth century has women as respectable home-dwelling mice one moment; the next, as towering intellectuals capable of all that men are. And by the close of the century, they are back to being cloistered by the punitive ideas about their feminine essence that so enraged Mary Wollstonecraft.[25] It's not a surprise the century closed that way, along with most others, nor that we find ourselves in such a negative moment for and about women. John Stuart Mill found that while public opinion, or any given crowd, believes its judgements are rooted in the wisdom of 'universal experience', the only universal is the urge to 'extend the bounds of what may be called moral police, until it encroaches on the most unquestionably legitimate liberty of the individual.'[26]

## *The Great Amnesia*

Those who have lurched towards domesticity don't know, or have forgotten, a lot of important background information. Like the fact that the 'sexual revolution' wasn't some starting gun for a new progressive world order of casual sex, birth control and willy-nilly morality. It was a long time coming and can't simply be blamed on selfish, pot-smoking, anti-marriage horndogs. The truth is that premarital sex and generally looser attitudes to sex before marriage were on the rise long before the 1960s – and coincided with the long fade away from Christianity and towards secularism.

Indeed, the extent to which a 'sexual revolution' even happened in the 1960s, rather than over a much longer period, is a great debate in modern British history. A crop of notable historians in the field agree that the stereotypical idea of the sexual revolution 'rests on very little hard evidence', that much of what is assumed about the sexual revolution is actually based on a 'myth of permissiveness' in the 1960s, and that there is actually strong evidence of rapidly decreasing rates of virginity in single women from the start of the twentieth century.[27] Meanwhile, the definitive study of 'the long sexual revolution' finds a 250-year history of sexual change, with an increased use of contraceptive methods, and a particular uptick in non-reproductive sex in the late nineteenth century while elsewhere we find that even the relationship between fading God-belief and a sharp uptake in liberal attitudes to sex isn't clearcut – lots of single women became more sexual even before losing their religion.[28] So while it would be odd to argue that there was no dramatic change in sexual culture thanks to the pill and abortion, or that Britain went from being pretty religious (at some point) to pretty secular (by the 1970s), the rosy vision of a chaste, Christian paradise lost through the pill's effects is blatantly false.

As well as peddling such historical inaccuracies, it has also become voguish among the chastity belters to argue, as some did in the

1970s and 1980s, that the pill benefitted men more than women, robbing women of a decent excuse to say no. The historian Hera Cook painstakingly gathered historical evidence on contraception and fertility practices and politics from 1800 onwards. In her introduction, she writes with frustration:

> Historical analysis of change in heterosexual women's sexuality has often remained trapped in debates that began in the 1890s. Some feminists continue to argue, even in the late twentieth century, that contraceptive technologies can be seen not as emancipating women but as making women available to men and ensuring they alone bore the responsibility for preventing pregnancy. This argument has been extended to include the notion that contraception was part of making sexual pleasure rational and scientific – and therefore bad.[29]

Cook goes on to recall a particular moment in which a speaker at a research seminar in the mid-1990s announced authoritatively that the pill had not given women greater sexual freedom, rather the drug had merely made them subject to male sexual demands. ' "Not all women," I responded. Many younger women of my generation, including myself, enjoyed extensive sexual experimentation. Only a decade or so earlier such casual, low-risk sexual activity had not been possible for young women. Many thousands of intelligent, self-possessed girls had "fallen pregnant" and been hustled out of sight into institutionalised mother and baby homes . . . or risked unsafe illegal abortions during the 1950s and 1960s.'[30]

It is hard to fathom anything controversial about this state of affairs, or the benefits to women of what came next. And yet: here is Mary Harrington: 'In my view, the sexual revolution was not the beginning of feminism, it was the end of that feminism. It killed that feminism stone dead, because . . . the feminism of freedom won. The feminists of freedom who just wanted all people to be interchangeably, indistinguishably human were the ones who won the battle. And they did so via another technological change, which was the arrival of legal birth control and subsequently of abortion.'[31] Harrington must surely know, but somehow overlooks, the fact that the sexual revolution was not the moment birth control began to be widespread: it was just the moment it became safe and reliable. For hundreds of years, couples – and individuals – had practiced it, only in anxiety-producing, unreliable and uncomfortable ways – from thick 'sheaths' to withdrawal to attempted abortions with coat hangers that resulted in death from infection. And despite the fact that throughout the nineteenth and early twentieth century men's methods – withdrawal and condoms – were the most widely used and men had far greater knowledge in sexual matters, contraception is almost always treated as solely a woman's issue. And that is what is happening again: once again women are the eye of the anti-contraceptive storm. Used, abused, precious, mothers-in-waiting. In the master interpretation that spans the political spectrum: the sexual revolution and introduction of the pill just made women men's fools, men's vessels – and made sex worse, to boot.

This only works if you refuse to look at what came before. Just the desire not to conceive was a massive vale of tears. Letters to Mary Stopes, the birth control reformer, are a useful reminder of the sheer desperation that comes with poor contraception and unsafe-only abortion options. They're heartbreaking.

'I am a young mother of two beautiful children a Girl . . . and a Boy. I had terrible times for both . . . the doctor told me when my baby boy was born I wasn't to have any more children . . . and I am now dreading the thoughts of having any more children . . .' Another woman, who had seven children, one dead and two with consumption, whose husband was a labourer, wrote: 'I don't want any more children and it seems how careful I try I seem to fall wrong . . .' Another was buckling under too many pregnancies, which still kept coming: 'I get no sleep and break down many a time because I wonder will the child be alright in brain and limb, also I suffer agonies at birth . . . will you send me your birth control method so I will have no more if God spares me to live.'[32] And so on, and on.

You don't have to go back to the 1920s for such horror and anxiety. It is happening in America right now. Many Republicans seem to want a return to the kinds of figures from the 1980s, in which 30 to 50 per cent of all 'maternal' deaths in Latin America were caused by sloppy illegal abortions or complications following abortion attempts. Perhaps they'd also appreciate a return to India in 1980, when every ten minutes, a woman died of a septic abortion. The catalogue of horror goes on: 'illegal abortion is the leading cause of female deaths in Caracas, in Peru 10 to 15 per cent of all women in prison were convicted for having had illegal abortions; 60 per cent of the women in one Lima prison were there for having had or performed illegal abortions.'[33]

It's true that there is a seamy half-light to the post-1960s contraceptive and sexual revolution – and this is what the new reactionaries are focusing on. In pornography, featured in a new raft of erotic or smutty men's magazines, this effect was most visible. *Mayfair, Men Only, Playboy*: these magazines were queasy-making champions of Pill-based contraception. They reduced women's liberation – and the sexual revolution – to miniskirts and the promise of titillation and access; asserting that women enjoyed this economy of low-lit fleshly pleasure as much as them was a convenient gloss. And when it turned out that feminism had other ideas – despite the models, bunnies and 'pets' they featured insisting they did not want to be men's equals because it wasn't sexy or natural – they reacted with viciousness to women's liberation.

During MeToo, there were strong echoes of this grotesque alliance between 'feminist' men (men who insist they love female empowerment and unleashed sexual freedom) and the coercive, pathetic behaviour they exhibited – either as a faulty interpretation of what women want, or deserve, or simply showing truer, uglier colours. And so we see cycles of toxic masculinity echo down the generations. But that some men abuse women straightforwardly, or under the cover of sexual liberty, does not undermine the value of sexual liberty – or mean that the culture needs to row back on the protections of such freedoms. Obviously.

Also, there is always much between the lines. Even the lines of data showing the popularity of the pill. Prescriptions in the UK have fallen by 46 per cent with a doubling in progesterone-only, long-lasting contraception.[34] Some women implant coils. Others practice versions of what has sufficed for centuries. I am one of those women. Already emotional, the few times I have tried the pill or any hormonal contraception at all it felt like bad news. While the minipill, or the progesterone-only pill, didn't alter my feelings or mood, it caused me to have my period most of the time. The non-hormonal copper coil caused such agony before my normally-painless period that I once had to sit on the middle of the pavement, wolfing down five ibuprofens. I had it removed after three months. I quickly deemed agony, mental disturbance and extended light bleeding as an unacceptable price to pay to have unprotected sex – which feels nice, but not so much nicer than a condom that it's worth all that. I then took up condoms with a new partner, disciplined withdrawal in a monogamous relationship where both of us had had STD tests, and finally, advanced ovulation monitoring, and all worked as I wanted them to, but only because the rest of the edifice was in place to reassure me that if they didn't, I wouldn't pay a heavy price. I could (and did/would still) take the morning-after pill, of course (still far too expensive in order to warn women off using it as a contraceptive – which is, however heartless it sounds, their right), and I could have an abortion. This knowledge has been nothing short of integral to my ability to function for the past twenty years and I know that I am far from alone in this.

## Chapter Three

## 'But the Science Says!'

## *The uses and abuses of evolutionary biology*

### *Why 'Hardwiring' is Mostly Bollocks*

The complaint of the new anti sex-liberation vanguard isn't just that aspects of hookup culture make some women miserable. It's that it's a form of universal violation of all women, because nature. To bolster this position, we are seeing the heavy reuse of sexually determinist arguments from sociobiology, which have been either weakened or fully discredited in last few decades by the application of more rigorous and sophisticated science. 'To confuse human (cultural) sexuality and (natural) reproduction is classically un-scientific,' wrote the anthropologist Jonathan Marks in 2013. 'Of course sexuality is for reproduction – if you're a lemur. If you're a human, sexuality is far more than for reproduction; that is what evolution has done for human nature.'[1]

The rediscovery of biological 'realities' is deeply flawed, whether by the new reactionary feminists, the minions of the manosphere, the new Catholics, post-liberals, or anti-progressive academics with mass right-wing followings or the growing army of YouTube and TikTok influencers preaching to millions while railing against feminism. In fact, rethinking the legacy of the sexual revolution and concluding that it's a gross inversion of what women evolved to be or do is not a clever position at all. It is one held by the 'female Andrew Tate' Hannah Pearl Davis (2.5 million YouTube followers; 470,000 X followers as of late 2025), who thinks women should not have the vote; the Canadian alt-right activist Lauren Southern, who thinks women are 'not psychologically developed to hold leadership positions'[2], and Boise State professor Scott Yenor, a men's rights activist who hates how America 'endlessly celebrates careerist women'.[3] We are at a point where wellbeing influencers valorise 'Vatican roulette', scaremongering about hormonal contraception – because it's not 'natural'. I spoke on the phone to Susan Faludi, the author of the feminist classic *Backlash* (1991), about the new backlash. She said she was staggered by the number of young women in America posting about all the mental capacities they felt they regained once they came off hormonal contraception: 'The science does not back any of that up!' she said. No indeed. The science does not back up much, if any, of what this growing movement is calling for.

Not that this is new. The deployment of biology to suit highly biased gender agendas has worried feminists of a more traditional cut than the 'trad femmes' of today for quite some time. Long before the study of hormones and neuroscience became supercharged, female writers were noticing the way sexually deterministic rhetoric is used to reach conclusions not suggested by the facts.

As Marilyn French notes:

> While drawing their examples mainly from certain mammals, male authors did not hesitate to extend their arguments to prove 'the inevitability of patriarchy' among humans. A reading public that revered men touted as eminent scientists did not perceive the serious methodological flaws and factitiousness of their

arguments. Authors sophisticated in using 'objective' fact to mask preconceptions of male dominance, or perhaps blinded by their own over-riding need, made unsubstantiated extrapolations from animal to human life. These works of pop anthropology prepared the ground for sociobiology, which arose soon after the second wave of the women's movement . . . Sociobiology is evoked to challenge feminist assertions of human equality. It tries to justify male dominance among humans by showing that male dominance, rape, and infantilised females exist among animals. **Again, the material is carefully selected, slanted, and often false** [my emphasis].[4]

This is strong stuff, provocative stuff, but it feels right to any woman who has ever been flummoxed and irritated beyond belief – as if having her face shoved into a wall – on being told that she is a certain way, and can't pretend otherwise, because she's a woman, when she knows this is rubbish. And then, on proclaiming that her lack of interest in maths is down to personality not sex, or her lack of confidence in physical combat is due to lack of training not some kind of innate gentleness or caution, or that she enjoys casual sex, is told she's lying to herself, and anyway, while there may be some exceptions, there is a bell curve, a normal distribution. Always the bell curve, as if that magic phrase explains the underlying reasons for that distribution. The bell curve is a description, not an analysis, but it is constantly used against those who dispute that gender norms are a straightforward function of biology.

Let me clarify my own position on feminist theories of science. Much of this material is interesting, but some of it is total bollocks and ends up reinforcing regressive ideas about women and what they are capable of. As an MPhil student of gender studies at Cambridge, I was amazed and intrigued by a body of literature arguing that the natural sciences themselves – the methods by and language in which they are studied and their findings reported on – were a function of patriarchy.[5] How could the laws of physics be patriarchal? Yet this idea – that natural scientific knowledge, down to the very laws that govern physics or chemistry – are 'sexed' is one of the key planks in Judith Butler's book *Gender Trouble*, which argues that biological sex, not just gender, is a mere social construct. Her argument ended up being much more influential than one would ever have thought possible, given the book's impenetrability, because the basic idea stuck and travelled and ended up laying the foundations for the trans-dominated epistemological revolution that we are still clambering out of. These ideas are intoxicating for the left, because they seem to promise a total rewrite of all norms and held assumptions.

Clearly, then, I am not someone who thinks 'science' itself is mere social fabrication – especially the hard sciences. The laws of physics are the laws of physics. Cells are cells. Cutting-edge research in molecular biology and genetics and so on is just that. But I do think that when it comes to the softer, dare I say pseudo-sciences of sociobiology and evolutionary and developmental psychology, far more human spin is present. Right now, that spin is being added on both the political left and right – on the left to cherry pick studies that suggest biological sex isn't real, or obesity isn't dangerous; on the right to sustain equally big, false worldviews about nature and women's proper role.

## *Women are not Ducks or Baboons*

Now, advancing their cultural-medical-social-political aims, the right is busy rehabilitating work that features the dubious leap from animal to human behaviour (the sexual practices of ducks and insects have been used to interpret men's alleged predisposition to rape). Therein lies the obsession with and over-emphasis on testosterone's powers, without appropriate counterbalances, including much interest at all in female hormones, and the insistence on 'hardwiring'. All this despite the fact that even a basic comparison of cultures over time points to the plasticity of the human brain and the variability of norms. With a late twentieth century/early twenty-first century twist on the mentality of those Victorians who wrote books about female 'nerves', 'hysteria' and 'puerperal [ante-and post-natal depression] insanity' or who lauded the 'angel of the house' archetype of femininity, we are now hearing about how it is in evolution and hormones that we should look to understand women's proper sphere, and that the clue to their happiness – and safety – lies therein.[6]

Hailing evolutionary biologists as luminaries, the new feminist (and non-feminist) right wants to prove that women are biologically ill-suited to the range of sex that men enjoy: at the cellular, 'hardwired' level, casual sex must be bad for them and so, therefore, must all its consequences (abortion, the morning-after pill, being ghosted, dumped or otherwise dropped after sex). 'Both reactionary feminists and manosphere red-pillers [very-online men who hate women and blame them for what they see as female tyranny] are often committing exactly this fallacy, assuming that everything natural must be good, and that things that are more prevalent in the modern world [than in the past] – contraception, divorce, surrogacy, etc. – must therefore be bad,' says Stuart Ritchie, an academic psychologist. 'That's not necessarily to defend any of those modern things, but just to say that the arguments used against them are often very weak and fallacious – and that might be the main overarching thing reactionary feminism and the manosphere have in common.'[7] Needless to say the manosphere, bristling with obscene, sometimes violent misogyny, is a hideous bedfellow for anyone calling themselves a feminist.

One illustration of how anti-sexual freedom movements build on evolutionary biology can be found in the content of – and reaction to – a 2000 book called *The Natural History of Rape*, by Randy Thornhill and Craig Palmer, two evolutionary psychologists. The book argues that male rape of women is a Darwinian adaptive feature activated out of a primarily sexual urge to reproduce when that capacity feels threatened. While the authors are careful to state that it does not mean they will do so, men are – if Darwinian principles are applied in the way Thornhill and Palmer apply them – nonetheless programmed to attack young women of fertile age. They recommend that young women shun revealing clothing – and, in a prescription adapted by Perry, avoid being alone with non-familial men who aren't your partner. Hugely controversial and widely criticised, the book triggered such high emotions that its authors were harassed and threatened. In a more civil domain, many of its core arguments were also debunked. The authors defended their work against the barrage of criticism in a back and forth furore that lasted years.

Feminists were widely blamed for the negative reaction to the book and were accused by the authors of an anti-Darwinian, anti-science insistence on bending the laws of nature to suit themselves. Indeed, the discrediting of 'feminist' reactions to such arguments is a crucial part of Perry's *The Case Against the Sexual Revolution*. She writes of discovering and devouring *The Natural History of Rape*, which is 'not a book that feminists are supposed to like. It isn't even a book that feminists are supposed to read' (except that to make their critiques, many feminist researchers did read it). But when Perry came across it, she 'read it compulsively, all in one sitting, and was left by the end feeling both disconsolate and oddly satisfied'.[8]

In the critique with which she follows up this eureka moment, Perry glosses the argument within certain evolutionary biology circles that the feminist understanding of rape is that it is a crime primarily of power, degradation and violence. This understanding is largely attributed to Susan Brownliller's comprehensive study of rape's history, *Against Our Will* (1975). Perry pitches Brownmiller's work as feminist propaganda, a rewriting of biological urges in feminist social terms. But, in fact, *Against Our Will* is a rigorous, painstakingly researched and argued history of rape, leaving anyone inclined to see men's sexual attacks on women in primarily natural terms at least considering the role that human culture, including theology and religion, has played in its continuing widespread prevalence.

Feminism, a baggy term that loses meaning by the year, merits many critiques across many disciplines, and its fringes can be especially unhelpful. But the contribution of feminism broadly understood since the suffrage movement and before includes the illumination of the foul-play, agendas and falsehoods inherent in things formerly assumed to be 'common sense' – from women's place being in the home to the natural justice of rampant sexual double standards. From here has come a new language and moral rubric whose effects, while hard to pinpoint politically and legislatively, have at the very least *contributed* to the overhauling of women's rights in the West. So if a partial critique of feminism is merited, the reflex of reactionary gender politics to blame feminism for everything is regrettable and misleading.

Critiques of *A Natural History of Rape* came from a wide variety of sources. Dr Jerry Coyne was the leader of a pack of scathing peer responses to Thornhill and Palmer's work but hardly fits the caricature of a raging women's liberationist. An evolutionary biologist at the University of Chicago with a PhD from Harvard, Coyne is a specialist of the evolutionary genetics of the fruit fly and a staunch opponent of theories of creationism. Of the argument that rape is a Darwinian evolutionary trait, he said: 'This is the worst efflorescence of evolutionary psychology that I've ever seen. It's irresponsible, it's tendentious, it's an advocacy article and the science is sloppy. There are some aspects of human behaviour that are fairly clearly evolutionary. But that's a long way from saying that rape is adaptive in males.'[9]

Others pointed to a 1998 study from the US National Institute of Justice and the Centers for Disease Control and Prevention finding that roughly one in six women were raped in America in the course of their lives, but only 14 per cent were attacked by strangers. Kim Gandy, CEO of the National Network to End Domestic Violence, said that 'the research that's been done – and we are talking about research with thousands of convicted rapists, thousands of victims of rape – demonstrates very clearly, from a sociological point of view, that rape is a crime of violence. It is a crime of control, it is a crime of power, not a crime of passion. It's insulting to both men and women to say that women ought to have chaperones and wear high necklines in order to prevent rape.'[10]

But what researchers choose to study and the conclusions they draw, occur within culture and are quite often politically inflected. Cultural prejudices can be as strong in the research agendas of evolutionary biologists studying male sexual proclivities as in any other professional context. Pointing this out hardly makes you a feminist dupe. I certainly didn't feel I was reading the work of feminist ideologues when I looked into some studies critical of the strand of evolutionary psycho-biology advanced by Thornhill and others.

Malin Ah-King, an evolutionary biologist at Stockholm University, has written about the received narrative of 'sperm competition versus female cryptic choice'. Operating as she does within gender studies and biology, she is affiliated with a field (gender studies) that in recent years has been prone to disturbing distortions but it appears she is more concerned with the possible biases within existing literature than banging the drum of 'feminist consciousness'.[11]

She writes: 'Evolutionary biologists have bit by bit moved away from perceptions of females as coy and passive, towards acknowledging that females can have active sexual strategies, be fiercely aggressive, dominant and variable among themselves.'[12] It doesn't seem like truth-blind feminist didacticism to question why insects are chosen to support 'sexual conflict' theories that are always about how sex incurs a cost to females only, or flagging that the emphasis on male reproductive competitiveness has occluded the evolution of scholarship on female reproductive behaviour.

Plenty of serious scientists who are not particularly or obviously feminist have highlighted major flaws in evolutionary biology in general. It's not that they hate men or don't believe in nature. It's that the methodology used to present 'findings', which then have major implications for culture and society, such as arguing against 'the sexual revolution' and even legal defensive strategies for rapists, requires staunch scrutiny.

Indeed, the main debate within the field about whether rape is an adaptive strategy isn't to do with whether feminists are right to think about rape as power and violence rather than motivated by male lust. It's about the damage already done by evolutionary psychology detaching itself from findings in human genetics, cognitive neuroscience, developmental psychology and paleoecology. This division means that plenty of evolutionary studies simply ignore evidence from other fields that makes it clear that humans play an active constructive role in co-directing their own development and evolution.[13] According to some, the detachment from the latest findings in other branches of science makes evolutionary psychology so outdated it should be of mere 'antiquarian' interest.[14]

*The Seven Sins of Evolutionary Psychology*, co-authored by Jaak Panskepp, the pioneer of the study of the neurology of emotion, is one of the most influential critiques of the evolutionary school of sex research so central to Perryite thought. It is no feminist tract either.

> Many investigators, including ourselves, feel that evolutionary psychology has recently gone too far in its epistemological

agenda, as it attempts to uncover the brain 'mechanisms' that constitute 'human nature'. Although we applaud the willingness of evolutionary psychologists to open up the Pandora's box of innate faculties within psychology once more, we fear that the parochial tendencies of many current views may promote needless controversies reminiscent of those that characterized the sociobiology wars of the past quarter century.

The paper reviews the shortcomings of a methodology that is curiously detached from biological findings in mammalian brain research.

For the past dozen years [evolutionary biologists] have been asserting, often with a tone of revolutionary fervor, that our ability to peer into the hazy crystal ball of 'recent' human ancestry will help us fathom the intrinsic nature – the evolutionary epistemology – of the human brain/mind. We, as well as many other scholars who have long accepted evolutionary principles as being ontologically correct, are forced to question this new and potentially virulent strain of dubious Neo-Darwinian thinking. Without a strong linkage to neuroscientific research, evolutionary psychology has no credible way of determining whether its hypotheses reflect biological realities or only heuristics that permit provocative statistical predictions.[15]

In other words: much of the field beloved of those trying to prove the naturalness of a traditional society is agenda-driven pseudoscience.

The authors conclude, without a sniff of feminist zeal, by highlighting the pitfall into which Thornhill, Palmer and also their most vicious critics fall.

What makes humans unique, perhaps more than anything else, is that we are a linguistically adept story-telling species. Evolutionary psychologists also have many intriguing stories to tell, but if we are committed to a deep evolutionary view, their current speculations should not be accepted as credible foundations for our fundamental nature. The only massive cortical modules we should be convinced of at the present time are our vast linguistically based foresight and hindsight abilities, which mediate our compulsion to tell tales to each other.[16]

Cordelia Fine, neurobiologist and author of *Delusions of Gender* and *Testosterone Rex*, is someone that the reactionary right heavily criticises as a deluded feminist extremist trying to argue away obvious differences between men and women. But Fine cuts to what is a rather important chase, feminist or not. With some notable exceptions, researchers cherry picked results from the mid-century fruit fly study of the British biologist Angus Bateman, which became the bedrock of the idea that men drive sports cars for the same reason peacocks have enormous tail plumes: to attract as many mates as possible. Bateman's study pointed in a variety of directions, but most researchers relied on his data from graphs five and six, 'usually as an explanation of why males are promiscuous and females are coy and choosy'.[17] However, when Bateman's data was considered in its entirety, researchers noticed that it contained evidence of the reproductive benefits of female promiscuity. The data showed a correlation between reproductive success and an increased number of mates for both males and females. Other studies in the 1970s, including of baboons and lions, also showed striking female promiscuity. As Fine sums up: 'Since it only seems fair that women, too, should have access to evolutionarily flavoured "the-whispering-of-my-genes-made-me-do-it" excuses for cheating on a partner [or promiscuity], proposed gains include genetic benefits, healthier offspring, and the opportunity to set up sperm competitions that weed out inferior specimens.'[18]

Crucially, there is a limit to how interesting or useful analyses of obscure salamander breeds or baboons are in thinking about human sexuality and preferences along gendered lines. Humans are different. They have not been subject to the same design features, or processes, as baboons and fruit flies, largely because they exist in a social world whose psychological, economic and cultural facets – and language – give us a completely different ecology of desires, motives and choices. It's not as if 'sex, in the normal course of events, is separate from, and untouched by, identity, reputation, gendered norms, notions of "conquests" and "sluts", peer pressure and prestige, power, economics, relationships, culturally shaped sexual scripts, body shame, or any other complex part of one's inner or outer life,' in Fine's words. 'Sex stripped of everything human sounds more like . . . mating, and it's not clear how much of that humans actually do.'[19] Especially given how little sex is sought, by men or women, in the context of ovulation windows – and how far, on some very basic examination of data about men's own sexual behaviour, such as patronage of prostitutes and experiences of casual sex, the psychological and emotional quest for meaning and intimacy governs the sexual choices of both sexes. We all know this. So why let the garbage science creep in and take over? Women deserve better.

## *Biology is not Destiny. You Are*

This is a particularly opportune moment for reactionaries to dismiss critiques of simplistic, oppositional categorisations of male and female sexuality as so much head-in-sand burying because feminism has become mixed up in people's minds with the worst excesses of trans ideology. Mary Harrington writes that women have been forced into a 'template' that offers the '"right" to medical interventions that would "liberate" us from unchosen embodied obligations.' The price for doing so, she says, was to deny biology as destiny:

> ... accepting as the default paradigm for what 'human' means a now supposedly gender-neutral template person shorn of female specific reproductive vulnerabilities, potential or obligations. And the feminist campaign to grant women the 'right' to this form of personhood, and thus prioritise autonomy even to the extent of killing an unborn child, settled the century-and-a-half of back-and-forth between the feminism of care and the feminism of freedom, decisively in favour of freedom.[20]

The use of the phrase 'killing unborn children' instead of 'right to safe and legal abortion' tells you all you need to know about how radically religious this mode of thinking about 'freedom' is.

Perry, meanwhile, attributes the durability of rape in part to a wilful misunderstanding of its causes which, she says, are rooted in an insistence on 'socialisation theory' – the belief that there are no innate psychological differences between men and women. Actually, this assertion is difficult to find in critiques of evolutionary explanations for rape. Hardly anyone actually insists there are 'no' innate psychological differences. Rather, what comes through is that the causes of group sexual behaviour remain a complex question, far from resolved. The rebuttals, including from fellow evolutionary biologists and hard-boiled hormone researchers, make the more convincing case that the data that has been drawn on so far, widely seen as cherry-picked, does not actually demonstrate what such 'psychological differences' would be.

There may be psychological differences that happen to split along sexual lines, but also there may not: the social interference has been so great for so long, it will take far more inquiry and methodological experimentation and data analysis to begin to even know which questions to ask, and how to isolate relevant answers. Moreover, it is perfectly reasonable, as many scholars have done, to question whether differences are best studied in terms of opposite sex at all, or more useful when seen in terms of typologies that span sex.

Given the stakes involved in marshalling the authority of some observed male behaviour in mallard ducks and dragonflies in order to diagnose social problems, it's worth being careful. Actually, it's essential, given that findings from recent molecular biology point to 'a much wider range of possible evolutionary mechanisms' than have informed the assertions of the evolutionary psychology gang so far. Crucially, new findings point to the importance of responses to the environment, which are triggered by experiences, not deep hard-wired evolution.[21]

Still, to see if I was falling for the whole 'sociobiology is used to justify male dominance and the partiality of women's personhood' line out of emotion and contrarianism rather than cool-headed rational evaluation, I spoke to Rebecca Jordan-Young, a professor specialising in the cultural history of hormone research. I first came across Jordan-Young in 2013. I had long found it annoying – and wrong – that 'science' was being marshalled to 'show' that women and men were 'hardwired' in a particular way (just as bad, in fact, as feminist scholarship calling natural scientific laws patriarchal).

In the preceding decade, bestselling books like *Why Men Don't Listen and Women Can't Read Maps* and *Why Men Don't Have A Clue* by Allan Pease and Barbara Pease (Australian 'body language experts' who once gave a body language seminar at the Kremlin, to Vladimir Putin) had created an irritating background buzz. In fact, the 2000s was a decade dominated by Peasean evolutionary biology; the pair wrote half a dozen other books in a similar vein, including *Why Men Can Only Do One Thing at a Time & Women Never Stop Talking*

(2003), *Why Men Don't Have a Clue & Women Always Need More Shoes* (2005) and *Why Men Want Sex and Women Need Love* (2009). In a more serious register, Simon Baron-Cohen, professor of developmental psychopathology at Cambridge, was writing papers about how women's brains were less suited to maths and more to caring. When I spoke to Jordan-Young, she referred to these findings and Baron-Cohen's methodology as 'laughable'.

In this strange moment – one filled with dating books like *Men are from Mars and Women are from Venus*, or *Why Men Love Bitches* – I couldn't help but notice that my own traits, and those of many of my friends, including assertiveness, competitiveness, (controlled) aggressive urges, strong logical abilities, professional ambition and a buried, possibly absent maternal drive, simply didn't fit the narrative. We could read maps just fine. Many men we knew listened perfectly well. We were risk-takers, albeit with little appetite for physical risk, for instance starting fights (but then, we didn't know many men who were into that either), and a number of us had both a dual taste for the casual sex we were apparently not 'wired' to want, and a long-term yearning for love at the same time. It seemed obvious that the two could go hand in hand, and most of the women I know who shagged around (happily or unhappily) are now married with children and a house. This fits with no fewer than '17 waves of prospective data from the National Longitudinal Survey of Youth's 1997 mixed-gender cohort that show the association between non-marital sex partners and marriage rates is temporary [and] cast doubt on recent scholarship that has implicated the ready availability of casual sex in the retreat from marriage.'[22]

And so it was with great interest – and a sense of relief – that I stumbled upon a quiet but important strand of academic psychological research that calmly, and through data, showed how the very edifice on which many of the deeply-held assumptions about 'hard-wired' male and female behaviour – whether acquired through studies of testosterone or observations of animal behaviour – were simply rooted in bad methodology. One of the most comprehensive of these came from Jordan-Young, whose 2010 book *Brain Storm: The Flaws in the Science of Sex Differences* exposed the fallacies in the data proving that male and female brains are meaningfully different. Jordan-Young spent thirteen years analysing hundreds of studies of prenatal hormone exposure in humans conducted since 1967, when such studies were first applied to humans. She had been piqued and puzzled by such grand findings as those contained within neuroscientist Simon LeVay's 1991 study that pinpointed male homosexuality in a particular area of the hypothalamus or suggested in former Harvard President Lawrence H. Summers' comment that a difference in aptitude – not anything cultural or social – best explained the discrepancy in the number of male and female scientists.

Jordan-Young is slender and pretty with a pixie haircut. Her intelligence crackles down the line in her focused, articulate and highly thoughtful manner. I reach her in her study in New York. When I put to her my sense of perplexity and anxiety at the direction of travel among the new vanguard of young people seizing on the idea that women have only been damaged by consequence-free sex, because 'hardwiring', she leans back knowingly.

'There are so many ways to take apart hard-wiring that on one hand it feels like it's almost too easy,' she says with a laugh. 'It's like, oh, it's boring. On the other hand, it's unbelievable how tenacious this set of arguments is. And I think that's because it's doing something right. It's not because the evidence is so great or because the logic of it is so sound. It's clearly not. But it's doing something and it's resonating in a way that evidence is not enough to dislodge this, obviously, or it would have been gone a long time ago.'

Jordan-Young muses over where to begin with contemporary reactionary ideas of women as less lascivious than men and innately exploitable by them.

Just stretching the historical view a tiny little bit, staying firmly within the West initially, the sexual history of the early modern period and the pre enlightenment period shows us that it was an absolute matter of fact, a taken-for-granted, well-acknowledged fact that women were much more licentious than men. And that women, because of their lesser rationality, were much more governed by their passions and were much more susceptible to all kinds of excessive appetites, whether that was sexual or overeating or, you know, getting too obsessed with one thing or another thing. And then, within 150 years, that had absolutely flipped so that the common wisdom, what everybody knew to be true for all time was exactly the opposite. All you need to do is know some history.

Jordan-Young does not say that there are no differences in the impact of antenatal sexual hormones, but, writing in *Brain Storm*, says that it's rather that the science 'attributes an unrealistic specificity and permanence to [them], as well as a demonstrably false inevitability and uniformity to sex differences ... Even in rats, early hormone exposures do not create a solid foundation on which behavior must forever stand.'[23]

Back on our call, she proffers suggestions on how to refute hardwiring claims:

Another route is to get really particular about the construct that people believe is actually hardwired. So what is it that's hardwired? Is it, you know, something about attaching sex to maternity? Is that the thing that's hardwired? The idea that we might not think that we're driven maternally, but that's really what's driving our sexual needs, etc.? I don't buy it. Women throughout history have been doing as much as they could to minimize childbearing in many, many, many circumstances. Not everybody wants the same minimal number of children, obviously. But the notion that our actual erotic drives are tied to some inchoate desire to reproduce just doesn't actually fit what women do.

Quite. You only have to look at the desires and behaviour of modern young women at peak fertility to see that motherhood is as far from being the immediate framework guiding sexual choices as is tilling potatoes. Though even the spree of experimentation, whether out of a sense of cultural pressure or duty, or genuine zest, displayed among young Western women could be converted into a pre-maternal frame: you have to try out lots of mates to find the right one to breed with. Interestingly, there is a distinct lack of studies exploring this hypothesis for women, which I find odd. After all, it fits with a truism of app-enabled dating: you've got to throw a lot of shit at the wall if you want anything good to stick.

What we do know is that numerous studies of female sexual desire point, time and again, away from any single motivator for arousal. That is: women's sexuality is overwhelmingly governed by things that are nothing to do with finding a nice steady/alpha male to give them babies and protect them. Women are so all over the shop in what turns them on that some scholars have even suggested the whole idea of category-specific arousal (e.g. being aroused only by women, or only by men) doesn't apply to women.

The specific patterns of female desire may or may not be worth pinning down (can't say I care much if a monkey, man or woman is found to activate vaginal lubrication) but even these studies are threatened by the incredible power of confirmation bias. Take studies measuring vaginal lubrication. Such moistening is a form of sweat, and can therefore be an indicator of fear as well as arousal. Jordan-Young notes the enormous – and subjective – number of ways in which physical phenomena and group stimuli are decided upon for study. 'There are all kinds of decisions that are made that are based on what you think the correct outcome is. And if you test it and you get the wrong kinds of associations then you go back and you keep tweaking your model till you get the kinds of measures that look like they're doing the right thing. You have to already believe something about masculinity and femininity before you come into thinking about how these things work.' So, many of these studies appearing to shed objective light on 'male' or 'female' sexualities are actually answering questions and corresponding to models that agree with the beliefs of the researcher.

Jordan-Young's fine-tuned irritation with cherry picking the evidence becomes ever more apparent. 'There's so much work right now that makes it absolutely clear . . . the diversity [of sexuality] . . . the behavioural repertoires . . . are just extraordinarily varied. And so it takes a determination to move through the animal kingdom in a way that you want to support your story instead of like actually saying, what is the range of things that I see here?'

History and the problems of study construction are fatal flaws in assertions about 'hardwiring'. A third is simply what women have said and say about what they want and enjoy. To conclude, says Jordan-Young, that 'the sexual revolution writ large was bad for women you have to actually completely ignore and discount the testimonies of many, many, many women. In lots of ways it's been fantastic.' We live in writ-large, anti-rational times. Which means we better get at least some of our writ-large hot takes right, and make sure the wrong ones don't just swirl unchallenged around the ether, swimming into sensibilities, discourse, norms, policy and, ultimately, right into women's bodies, horizons and choices.

# PART TWO

## *The Business of Bodies*

## Chapter Four

# Trad Femmes and the Menstrual Left

Part One focused on the dangerous fallacies of the chastity belt right and its attitude towards the gains of the 'sexual revolution', wrongly imagining them to be a trigger for all kinds of unnatural sin and misery. We also considered the new reactionaries' unfortunate thinking about motherhood and economic ambition. In this chapter, I want to circle back to the left, mentioned in the last chapter, and look more closely at the norms, discourses and beliefs that have taken hold among 'progressives'. For, taken together with the right's increasingly powerful trad yearnings and activities, the anti-girlboss direction in which the lefty gale is now blowing has provided the kindling for the bonfire of actually liberal attitudes. Thanks to the left, it's no longer cool, or even acceptable, to embrace success, even with caveats. Because if you do, it sounds like you're complicit in 'the system' instead of being an ally, or realistic, about its victims. It's better strategically, socially and professionally to lay claim to all the bad things, the pain and injustice of being a woman. Disempowerment is now empowerment, and this is a shame, which I hope to counterbalance here.

The left's an interesting one in relationship to our bodies, our sexuality and our existence within a society, full stop. Key to its ideas is that a utopia is around the corner, achievable through revolution violent or peaceful, and until that is achieved, a malign society is always looking to get one over us. For feminists, there is the fixed but also nebulous spectre of patriarchy – a one-size-fits-all blame-bag for social woes, and a lynchpin of the idea that we are being 'exploited'. It's not that we are never exploited, but are we all always being exploited by the system? There is plenty of evidence to suggest the answer is no.

## *Neoliberalism Emancipates Women*

It began about a decade ago. I mean that politicised sense of all-encompassing shitness, residing not in specific outrages but in the fabric of society as a whole. In the 'system'. And particularly in 'neoliberalism', a word that had gone nuclear within academic circles by then, usually as a byword for globalised markets and the gig economy.

This burgeoning sense of the pervasive shitness leaching off the economic system in which Western women find themselves began to be expressed in sentences like this one from Tracy Clark-Flory, a milennial American sex writer and memoirist. '[The] neoliberal narrative of personal sexual empowerment is incredibly prevalent. It totally dominates within . . . mainstream pop feminist messaging. It really shifts the focus away from the need for collective struggle and collective gain. And when young people grow up with that narrative, when they find their own sex lives lacking, it can very much feel like a personal failure as opposed to a cultural and political failure.'[1]

Or this conviction, expressed by the prolific commentator Grace Blakeley, born in 1993: 'Economists from all schools . . . completely fail to account for the subjugation of women under capitalism, and the importance of social reproduction (often seen as "women's work") in the maintenance of wage labour.'[2]

No wonder, then, that when I say 'neoliberalism is great for women' I am looked at like I have just praised the Unabomber. Which of course adds to the pleasure of saying it. But I say it with sincerity, nonetheless. I actually think that neoliberalism – the successor of normal economic liberalism that means globalisation, more financial deregulation and the greater opportunities as well as precarity that go with that – is especially good for women. Hear me out. First, neoliberalism itself. It's bandied around like it has the most obvious meaning in the world, but most economic philosophers acknowledge both that it is a messy term, and also that it is not what its detractors accuse it of being: namely a programme or ideology for how to live focused on pursuit of profit and competition to the exclusion of all else. Hayek and Friedman, the two theorists most blamed for the embedding of neoliberalism, both denied that the good life means wealth maximisation, and argue instead that economic and political freedom is the pre-requisite for people answering the question themselves of what constitutes the good life. Hayek even believed that a good society needed people to act on fundamentally religious principles.

There is another way that helps us deduce that neoliberalism is good for women, and that is by looking at what the people who hate it think. They think, or say they think, that all our sexual and moral woes are systemic and capitalist ones. Enslavement to a demonic market has perverted us with the idea that motherhood is compatible with careerism when of course it can't be because careerism itself is a patriarchal capitalist concept. Hands off motherhood! Though motherhood is also something that's foisted on us and turned bad ('mother's load') due to the fact that it takes place within a patriarchal neoliberal system! And so on.

And yet, the three most positively transformative forces of all for women in the modern West have been market forces, or 'the market', medical developments and liberalisation, so that women's insides are no longer a looming death sentence should they wind up with a pregnancy they don't want, or sex that they prefer to keep non-reproductive. In the US, Christine Emba's *Rethinking Sex* was a clarion call to eradicate casual sex in favour of something more wholesome. Tracy Clark-Flory's memoir was hailed as 'grieving the idea that the sexual revolution had been fought and won', and it concludes, amid tales of the outer reaches of consensual sex, that 'We're in this space of neoliberal, individualistic, commercial feminism that really emphasizes women fixing themselves, and I think that takes us away from the collective solution. And I want to acknowledge that unfairness. To have us cut ourselves some slack and realize: It's not you.'[3] (Clark-Flory ended up happily married and a mother not long after turning thirty; Louise Perry, Mary Harrington, Kathleen Stock and reformed slut (self-billed) Bridget Phetasy are all married with children, clearly not too badly damaged themselves by the neoliberal-inflected sexual culture they blame for a fatal erosion in both women and men's ability to find mutually fulfilling love and all good things. Indeed, if what they say is true, then each of these firebrands have pulled off the impossible: loving commitment, children and family lives that satisfy their values and ambitions).

So again. Freer markets, freer women (in all senses). Incendiary but true. Harriet Taylor Mill had this to say about women's financial dependency. 'Wretches [men] unfit to have the smallest authority over any living thing, have a helpless woman for their household slave. These excesses could not exist if women both earned, and had the right to possess, a part of the income of the family.'[4] Women now regularly earn money and have the right to possess income, but that doesn't make this old point of view irrelevant. On the contrary, it forms part of the intellectual history of the changes – including the ever-closer links between liberal markets, women as valuable economic agents and women's rights – that are now so casually deplored across the political spectrum.

Crucially, the arguments made by the Mills serve as a reminder of what it was like before the alleged curse of late capitalism, when women's economic potential was overpowered by beliefs about the primacy of femininity and a woman's brain's unfitness for man-style work. Taylor Mill writes of:

> ... the numbers of women who are wives and mothers only because there is no other career open to them, no other occupation for their feelings or their activities. Every improvement in their education, and enlargement of their faculties, everything which renders them more qualified for any other mode of life, increases the number of those to whom it is an injury and an oppression to be denied the choice. To say that women must be excluded from active life because maternity disqualifies them for it, is in fact to say, that every other career should be forbidden them in order that maternity may be their only resource.[5]

And yet, here we are, Instagram a-churn with cutesy, mass-followed accounts with, for instance, strawberry frosted cake filling the screen and the text: 'When your husband says you can finally get that evergreen KitchenAid mixer you've been dreaming of'. She could get that mixer, and plenty more, without her husband's permission, but she doesn't want to. Why?

## *Angels in the Home That Never Were*

As plenty of scholars have indicated, the history of women's economic activity is not a straightforward tale of domestic confinement. At the same time, the historical evidence provided in detailed local studies also contradicts the lazy arguments about capitalism being particularly bad for women. Things were always a mix of bad and good for women (mostly bad), before and after industrialisation. The historian

Amanda Vickery's influential 1993 take-down of the 'separate spheres' lens that ordered so much historical scholarship of women's lives in the eighteenth and nineteenth century – 'Golden Age to Separate Spheres?' – offers indispensable insights. In it, she destroys 'the unquestioned belief that the transition to industrial modernity robbed women of freedom, status and authentic function'. Unlike those who advance their assertions by cherry-picking data, Vickery had spent years examining the records of English parishes, putting her in a position to take account of 'the different histories of sheep-, corn and wood-pasture farming, the contrast between the well-studied south-east and the under-researched north-west [of England], and the different experiences of families with a skilled and unskilled head . . . the worsted handspinners of Yorkshire and the lacemakers of Devon.'[6] Here is her overview of the flawed narrative.

> According to customary wisdom, sometime between 1600 and 1800 a wholesome 'family economy' wherein men, women and children shared tasks and status gave way to an exploitative wage economy which elevated the male breadwinner and marginalized his dependents. The commercialization of agriculture and the enclosure movement strangled the informal livelihood contrived by many labouring families on the land. The housewife lost her ability to contribute through husbandry, while female field workers who had previously worked shoulder to shoulder with their menfolk were suddenly marginalized in sporadic, demeaning and low-paid agricultural occupations. Meanwhile, the mechanization of industrial processes took manufacturing out of the early modern home and into the modern factory, separating for ever after the home and workplace.[7]

So goes the traditional narrative, still in use by those seeking to scandalise the effect of industrial capitalism, followed by late modern capitalism or neoliberalism, on women's essential sense of purpose, value and happiness. But as Vickery shows, women did all kinds of work, depending on their class, whether that was operating the business of the home by letter-writing and running the house, working in family enterprises, service, or in a shop – before and after the industrial revolution. But it didn't make their lives better before, and worse after. Because without any pretence at equal rights, meaningful change for women was limited. As Vickery notes, before the twentieth century, women did not enjoy the full rights of citizenship – including the right to vote.

In short: women were hardly ever simply 'angels in the home', whatever the literature of the eighteenth, nineteenth and twentieth centuries suggests. But their professional horizons were severely limited and this entrenched their powerlessness, boredom, subservience and misery. Even where women's work outside the home was widespread, most historians now agree that it would be difficult to squeeze from the grind of their daily lives any evidence of independence or other transformation in their social status and prospects. At no time in the pre-industrial past, writes the historian Duncan Bythell, 'was there a "golden age" when women were not confined – either by prevailing notions or "separate spheres", "complementarity", or "partnership", or by the institutional structures and mentalities created by patriarchy – to marginal, unskilled and poorly paid work.'[8]

The debate about whether the market fundamentally ends up exploiting women or empowering them has occupied historians for decades, ever since – in the post-war period – the lives of women, and ordinary working women at that, became worthy objects of research. It is true that the nature of work changed in the nineteenth century with growing mechanisation and an expansion of certain types of work performed outside the home: the boot, shoe and hosiery industries were among those that, while fuelled by mechanised factory work, still required intricate at-home 'fancy work'.[9]

The old problems of underpayment and devaluation compared

to men and the 'double shift' of paid work and housework, continued throughout European history, even if some of its outward manifestations appeared to worsen in the nineteenth century. In Britain, the marriage bar – either not hiring married women or firing them once they got married – persisted from the late nineteenth century to the 1970s; in the US it began earlier and was only terminated by the 1964 Civil Rights Act.

Among historians intimately acquainted not just with broad notions of 'the industrial revolution' and 'exploitation', but with the contradictions between the ideology of the male breadwinner, advanced by (male) trade unions towards the end of the twentieth century, and the granular occupational patterns of, say, (women-intensive) Bedfordshire's straw industry or the dairy farms of Buckinghamshire in the 1850s, there is unresolved complexity. 'Do we characterise the migration of women to towns as a sign of the "crushing effects of industrialisation", or a reflection of "women's economic initiative"?' asks Duncan Bythell. 'Should women's work be defined as a feature of the "survival strategies" of an oppressed underclass, or as occupations and employment?'[10]

Such questions should at least put the brakes on the assumption that ever since the industrial revolution women's lot has gone downhill, as the horrible stamp of market forces, an imprint of patriarchy itself, pressed ever more cruelly on them. Undoubtedly the working world for many women in the nineteenth and early twentieth century was brutal and relentless. But as is obvious from the history of women's work, the problem wasn't – and isn't – women working and being mothers, or being crushed by an ahistorical capitalism. Rather, the problem was the toxic combination of poverty, underdeveloped thinking about women's professional and political capacities, their physical capabilities, and, of course, a market that was both over-regulated and under-regulated in all the wrong places. The problem was the routine degradation of women's efforts in the public sphere, and shoddy and unequal remuneration for their work in the commercial and domestic spheres.

Remuneration isn't the best measure of the possible satisfaction gained in getting out the house, seeing workmates and earning something – which many weavers, hosiers, dairy women – felt. But it is a crude indication of how women are valued. And in the twentieth, nineteenth, eighteenth centuries and before, this value, expressed in derisory pay, was calculated on ideas based in miserable confusion, misogyny and religion. Compare to the 2020s, when the gender pay gap has actually all but disappeared (3.2 per cent or below) for people in their twenties and thirties, re-emerging in the forties as women still pay a price for motherhood – a price paid happily by those who want to 'lean out' of professional life and 'lean in' to flexibility that prioritises motherhood. But, while the gap goes up after age thirty-nine (by 10.9 per cent), the point at which earnings tend to leap for those who stay in the game full-throttle, there has been a sharp fall in the gender pay gap in high-echelon occupations. According to the Office for National Statistics, 'the largest fall in the gender pay gap since [before Covid] is among managers, directors and senior officials.' I note with particular satisfaction the squeezing of the gap in categories including 'process plant and machine operatives', 'skilled trade occupations', and 'technical operations'.[11]

Given all this – the proven humiliations and miseries of the pre- *and*-post-industrial period; the incredible improvements in women's autonomy, wellbeing, independence and freedom since the last of the legal bars on women's ability to learn and work in whatever area they choose; the recent era in which women have been able to be mothers with successful careers in professions once exclusively male – given all this, how odd to find that a 'new' vanguard wants to resist capitalism, row back abortion and contraception and otherwise return women to their (inaccurately conceived) essence as mothers. It seems terribly obvious that the better use of time would be improving, not wishing away, the most dynamic, promising system the world has ever known: capitalism tempered by the liberal democratic states in which those of us in the Anglosphere are lucky enough to live.

## *Patriarchy is No Longer a Thing*

But if, like the feminist scribe Laurie Penny, among others, you believe that patriarchy is what 'all of us are living in' then you will struggle to even notice the transformations in women's horizons that have changed everything.

Let's look at this 'until patriarchy is gone, nothing can be good for women' argument. Patriarchy is neither a made-up progressive buzzword nor the system through which we should parse our whole world. It is not a good explanation of the economic forces at work, nor of the professional and educational options facing women. It's not really appropriate for the romantic or social spheres either.

Patriarchy is a real thing, still ruining much of the world, though thankfully – for all its imperfections – not the West. Patriarchy is not actually what's going on when a boyfriend behaves with systematic selfishness or entitlement, or when you have an infuriating, and unfair, encounter with a man at work. Or any number of bad experiences or circumstances, even serious ones. Patriarchy is 'a system of interrelated social structures which allow men to exploit women'[12], and provides a totalising dynamic whereby some men control a society's money and institutions, a group to which all women are subordinate, legally or practically. Women are not in that situation now, in the West, and I believe that, while difficult, it is possible to distinguish between uneven societal pressure and the rule of law or the pervasive, iron-clad norms of old. It is liberating, I think, to make that distinction.

To better understand how patriarchy is not what we are living in anymore, I've always found the historian Judith Bennett's idea of 'patriarchal continuum' helpful. To describe the system by which women have historically been kept down, whenever they rise up or prosper, Bennett uses the example of Medieval brewsters: women who ran and grew the beer brewing industry in England between 1300 and 1500, before they made it too successful and had to be banned from working in it.[13] A similar dynamic was visible in the early computer coding industry. Considered trifling or secretarial work, women regularly worked in this field. As soon as computer programming became important, the old dynamics swung into gear and it became a male-dominated business, unfriendly and therefore off-putting to women.

Some version of this has always been in play: as soon as women make gains, they are forced to pay for them. Something of this is visible in the way women themselves are turning away from economic ambition now that they have the chance to run with it.[14] But in terms of an actual patriarchy, we have recently – but truly – escaped.

The Married Woman's Property Act of 1882 was the first to chip away at the formal edifice, allowing women to hang on to their own wealth even after marriage. Of course, even when the law appeared to protect women's rights to self-determination, the reality was quite different: street life was aggressive, intimidating, and dangerously predatory in ways that make today's streets seem utopian. Prostitution criminalised, stigmatised and vilified women, while protecting clients at the women's cost. This was the injustice that galvanised the first major wave of feminist campaigning, which traversed an ideological spectrum from the vehemently and religiously sin- and purity-focused, to the more nuanced sexually liberal.[15]

But patriarchy doesn't exist anymore, at least not in the ways that it was enshrined in law and custom even in the West until about 1991, when rape in marriage finally ceased to be legal in the UK. It's not the case that there are no problems, no sexism and perfect treatment of women's health: childbirth is still an unholy mess. Maternity still poses unresolved paradoxes and strains that fall hardest on women. Women are still violently attacked by men. Women's cancer and other sex-related diseases are still shockingly prevalent. But we need a new frame of analysis; to move towards a 'job not yet done' paradigm, rather than a 'we will always already be screwed because we are women and because capitalism and patriarchy' one. In fact, given that patriarchy is a collectivist, kin-oriented system (most literally represented by the authority of the patriarch), it is the socialistic society imagined by most left-leaning feminists and other progressives that is the far more obvious host for patriarchy than a system that enables and encourages individual autonomy and independence. The mistake, made everywhere and always by capitalism's feminist critics, is to say that the desire to make money in order to enjoy individual autonomy, and engaging in the pursuit of that feeling of the metaphorical wind in one's hair, somehow erodes other aspects of personhood. In fact, it makes them, and especially family relationships, more pleasurable and less like drudgery, and opens up real possibilities for doing good. Plus you'll never have to ask your husband to let you get that KitchenAid mixer.

### *Capitalism is a 'Faux' Problem*

'Capitalism', which has never existed in a pure state, has not just been good for women – it has dramatically overhauled their whole horizon of possibility and will continue to do so. The more capitalism is allowed to operate without gender discrimination, the better it works for everyone.

'Capitalism' is a faux problem. Back in the 1960s, when the modern wave of anti-capitalist social movements began, anti-capitalism was just the accepted vogue. After all, the sexual liberation movements began life being wedged into the heart of a broader leftist politics concerned, particularly in the UK, with class and wages. The feminist movement in the UK was founded by women who had grown fed up of being sidelined by men in groups such as the Vietnam Solidarity Campaign, the Revolutionary Socialist Students Federation, the Young Socialists and the Campaign for Nuclear Disarmament: socialism was in their political blood. And because those feminists and other liberationists, such as gay rights activists, had real fish to fry, one might allow the (confected, often hypocritical and highly privileged – though sometimes cerebral and well-argued) debasement of capitalism to pass. In the US, unlike the UK, the women's movement tended to be more radical than socialist anyway, more concerned with the direct results of male domination and entitlement on women than the political economy surrounding it.[16]

Now it is 'neoliberalism' that is blamed for all evils. Let us return here to the definition provided for neoliberalism by the Plato encyclopaedia, hosted by Stanford University. We saw before that neoliberalism's godfathers, Hayek, Friedman and James Buchanan never advocated replacing ethics and morality with the pursuit of profit in order to live 'the good life'. In terms of a positive definition, it is that 'society's political and economic institutions should be robustly liberal and capitalist, but supplemented by a constitutionally limited democracy and a modest welfare state'.[17] This is much more moderate and less total than its detractors insist; especially given that no country has come anywhere close to achieving it. Neither Europe, the UK or the US have a 'limited democracy' and the former two have nothing like a 'modest welfare state'. And yet, central to the widely-understood definition, or sense, of neoliberalism is that it is an all-encompassing philosophy, and thus as responsible for the thoroughgoing commercialisation of women's bodies, indeed of feminism itself, as it is for the banking crisis of 2008.

'Neoliberalism' is usually only deployed by left-leaning academics, think tankers, journalists and maybe some YouTubers and TikTokers, circles within which neoliberalism is widely agreed to exist as a system that worships the market to the exclusion of humanity, animated by the revived spirit of global business and deregulation that was blamed for the financial crisis. In the columnist Stephen Metcalf's words, post-1980 neoliberalism saw 'society as a kind of universal market (and not, for example, a polis, a civil sphere or a kind of family) and of human beings as profit-and-loss calculators (and not bearers of grace, or of inalienable rights and duties)'.[18] The symptoms of this anti-bearer-of-grace attitude are austerity (a desire to balance government books by shrinking state expenditure, such as we saw after the financial crisis in 2008), tax cuts and deregulation. In the UK, the latter is correctly attributed to neoliberalism's infamous witch Margaret Thatcher. Yes, Thatcher deregulated markets, but she also cut the highest rate of tax from 80 per cent to 60 per cent, the basic rate from 33 to 30 per cent, and increased state spending – hardly the work of a die-hard market-worshiper blinded by profit-and-loss metrics.

But 'neoliberalism', we are told, goes further, seeping into our very bones. It is nothing short of 'a name for a premise that, quietly, has come to regulate all we practise and believe: that competition is the only legitimate organising principle for human activity,' as Metcalf says, dramatically.[19] But as anyone who has lived pretty much anywhere on Earth will tell you, even in hyper-marketised places, like Dubai, Florida or Monaco, this description has nothing to do with the way life as a whole is 'organised'. There is competition for schools and the best jobs – but that's as much to do with increased pressure on resources through population growth and the expansion of higher education than some kind of total takeover producing an entirely marketised mind. Indeed, it would take a lot more than a partly globalised, but still quite regulated, financial market to extinguish our humanity so thoroughly that nothing, from parental love to curiosity to irrationality to dissent, remained but the charred husk of a vast competition monster. Even the monolithic nightmare in Orwell's *1984* and, indeed, the real-life Soviet regime, failed to do this.

Generally, I am not a fan of the idea that that which purports to offer women freedom actually merely represses them further, by – for instance – driving them to make money posing in lewd and nude postures on OnlyFans or, through social media, goading them to constantly improve their looks through expensive, damaging procedures and buying more and more make-up. Kim Kardashian's 'work' and wealth, or women pole dancing for 'empowerment', are, for them, the ultimate hoax; the terrible co-option of all that is good for women, and feminism itself, by market forces that are inexorably misogynistic.

There is, of course, truth mixed in with this analysis. It's hard for many of us to look at the women dying from Brazilian butt lifts gone wrong, or defaced by too much filler, or indeed cavorting seductively before the camera for their panting fans the world over, without wincing. The bigger issue is pinpointed by the sociologist Arlie Hochschild – pioneer of the idea of 'emotional labour'. She makes the fine point that 'intimate life' and indeed feminism is co-opted, certainly in America, by 'the commercial spirit'. Her argument is persuasive that there is a parallel between the escape of religion from its 'cage' (hard praying) into the 'spirit of capitalism' (hard working) and feminism's escape from the 'cage' of a social movement (consciousness raising, campaigning) into the 'commercial spirit of intimate life' (e.g.: Bumble, pre-nups). As Hochschild points out, just as market conditions 'ripen the soil for capitalism', so a 'weakened family prepares the soil for the commercialised spirit of domestic life'.[20] The category of 'domestic' includes romantic relations as well, and it is a shrewd and subtle fact of modern life, and late capitalism, that the two become intertwined. But acknowledging, or even investigating, how market logics shape the intimate sphere does not mean we ought to see women's false consciousness, or the exploitation of women and their sexuality, in every dating venture.

## Chapter Five

# Why Money and Capitalism are Good for Women

### *Purity Economics*
#### *The theological origins of leftist money angst*

If we zoom out further, we remember that it has always been tempting to bash money, wealth, markets, greed. Whole worldviews have revolved around doing so. Just ask the Jews, who have been on the receiving end of thousands of years of it under false charges of possessing and controlling a suspicious amount of all of those things. Following suspicion among the Greeks, who saw money-making in opposition to virtue, the yearning for a society that forces 'grace' and 'family' and 'inalienable rights and duties' on people (a collectivist vision), rather than encouraging profit-making and property accrual (individualism) became essentially religious. It's Christian (You cannot serve both God and money, says Matthew in the Bible) but not exclusively. Judaism, too, is preoccupied with family and concepts of legality and moral justice. But for most of history, Christian Europe was a place with terrifying enforcements in place to punish those deemed to have stepped away from a life of virtue into one of vice and greed; Jews' forced role as money lenders helped to keep them as permanent targets, the money-grubbing, grasping scum against the virtuous, civic-minded Christian. Those Christians who accrued great wealth were expected to make showy donations to the Church, though the tension between market and God was never quite defused.

The question of how far the left has ever escaped from Christianity, and its unease about money, is open to discussion. In his seminal essay 'Religion and the Origins of Socialism', the historian Gareth Stedman Jones outlines the Christian relationship to socialist movements in Europe in the nineteenth and early twentieth centuries, arguing that they evolved theocratic cosmologies in direct response to growing secularism; socialism 'presented itself as the universal replacement for the old religions of the world built upon a new "science"-based cosmology and a new ethical code.' In fact, socialism – French in particular – drew explicitly on the democratic nature of Christ.

'Not only was Christ a man of the People, preaching equality and fraternity, Christ was the People . . . the divinely appointed embodiment of the democratic people.' This was the core belief held by most leaders of the French democrats during the revolution of 1848. In the twentieth century, socialism, or communism, could be just as theocratic while renouncing Christian theology, as when 'dialectical materialism . . . served to provide a distinct identity to a new theocratic regime obsessed by internal enemies and surrounded by hostile powers until its final collapse at the end of the 1980s.'[1]

The relatively unacknowledged theological kernel to much of the politics that underscores the left's grinding suspicion of money-making systems can be found in many places. The introduction to the Communist Manifesto contains theocratic assumptions. Christian socialism was also a key influence on J. S. Mill, while

Henri Saint-Simon, one of the founding fathers of Christian socialism, was a major influence on Mill and his ideas of a 'social physics'. Saint-Simonianism was both hyper-patriarchal and also gave rise to a Christian-spiritual feminism in which the next messiah was a woman. Over the course of the twentieth century, socialism morphed more fully into a secular progressive cause, its older forms disintegrating as the horrific real-life implications of the creed were revealed everywhere from Hungary in 1956 to Tiananmen Square. Socialism was reborn as a more nebulous, identitarian movement. Tempered by growing individualism and a more mobile younger generation, it spread itself through a range of causes, from equality for women to those of sexual and racial minorities, in addition to labour and the distribution of money.[2]

While socialist feminism had been a key strand in the early twentieth century as activists tried to get women a modicum of equal pay and treatment in the trades, where they were brazenly exploited compared to men, in the post-1960s period, the 'personal' became the political, widening the scope of progressive capitalist critiques into much larger domains of female identity and daily life.

Now we have a bit more context for why 'neoliberalism' started on its merry way to being the gateway to critiques of the alleged hubris of those who believed that wealth creation and the entrepreneurialism of some can spread to all. How it became the go-to basket of evils for those who believe wealth is a zero-sum game: that someone's gain is another's loss; that indeed the gainer plucks food from the mouth of the poorer. And why the term is basically a clever-sounding fig leaf for conspiratorial thinking about people who make money – that they must be either corrupted by, or corrupting, a system.

## *The Twin Evils*

Left-wing feminism imagines the world as a social hierarchy that puts women below men, and sees men's gains as feeding off women's resources – a zero-sum characterisation of things. One person's gain is another's loss. It is no surprise that one zero sum way of thinking translates neatly to another – especially when something as big and blobby as global systems of wealth creation provide the analytical frame. Take the way in which gender studies reading-list stalwart Nancy Fraser reflexively and nimbly connects the two in her iconic essay, 'Feminism, Capitalism and the Cunning of History'. Instead of contemplating the possibility they might be disconnected, or different things entirely, she spots a 'disturbing convergence of some of [feminism's] ideals with the demands of an emerging new form of capitalism – post-Fordist, 'disorganized', 'transnational'.[3]

And so when we begin to unpick or question the uniform assumptions of the millstone 'patriarchy', we see that a lot of it is about money angst – even though the sins of patriarchy are not necessarily the sins of capitalism.[4] And yet the two have remained closely connected in the feminist mind since the 1960s (and before). The historian Sheila Rowbotham, one of the founding intellectual powerhouses of the British women's liberation movement, argued that it was capitalism that had kept women exploited and maltreated at home, serving industrial systems run by men by performing family-creation and maintenance labour; and that, more generally, capitalism, in oppressing the working class, had oppressed women particularly, forcing them to sell their labour and do the double shift of unpaid domestic work too. As Dijana Jelača, Nikolay Karkov, and Tanja Petrović write in a special issue about women in socialist south-eastern Europe: 'For readers versed in the tradition of North Atlantic feminist theory, the intersection of "socialism" and "feminism" is relatively uncomplicated. As a rule, the theory proffers a critique of the "double oppression" that women experience under patriarchy and capitalism, with the exact relationship between these two systems then up for debate.' They continue by saying that feminists like Nancy Fraser, who so glibly assume that feminism and socialism are bedfellows, make scant reference to actual socialist societies. Therefore, 'the socialist feminist project continues to boast more than a few adherents to this day. [But] the herstory on the other side of what used to be called "the Iron Curtain," however, has unfolded quite differently.'[5] Indeed.

More broadly, these ideas about capitalism and patriarchy as twin evils were adopted with far less critical and historical rigour than we might have imagined. This is clear when we move from the metanarrative of feminist intellectuals to the micro and particular. Even feminists in the 1970s and 1980s running feminist businesses were hobbled by immovable antagonism towards money making. Cambridge professor and historian of feminism Lucy Delap has studied the attitudes to business of the collective who ran *Spare Rib*, the UK's only feminist magazine, founded in 1972. Those attitudes were abundantly clear when, in 1977, *Spare Rib* – still the organ of British feminism – was calling the Conservative Party Women's Conference that year nothing more than 'a meeting of small capitalists'. This critique focused not on women as business-people – which was barely mentioned – but on small businessmen as exploiters of the unpaid labour of their wives.[6] Róisín Boyd, who worked in the *Spare Rib* collective in 1980, told me in an interview in 2018 that 'business was seen as Tory, if you were in business you were right-wing'. As many of these feminist businesswomen later admitted, the only people to gain from their socialism were their competitors.

Still, it was fun while it lasted. In the July 1979 edition, one of *Spare Rib*'s editors, Rosie Parker, argued that the magazine had always wanted to draw 'attention to the way business profited from women's constantly encouraged consumption and sexual objectification'. The magazine during that period was relieved of the need to make a profit, or take revenue too seriously, thanks to the funding of the Greater London Council (GLC), which, says Delap, 'seemed to require a more explicit repudiation of business and profits'. A *Spare Rib* application to the GLC stated unequivocally that it 'had no intention of becoming "profitable" in the sense of accruing profits which are awarded to individual members'. The ambivalent if not downright hostile attitude to market forces included advertising. The magazine ran lots of ads for women-run businesses and operations that fit the ethical mould by being not-for-profit, or state-funded, and readers were alive to those that didn't fit this model or seemed to be charging 'too much'. Thus when adverts for a women's retreat called Hen House appeared in 1989, with a weekend in Lincolnshire for £126, feedback was scathing. 'It is insulting to women with little access to sufficient money,' wrote one reader. 'It has taken a long time to get working class women onto the 'feminist agenda'; places like the Hen House make me angry.'[7]

This, of course, was because of the firm belief in a causal link between profit and markets – capitalism in short hand – and exploitation, moral degradation and necessary betrayal of the cause. In shunning profit, the *Spare Rib* collective talked about getting enough to pay 'fair' wages, show 'respect for skill' instead of money, and to instil trust, which, again, market bonds must surely corrode.[8]

The magazine was interesting for more than ten years, and a meaningful enterprise that was essential reading for feminists, budding and otherwise. But without proper hierarchies, management and accountability – all of which could have been stapled down with good, staggered pay, rooted in a well-thought-through business practice – *Spare Rib* imploded slowly and gruesomely, through in-fighting, sinister race politics that fostered open anti-Semitism, politicking and competitive victimology. At the end, when GLC funding had been withdrawn (Thatcher shut the GLC down in 1986) the shabby production and editorial standards that went with a complete lack of money killed off all remaining appeal. *Spare Rib* provides a neat example of how the aversion to capitalism baked into left-wing and feminist ideology has not always instantly and necessarily interfered with certain feminist ventures; it was possible to disseminate experimental but important writing before the internet.

But the 1970s were a particular moment when state funds seemed to rain down from the sky, and the arts and heritage industries were briefly able to break loose from the old boring business model of profit and loss. When that moment ended, however, British feminism's discursive infrastructure swiftly dissolved: magazines shut, and those who ran other worthy enterprises had to find jobs that paid properly. It is no coincidence that the UK feminist movement ran out of funds, and steam, at roughly the same time. In the US, by contrast, the feminist movement had always had a more integrated approach to dirty old capitalism. Its *Spare Rib* equivalent, *Ms.* magazine, made money enough through courting profitability to adapt and survive, with a roster of celebrity contributors that continues to today.

In short, being 'anti-capitalist' in a crude sense – shy of the pursuit of profit, being against hierarchy and market competition – weakened, in the long term, the movement's presence and cohesion, and arguably fostered more social fractures, such as bitter in-fighting.

There was, and is, a tension, of course, between workplace feminism and more purist, activist or intellectual forms. *Spare Rib* was influential in many ways, something of a litmus test of the health of a rather baggy and diverse movement – but it occupied a different sphere from the politicians and lawyers working on women's divorce rights, or businesswomen forming fledgling women's networking and support groups.

## *'Real' Feminists Vs the Shills*

Today, despite the loathing among progressives for former Facebook COO Sheryl Sandberg's idea of women 'leaning in' to get ahead at work, her book was a bestseller and has been in sync with workplace policies such as egg freezing on the company dime, in-work nurseries and boosting quotas for women on boards and in executive positions. But still, the intellectual vanguard, those who still set the parameters of 'real' feminism (as in that which is not contaminated by neoliberalism) dismiss all gains, so long as they are measured in metrics of money, physical freedoms and political and financial power, because these occur within a market framework. No matter how much evidence emerges that the urge to make money within regulated but liberal markets is actually good for women – all women, of all classes, sexual identities and marital status – the antimoneyism persists in feminism.

This perplexing, counterproductive dogmatism is particularly evident in the most respected and trendsetting of journals. This piece in the 2019 edition of leading left-wing journal *Jacobin*, for instance, could have been plucked straight from *Spare Rib* in 1977. Headlined 'Why Capitalism and Feminism Can't Coexist', the author, *Jacobin* editor-at-large and sociologist Nicole Aschoff, trots through the usual buzz-word contexts: the financial crash and the emergence of populism have shown capitalism and neoliberalism to be 'in crisis' while the failure of Hillary Clinton to become president is apparently an example of neoliberalism's failure, rather than an outcropping of misogyny and rampant conspiracy theory among her opponents on the right. Sexist pig Trump's victory over Clinton, she says, gives the lie to the idea 'that feminist goals are best achieved by each woman striving to reach a position of power and success within capitalism'.⁹ This is an odd supposition, given Hillary's problem was palpably less to do with capitalism, which arguably tracks only adjacently to politics and is certainly not the same thing, and more to do with America's ongoing aversion to having a woman in power. In other words, Clinton's failure was a showcase of the injustice and persistence of a sexism that continues to penalise highly competent women simply for being women.

Turning her loss into a criticism of the very idea of female 'striving' makes no sense, unless you just don't want women to succeed in any of the mainstream arenas of politics, business or the law. I guess if you hate 'capitalism' enough, then you won't. This, alas, is a typical left-wing completism – until the whole system is changed and overthrown, nobody will be free.[10] Which is why the rest of Aschoff's argument turns on saying major areas of progress are worthless. She casts shade on widespread prosperity because it's only for some women and some people; feminism 'is about fighting for the good life for everyone' and capitalism isn't a system dedicated to that. Those who do well are bolstered by an elite that is inherently unjust if not malign (and certainly not meritocratic).

And then there is the climate, which, in this view, is a problem that can never be mended within any vaguely capitalist system, since the crisis was apparently caused by the super-rich. The truth, as in most areas, is that communism and the socialist bloc has been as bad, if not worse in terms of its environmental policies. Despite their haughty collectivism, they belched out fumes with careless aggression, because they cared less about individual wellbeing and health and in part because of 'the tragedy of the commons', which means that when property is communally owned and treated as a free resource, it is abused and overused without regard for the future. 'The attitude that nature is there to be exploited by man is the very essence of the Soviet production ethic,' writes the economist Marshall Goldman.[11] It's not a huge leap to imagine the socialist attitude to women, and the particularities of women's bodies, would fall short of the life-affirming.

And yet the conviction of young left-wing feminists that capitalism is the enemy of women – or rather, the women worthy of help, not those who are 'privileged' and white – fits with a broader demographic picture in which two-thirds of young people in Britain want to live under a socialist system.[12] Even in the more chest-thumpingly market-oriented land of America, more than half of people aged eighteen to twenty-nine say they prefer socialism to capitalism. And so we end up with simply ludicrous assertions like this one, from Muskaan Arshad writing in the *Harvard Political Review*, that 'equality with men isn't something we should aspire to' mainly because 'girl bossing' and other brash terms for female empowerment in a 'man's world' are just the pitiful desires of capitalist stooges.[13]

## *Kidnapped by the Market*

Because 'market forces' have seized on certain feminism-lite ideas and disseminated them in for-profit arenas like mainstream magazines and Michelle Obama merch, the whole conceptual edifice of ambition, success and wealth is fatally corrupted. Women who want what everyone has wanted throughout all of history – agency, remuneration or reward for hard work, and the enjoyment of the resulting freedoms and riches – are suffering a bad case of false consciousness. Arshad writes about how she looks back scathingly on her youth when she looked up to Indra Nooryi, who was the head of PepsiCo. Now she realises that because women who succeeded in climbing the greasy pole have not managed to eradicate the whole mass of female, indeed human, injustice as they go, their success is actually an insult to feminism. These women, in daring to pursue corporate success as individuals, have committed the grave sin of selfishness on a grand scale. And, as Arshad reminds us: 'the ethical value of their choices are defined by their impact on the collective rather than the individual . . . it becomes clear that choice feminism is morally reprehensible because of its selfish nature.'[14] That's Nooryi told.

Except you could just as easily argue, and with far more likelihood of being right, that it's actually only by participating in the commercial economy, as an entrepreneur or as a member of the workforce, that you contribute to the greater good as well as your own. Most sane economists agree that the modernisation of the West since the nineteenth century has led to the greatest improvements in living standards for all that the world has ever seen. They also argue that the yanking of the West into the world's most prosperous, powerful bloc in the period of its industrial acceleration was only achievable because of the relative freedom of its women, as compared to say China or the Islamic world. To make women merely the victims of the economic process of industrialisation or an ethic of selfishness, like Nooryi, is to sideline their noble, not shameful, role as economic actors – and to fundamentally misunderstand the relationship between healthy, innovative markets and women's access to power and liberty.

Ann Cudd, an analytical philosopher of feminism, president of Portland State University and former dean of Boston University, graduated in 1982 from Swarthmore College, one of the best in the country, with a double degree in maths and philosophy. Her grandmother was born on a midwestern farm in the late nineteenth century, had five children, travelled by horse-drawn cart, and had only the most meagre access to goods, services and healthcare. Still, her lot was better than those who came before: at the end of the seventeenth century, female life expectancy was around thirty years, with the expectation of bearing seven children, some or most or all of whom would die, and with a high chance of dying in childbirth herself. Cudd reflects: 'The massive changes in the lives of women and girls are due in large part to the development of capitalism . . . the main force in the advancement of society more generally'.[15]

Cudd makes the kind of argument that sends those immersed in academic discourse into frenzies of disgust. Yet the fact that: 'in the market, individuals are faceless, backgroundless utility functions, budget constraints and productive functions' is, as she notes, a very good thing, for it describes the 'purely economic rationale for . . . the nondiscrimination constraint' whereby people are considered 'as a bundle of assets and preferences abstracted from other aspects of who they are because it is [more] efficient'.[16] In other words, it's inefficient to stop women or other minorities doing, being, buying or selling something of market value just because they are women or other minorities. Clinging to just such restrictions, in the form of patriarchy, ensured society was poor, miserable and unfair for the vast majority. 'Capitalism, by providing an option outside kin and traditional community norms for independence and social power, can allow women the wherewithal to escape these constraints,' notes Cudd.[17] It's a basic point, fleshed out by the ongoing existence of women holding back from fleeing domestic terror because they don't have the means to be independent, or fear they won't be able to cope without their abusive partners. Equally, many women experience a transformation in self-esteem and ambition through the discovery of skills and enjoyment of work in the outside world, which also equips them to leave horrible home environments if they need to.

The left loves to talk about 'solidarity' – through protest and other collective actions. But, as Cudd points out, 'regardless of how good social bonds may feel . . . They are the very forces of unfreedom in many cases.' She specifically says that the bonds of solidarity 'both enable and constrain' and that she 'cannot think of anything that produces more anxiety than the requirement that I follow the norms of some particular community, without any opportunity to opt out of that community.' As she points out, this is most intensely felt by groups that have endured generations of oppression, such as women.[18]

When it comes to the left's disdain for women's fate within any kind of market-oriented system, there are some interesting overlaps with the illiberal right, discussed in Chapter One. In part, the left finds 'neoliberalism' problematic because it encourages commodified intimacy markets, with seepage through to all personal relationships, rather than nourishing the wholesome bonds the left (and conservatives) imagines circulate around a secure hearth and home. Both left and right also worry about the way the economic system seems to pressure women into downgrading motherhood in favour of ambition and careerism.[19]

They may quibble about the nature of the problem, but the conservatives and the anti-capitalist young feminists today agree on one big thing. Which is that work outside the home, servicing the god Mammon and masculine imperatives of greed, sullies women, either as mothers (say the conservatives) or as moral agents who ought not to be brought down by the unequal system of capitalism, and whose sexuality is all too often harangued by oversexed men (say progressives, feminists and again, conservatives). All three are concerned, in different ways, with the objectification of women, whether by men or by systems like patriarchy and capitalism. And for all three groups, an iron-clad taboo holds firm: money is the chief villain.

## Chapter Six

# The Politics of Pain

I know no woman – virgin, mother, lesbian, married, celibate – whether she earns her keep as a housewife, a cocktail waitress, or a scanner of brain waves – for whom her body is not a fundamental problem: its clouded meaning, its fertility, its desire, its so-called frigidity, its bloody speech, its silences, its changes and mutilations, its rapes and ripenings . . . There is for the first time today a possibility of converting our physicality into both knowledge and power.

So wrote Adrienne Rich, the feminist poet, in her 1976 book *Of Woman Born: Motherhood as Experience and Institution*. Rich was picking up on a core theme of the women's liberation movement: that the details of female bodily experience should no longer be kept quiet to satisfy punishing social codes of shame and decorum, and that only when women were able to freely discuss (and explore) their bodies, pleasure and pain, warts and all, would they achieve self-realisation.

This was one of women's liberation's most noble enterprises, rooted in a fundamental insight into the limiting and cruel nature of the epistemological regime that had long governed what was permissible for women to say, or know, about their bodies. Women's genital hygiene could be as appalling as their understanding of sex because they did not know what was 'down there' and dared not look too closely. A gynaecologist wrote with disgust in 1936 (not excluding men from censure): 'Every doctor who has to examine the genital organs of either sex must be struck frequently with . . . the dirty condition of the sexual organs . . . This is due, not to any innate perversity, but rather to ignorance and convention. Women who spend hours every day over their toilet, who take a complete bath once or more every day, who are manicured and pedicured . . . often display to their gynaecologist sexual organs bathed with foul discharges . . . '.[1] The other extreme saw women so convinced that their genitalia were dirty that they douched themselves to dangerous degrees. One woman in her twenties was recorded having 'presented with a severe vaginal and vulval condition as the result of douching four times a day with Lysol, in an excess of zeal for cleanliness'.[2]

Sexually, right through the mid-twentieth century, many women felt their private parts were off limits: in a general climate of paranoia about the evils of masturbation, women were more likely to say they had never done it. Eustace Chesser, the sex researcher, reported in 1949 that of six hundred women surveyed, only 30 per cent admitted to having masturbated, whereas of three hundred men, every single one said he self-pleasured.[3]

Unlike with men, female genitalia do require some study, with a hand mirror, to see it in all its complexity and manifold glories. The ability to shuck away shame and revulsion is also necessary. They had hand mirrors in the 1940s, but it wasn't until the 1970s that a revolution in women's relationships with their bodies and their sexuality was made possible, fostered through a new movement, with new language and new norms. And that movement had its work cut out for it. Women's relationships with their bodies remained highly mediated by male-dominated institutions into the late twentieth century. Medical schools retained sex quotas into the 1970s and only one in seven doctors was female, while gynaecology remained male dominated. As late as 1978, in the view of Nancy MacKeith, author of the *New Women's Health Handbook*, close self-examination of genital problems by women was seen 'by many people' as 'a sexual perversion' and an obscene interest in 'private parts . . . To some people a woman knowing her cervix and her vagina is too powerful a tool for her to cope with . . . she might get an infection . . . [become] dangerously frightened.'[4]

MacKeith was writing towards the end of a feminist decade that had begun, in and among other major developments, with the 1970 publication of the iconic *Our Bodies, Ourselves*, by the Boston (US) Women's Health Book Collective. Women's health groups began engaging in a highly physical form of consciousness raising, often deploying mirrors and sometimes probing with their finger, sometimes a speculum. *Our Bodies, Ourselves* evolved through careful discussion and data gathering, and was soon seen as 'validat[ing] women's embodied experiences as a resource for challenging medical dogmas . . . and, consequently, as a strategy for personal and collective empowerment'.[5] It was in this heady moment that Germaine Greer recommended women taste their own menstrual blood. 'If you think you are emancipated, you might consider the idea of tasting your own menstrual blood – if it makes you sick, you've a long way to go, baby,' she wrote in *The Female Eunuch*.[6]

It was also in this period that the sudden release in rectitude and secrecy, shame and ignorance around women's reproductive health led to a jamboree of complaints: detailed accounts of physical misery, not least at the hands of doctors and a medical establishment that still ignored, condescended to or simply maltreated women suffering from reproductive health issues. Half a century previously, the thousands of letters received by birth control activist Marie Stopes after her book *Married Love* appeared in 1918 were similarly frank, and full of tales of woe – but they were written in the desperation of closetedness and privacy, a geyser of experience clandestinely sent to a specific recipient. Stopes's correspondents were desperate for advice and relief but were generally not levelling political broadsides. And while agony aunts fielded more public epistles as the century wore on, these were usually less graphic and more to do with relationships than body parts.

This changed in the 1970s when the particulars of women's bodily suffering gained prominence, and those recounting them gained confidence, not just in pinpointing the details but in framing them in feminist, political terms. As a post-doctoral researcher on a project examining the feminist publishing industry, I looked into this new discourse of complaint and examined what it was doing for women and the movement. I was tasked with studying *Spare Rib* magazine, fulsomely referred to here in part for that reason. I was particularly interested in the letters pages because they represented an epistolary community of empowerment through the misery.

*Spare Rib* helped build its community of sufferers beyond the letters pages, by inviting women to write first-person features in articles such as 'Vaginismus: I Tried to Make Love But I Closed Up Completely', 'Abortion: Diary of a Nightmare', and 'No such thing as pain: Having your baby in hospital is supposed to be safe and restful ... Ruth Wheeler knows otherwise!'. Ailsa Irving, an endometriosis sufferer, started a self-help group and then a newsletter after writing a letter to the *Guardian* seeking others with the condition. Her article for *Spare Rib*, called 'Endometriosis: A Monthly Cycle of Problems', was a boldly synthesised description of the physical details of the malady with an unstinting description of the pain of 'debilitating abdominal cramps'.

But the crux of the community of disclosure, and the focus on female bodily discomfort and vulnerability, lived in the letters pages, where women sought not just to explore the feeling of politicising what had, just a decade before, been unspeakable detail about their private parts, but solidarity with other women and, quite often, information about conditions that the medical establishment had not answered. The detail was unstinting, even by today's standards, redolent of a juggernaut being released. 'Just over a year ago I had a wart – just inside the lips of my vagina . . .', wrote one woman in the *Spare Rib* letters pages in March 1982. A reader with an 'incorrect womb' told how she had been 'offered an operation to "correct" a retroverted uterus, mainly because 'for years I have suffered from fairly frequent stabbing pains during intercourse'. The procedure was elucidated in forensic detail, involving: 'lifting the uterus to a normal position and securing it with permanent sutures . . . leaving what the doctors describe as "a small scar below the bikini line".' This woman had failed to find the information she was looking for and now wanted 'the experiences and views' of 'any other women who have had this operation'. Another reader from Lancashire told how after starting to use the cap, she experienced secretions, inflammation and itchiness on removal, with 'pieces of skin discharged . . . I don't seem able to find the cause.'

In sum, women in the 1970s, emerging from the dark ages of discourse and knowledge about their bodies, a darkness with serious ramifications for their health and safety, were exploring and exploiting vital new terrain. This bit of historical context is vital for showing that there is a thin and complex line between wallowing and feminism – until very recently, the wallowing was indistinguishable, an essential part even, of the feminism. Women had to get real about their pain as well as their pleasure because the curtains had been drawn for way too long. Some over-compensation was part of that process and I am grateful to my foremothers for trying to create a world in which I can explain without shame or embarrassment what ails me to any medical professional – or friend, or indeed my mother (and even the occasional man).

## *I Am My Pain!*

### *How the politics of misery went from necessary to excessive*

But today, something different is going on in what we might loosely call the feminist left. There are some traces of the traditions of the women's liberation movement, but the general trend has morphed. On one hand, of course, there is more celebration of women's private parts and capacities than ever before. *The Vagina Monologues*, Eve Ensler's hit monologue from 1996 that still tours the world, was a shocking, exciting bolt from the blue. But now, TV and film regularly explores female sexual experience and sexuality. There is widespread and frank discussion of female orgasms from adolescence to post-menopause, and the word 'vulva' is known and used by little girls now, who understand the difference from 'vagina', another word they use easily. Neither of which was the case when I was little.[7]

But the flip side of this militant demystification of the female body has been something less freeing and celebratory: a new discourse of horizon-limiting victimology. It's as if to be a woman is inevitably to be a vehicle of pain and shame, with embodiment a vale of tears – and no positive side. But there is a positive side, such as the one explored in Marina Gerner's 2024 book *The Vagina Business* – it's just that it's not a trendy one, because it's a bit Sheryl Sandberg, a bit 'lean in'. Gerner, a young financial journalist, interviewed people who are innovating, researching and selling improvements in women's health, not narrating misery. The subtitle of her book is *The Innovative Breakthroughs That Could Change*

*Everything in Women's Health* and, as she explained in an interview, she hopes the book will empower readers while sparking more research and innovation in women's health.[8] I hope she succeeds.

By contrast, tapping the zeitgeist with their admirably sharp antennae, high profile women have used their platforms not to focus on breakthroughs, or girls in chess, or chemistry, or otherwise track girls' relative absence from physics and engineering, but to intensely focus on disorders of women's reproductive organs. Beautiful young women post on Instagram, in a maudlin but proprietary fashion, about 'my endo'; a popular French Instagram account goes by the handle @balance_ton_endo, where women share stories of their suffering. Davina McCall, Gwyneth Paltrow, Michelle Obama and Oprah have talked publicly about their experiences of menopause. McCall has presented several television programmes about menopause, while she and Lorraine Kelly put their faces to a campaign by the Menopause Charity, featuring posters headed: 'Lost your mind?', 'Lost your job?', 'Lost your strength?' and 'Lost your sex drive?' I'm all for making women more informed and less scared, feeling less like they're going mad and less alone, but must the campaign be quite so apocalyptic, quite so sure that there is empowerment in women thinking of themselves in such devastating terms, even when experiencing severe symptoms? Yet such an approach seems almost reflexive now, entirely in step with a broader move to focus on totalising emotional grievance, as much as on information and help.

It's good to have easy, stigma-free access to appropriate guidance on likely timescales of symptoms, and the ups and downs of HRT. But rather than benefitting from a new era of openness and medical interest, women are under pressure to succumb to the gloomy picture offered by the hashtags. For all our actual freedoms and openness about our capacity for sexual pleasure, we hear more about how we are ill-used and suffer. How we are victims of seemingly endless, painful diseases, from polycystic ovaries to endometriosis to adenomyosis to the gruelling difficulties of menopause and menstruation. There is much about women's sexual numbness, anorgasmia, libido challenges, vaginal dryness and anal damage following sex not really suited to our more delicate back passages. All of it is good to know about. But they doesn't the female experience make.

There are prominent stories of breast cancer, ovarian cancer and cervical cancer – I, like most people, have remained haunted by the brave and tragic young 'cancer babes' – Dame Deborah James and Sarah Harding (James was felled by bowel cancer; Harding by breast). I am not being glib when I say that it sometimes feels as if it's amazing that any woman remains alive past the age of fifty. And while there are way too many terrible stories of cancer affecting younger women (and men), with major scientific studies now focusing on the causes of this unsettling change, it cannot be the case that we are all doomed, and especially doomed as women. But the first-person stories of women being diagnosed with cancer, often shockingly advanced, are numerous and they are addictive; some prestigious news outlets publish one nearly daily. With the strange stalking of cancer so ambient in the cultural airwaves, a new type of fraudster has been spawned: the young women trying to get famous and rich by claiming to have cured her non-existent cancer through lifestyle. The most famous of these is Belle Gibson, the Australian woman behind the app The Whole Pantry, and the subject of Netflix's ghoulishly gripping docudrama *Apple Cider Vinegar*.

Then there is infertility, about which there is endless 'news', accounts of woe from those who have suffered, and warnings from medical professionals and politicians who seem to think women aren't aware of the fact that at some point in their early forties, their fertility options will dwindle substantially. The 'biological clock' is the 'neoliberalism' of women's medicine: the single most harmful piece of misused and under-studied science out there.

Those who ratchet up the stress about having babies in time say it is for women's own good – but they are being dishonest about the real issue, which is not that twenty-year-olds think they have all the time in the world, an idea that by thirty many of them are socialised out of, even though at that point they still have a decade or more at their disposal. Rather, it's the lack of understanding of reproduction, and how surprising and flexible it is, and how the statistics are manipulated into terror for those who may have perfectly good reasons for waiting.

When it comes to terrifying women about clocks and 'starting families', the maternity-obsessed right of course takes the lead – but issues with reproduction, especially those caused by underlying medical conditions, the pain, and painful expense of, assisted reproduction and the grisly experience of miscarriage (at whatever age) dominates progressive coverage of the 'biological clock'.

Much IVF angst, whether progressive or from the trad wife, nature-is-king view, is inflected with unease about marketised systems for helping women conceive. This discomfort and disapproval reaches its apotheosis in the consensus on both left and right that surrogacy is a grave sin – a clear form of exploitation of the utmost perversity. From progressives, there is actually something rather paternalistic in this, as well as contradictory. Whatever happened to women's right to bodily autonomy, including to sell our bodies in sex work (of which more later)? So often it seems as if anything related to reproductive freedom and technology for women gets turned automatically into something circular and bleak, a habit of mind bolstered by a growing body of scholarship.[9]

## *The Great Motherhood Whinge*

If they disapprove of the mixture of market, medicine and making babies, then the progressive literati love to expose postpartum depression and regret – it's become voguish to suggest that women may be psychologically dashed, permanently, by having children, and critics love a book that exposes the horrors of motherhood, especially new motherhood. The British author Rachel Cusk was a pioneer of this genre, with *A Life's Work*, which was an 'honest' account of the frequent hell of being the mother of two young daughters. Though this is child's play, as it were, next to the burgeoning obsession with 'matrescence', which is the transformation of women into mothers, via pregnancy and post-natal hormonal surges. There was Israeli sociologist Orna Donath's study, *Regretting Motherhood*, but more recently, there is the mix of memoir and science writing by Lucy Jones that became her much-buzzed book *Matrescence*, which brings together all the pet themes of those who chronicle womanhood today: especially the alleged neglect of and disinterest in the experience of new motherhood. I find this a profoundly odd perspective. From the perspective of other people, becoming a mother seems to be the single biggest and most fascinating thing I have ever done, garnering far more interest than my somewhat unexpected detour into academia and getting a PhD. But this book is about the true horror and hardship of things wrongly billed as joyful. Jones's work is strong and detailed, but what reviewers picked up on with glee, given a helping hand by the publisher, is the nefarious work of the 'systems' of patriarchy and capitalism in it all. 'Jones reveals the dangerous consequences of our neglect of the maternal experience and interrogates the patriarchal and capitalist systems that have created the untenable situation mothers face today,' its blurb states. Eh? The genre is wide-ranging and buzzing, from ex-Tory MP Theo Clarke's memoir about birth trauma to the hit American podcast

*Spread the Jelly*, from two hipster, newish moms of around my age, which is praised for its 'radical honesty' but which, if it was new twenty years ago for things like giving birth, really, really isn't new now. But we keep hearing that it is and that we need ever more of it.

Turning the downsides of motherhood into a career is a smart move; there are just so many things to complain about. In 2023, *The Nursery* was published, a novel about post-natal depression that was hailed by critics in the *New York Times* and *Atlantic* as shedding much-needed light on the bad sides of having a baby. Even the review presents motherhood in an exclusively negative light, as if we all agree. 'If motherhood brings with it the burden of our projected hopes, new mothers are especially hemmed in by wishful imagery, presumed to be ecstatically bonding with their just-emerged infants as they suckle at milk-filled breasts, everything smelling sweetly of baby powder.' Too often, the critic reminds us, 'the phenomenon of postpartum depression, for instance, a condition that affects 10 to 15 per cent of women, has been given short shrift in literature and other genres when not ignored entirely.' So women crucify themselves to get pregnant through exploitative medicine, and then once they have the babies, they're meant to be honest about how unremittingly awful and unfair the whole motherhood thing is. The construct of woman, on both the right and progressive left, is now very much seen as a lose–lose.

The gory register of bodily description is a key part of the 'radical honesty' motherhood memoir. The bestselling author Leslie Jamison's somewhat over-wrought memoir *Splinters* (2024), about the toll taken on her mind and body – and above all, her marriage, which implodes – of having a baby daughter, is unstinting in its detail about the physical aspects of motherhood, from leaking nipples to the blood clot 'the size of a small avocado, jiggling like jelly' that fell out of her on a bathroom trip shortly after her emergency c-section. If some reviewers tired of her relentless self-portrait as victim, despite her glitzy career as a famous writer and Brooklyn-based creative writing instructor, they also commended how she was 'Giving language to fundamental experiences of love, grief, and parenthood all too often skirted past.'[10] There it is again! The conspiracy of silence about stuff that we cannot stop talking about.

I can't help but compare all these to Margaret Drabble's beautiful first novel, *The Millstone* (1965), about a lonely, unsupported pregnancy with a first and unplanned child – and the searing bond and joy that the child, who is born ill, brings her young mother. It's too innocent for today's literary landscape; its straightforward gentleness and love would be viewed with suspicion. An edgier motherhood mosaic that interweaves politics and history is Marilyn French's novel *The Women's Room* about suburban housewives and mothers who go back to university in their late thirties and discover feminist politics. There is plenty in that book about the suffering and loneliness of new young mothers, but most of that is caused by the hostility and absence of bland and checked-out husbands. Once the women get used to their children, they become sources of intense joy, of course mixed with stress, sadness and anger. But we all know this; if we aren't mothers ourselves, most of us had one.

For young women in particular, social media has amplified negative force fields, from glamourising eating disorders and promoting under-achievement to the complex of trends that provoked the gender crisis. There is plenty of energy now expended on combatting the effects of such dangerous material. But much of it manifests in a drive to create still more and more 'space' for tales of emotional woe. The goal is to furnish young women with a politics of complaint and disempowerment.

I find this a sallow, weak echo of the transformative practice of consciousness raising of half a century ago. Selfies, Instagram pouts, 'what I eat in a day' and 'get ready with me' TikToks are all fine in moderation, but they're a quick slide down into a solipsistic rabbit hole that blots out real-world offers and opportunities, and even the will to consider or pursue agendas more interesting and fruitful than simply bodies and biology are everything or nothing.

Girls and women need to be sold on the promise that each person carries within their own person. The basic girl package is a brain, ingenuity and the ability to prosper and progress and create, and to carve out an exciting future. We don't need corny slogans, such as those Michelle Obama and other prominent merchants of saleable girl power manufacture for mugs and bags such as 'there is no limit to what we as women can accomplish'. We need challenge. Expectation. We need to learn, and teach, about real things that offer a taste for real freedom, the kind that goes beyond the bodies under our noses into the nurturance of our intellectual or manual capacities. In other words, we need 'flow', the term coined by Hungarian psychologist Mihaly Robert Csikszentmihalyi, which is a highly focused mental state conducive to productivity, and one that is considered the surest of all ways to promote thriving.

## *Fear*

### *Reversing the narrative*

So far we have seen how the feminist left seeks to reverse female bodily shame through a forensic approach to female embodiment that can tend to the negative, miserable and disempowering. We've also seen how the left's broad-spectrum dislike of 'neoliberalism' often entails the presentation of women as fundamentally objectified and preyed upon, due to the operation of the 'system' in its many guises, especially capitalism and patriarchy.

The umbrella problem that emerges from these ways of thinking is fear. Fear of violence, fear of objectification and fear of advantage-taking and trauma. Which translates into the sense that to be a girl or a woman now is both to be very afraid and very angry, to be wise to, but physically ill-equipped to fight the dangers surrounding us and the panoramic injustice.

In this debilitating scheme, all men are dangerous to women because of patriarchy. Women are dangerous to themselves, and to other women, because of patriarchy and capitalism.

If we are to boil down the substance of these fears, then the very important number one issue is male violence. In the polarised debate about how to deal with this nasty facet of masculinity, right-wingers see the bogeyman not just in the actions of male aggressors, but in the apparent reign of slut-loving, skimpy-top-wearing, hard-drinking 'liberal feminism'.[11]

In Louise Perry's estimation, the central principle of liberal feminism, is that a woman should be able to do anything she likes, including 'selling sex or inviting consensual sexual violence'.[12] Why shouldn't she do these things? Because, implies Perry, she's asking for rape and sexual coercion. 'Few liberal feminists,' continues Perry, 'are willing to draw the link between the culture of sexual hedonism they promote and the anxieties over campus rape that have emerged at exactly the same time'. And then these fools go one worse. In their haste to rebut the old canard that women in scanty outfits are 'asking for it', they insist the real solution is to 'teach men not to rape'.

But this can't possibly work because the 'horny men [they are alone with] are bigger and stronger ... and likely to have been raised on the kind of porn that normalises aggression, coercion and pain'.[13] Women can only protect themselves, she suggests, through being very afraid or suspicious or both, of the unchaperoned, boozed-up man – and acting accordingly. I find this sort of argument very dispiriting, and strangely unseeing, perhaps even cynical. Because we know that women in more segregated, anti-booze societies, which enforce modest dress on women, also end up being prey to violent sexual crime, a phenomenon to which I will return in Chapter Seven.

It's true of course that men tend to be bigger and stronger than women and are likely to have consumed more porn. And it's true that the best way to stop the kind of men who rape from doing so probably isn't trying to 'teach' them gently. But the answer isn't making women terrified or finger wagging, or telling them to 'get real', what did they expect and so on. It's to embolden and empower them, as literally as possible.

## *Deterrence*

So why don't we focus on, or at least contemplate, deterrence? Wouldn't this be the more literally empowering, and fairer, course of action? Surely it is men who ought to feel fearful of raping or being violent or coercive in any way that is not explicitly requested and actively consented to; it is men who ought to quake at the consequences of law and public shame. Fixing the former may simply be too much for our severely compromised justice system, and intimate crimes are notoriously difficult to punish. But there is another thing men might learn to fear: women themselves. Not everything comes down to strength and size. If that was the case there would be no female police officers capable of arresting hardened male criminals – and plenty do. I know two female crime-fighters, one British, one based in the Bronx. Both are extremely slim but strong. They're fearless even when facing huge drug-addled gangsters, which is the American one's bread and butter. This is a matter of a few weeks' training and unshowy confidence. I love riding the subway with the Bronx friend; I feel so protected.

When the MeToo movement began, I was a frequent guest on radio and TV to share my controversial view that the movement was not wholly positive. I thought it risked overdoing women's sense of danger and victimhood, without offering them anything stronger or more immediate than registering complaints later or public shaming on X. After all, for those without sympathetic audiences or bosses, the ability to respond decisively in the moment is even more important. And it's the same for the young women on campus who are alone with drunk and horny men.

And it's the same for someone like me. I have mercifully never been sexually attacked in any way by any of the hundreds of men of all types that I have been in close and unsupervised quarters with, but I feel uneasy walking home from the Tube late at night past piles of rubbish, dodgy side streets and men, only ever men, hanging around singly and in groups giving off sketchy airs. I am completely at an attacker's mercy, just like the college student at an ill-starred frat party, because I have absolutely no knowledge of how to defend myself. I am no threat to a would-be attacker whatsoever. He need fear nothing: he can assume immediate capitulation in the absence of other ideas.

But I have often thought about how good it would be for all girls and women, like me, to go through mandatory martial arts training tailored specifically to attacks from men, including knowing the perfect way to disable male genitalia which are, for all men's aggression, astonishingly delicate and exposed. It is so beautifully simple: if attackers thought there was a decent chance that a victim would go straight for his privates, I think we would see that what women wear and how much they drink and how sexily they parade in front of men would be far less of a problem. It would also be more effective than just waiting for men to learn the error of their ways. The types that attack women probably never will.

As I went around making these points, I garnered incredulous disapproval and dismissive snorts. That's because, in the mode of passive complaint favoured by progressive women, it is important never to do something that is not 'your job', especially that which counts as 'emotional labour'. Even just explaining something to someone else counts as not your 'job'. This was the inglorious, unhelpful nub of Reni Eddo-Lodge's book for the ages *Why I Am No Longer Talking to White People About Race*, which was an instant bestseller and reading-list stalwart.

But this is clearly unhelpful: it's not technically anyone's 'job' to do anything they aren't paid for, apart from ensure the children they create are cared for. And, as Perry rightly points out, the current state of play still allows too many women to be taken advantage of by brute force. So while it may not be our 'job' to stop men from being inclined to attack or ill-treat women, it would certainly be a useful and long-term service to womankind to do so. Also underlying the 'it's not our job' argument seems to lurk the assumption that it is somehow unnatural to ask women to respond violently to violence, that arming us with the skills to be scary is a joke of an ask. But why? Because it's not ladylike? Because, as a strong faction of the women's liberation movement protesting against nuclear armament also saw it, it's not how women, with all our earthy caring and mothering, do things? Because it's sinking to men's level?

This view unites people calling themselves feminists across the political spectrum, but it's still a learned perspective rooted in long-held beliefs about culture, not some 'natural' truth that inheres in women's softer (though far better protected) bodies and their capacity for motherhood. Indeed, as we saw in Chapter One, studies of the animal kingdom show that female aggression is real and in some cases more pronounced than in the male. In human females, there is plenty of aggression, and of course equal if not superior capacities for physical coordination and skill, that could be harnessed into making men think twice and thrice before trying their hand.

While the US and Israel have women in serious combat roles, there are fearsome female armies that make it even clearer that the old 'size and strength' argument is massively overweighted when it comes to self-defence. We know of several intriguing historical examples, from the eighteenth century all-women elite corps, the Dahomey of Benin, to the Nzinga of Angola who fought the Portuguese. More recently, we have seen women tank crews fighting against Hamas terrorists in Israel and dropping stealth bombs on Iran's nuclear facilities, an all-female elite combat unit in Norway, and the first British woman to pass the gruelling elite fighting course, the All Arms Pre-Parachute Selection, who concluded of her positive experience that women should be looking at the military as a career. Since 2011 there have been all-female and mixed Kurdish militias known as the Women's Protection Units (YPJ); by 2017 the YPJ had 24,000 members, a third of Britain's total professional soldiery. These militias build on the ideology of the Kurdistan Workers' Party (PKK), which is based in the writings of Abdullah Öcalan, who insisted that women must be liberated, with an equal stake in running and fighting for the revolution. The PKK (admittedly not the political orientation I would naturally tend to) established the first all-female guerrilla units in 1995.[14]

We are a long way from all that in the sticky student bars of Anglosphere universities and so we should be. But their example suggests that it is a choice, not a necessity, to emphasise women's physical vulnerabilities. In a world in which there are brave all-women Kurdish militias fighting Isis, we should be teaching girls and women – as I plan to do with my own daughter – that they are a force to be reckoned with, mentally as well as physically. Not a single woman need see herself as a passive victim, frightenable into submission by big scary men because of physical stature. Sure, some men are just too big and scary to beat, as they are to other men. But for the vast majority, a good first step is a confident blast of verbal fury and confident hostility, a mixture of glares and furious admonitions.

If that doesn't work, it can't be beyond our capabilities to learn how to plant a well-placed kick or punch or even bite to the groin.

And why can't we go even further than this? To disentangle, to punch, to headlock, to eye-poke? An article on a Krav Maga official website, called 'Do women stand a chance against men in a real fight?', states: 'A female fighter who dominates proper technique and remains calm and in control of herself, can overpower a larger and stronger male.'[15]

It's not that we want to have to do this. On the contrary. The socialisation has been so effective I actually can't even imagine pulling off a well-executed Krav Maga move in the heat of the moment, when my reflex is to freeze and feel mental paralysis. But such customs and habits of mind, body and society can change quickly. Knowing how to defend and attack, and men knowing we can, would be a huge deal for our sense of confidence, agency and freedom, all around the world.

The roots of this idea are, in fact, hundreds of years old. In her *A Vindication of the Rights of Woman* (1792), Mary Wollstonecraft, while frankly admitting to men's superior physical strength, attacked the way this one difference was magnified into a whole system that weakened women – and in which women, keen to curry male adoration through the appearance of delicacy and helplessness, were complicit. 'I earnestly wish to point out in what true dignity and human happiness consists . . . I wish to persuade women to endeavour to acquire strength, both of mind and body, and to convince them that the soft phrases, susceptibility of heart, delicacy of sentiment, and refinement of taste, are almost synonymous with epithets of weakness, and that those beings who are only the objects of pity and that kind of love, which has been termed its sister, will soon become objects of contempt,' she wrote.

The update I propose is that we don't victim-blame women *and* that we also recognise that narratives of weakness enhance a feeling of victimhood, resulting in more victimisation. We all have the choice and ability to push back.

GOOD SLUT

## *'All Women Live in Sexual Objectification the Way Fish Live in Water'*

It will be hard for women not to feel fearful if we retain the belief that we are still widely viewed as sexual objects rather than as full humans, and that each of these are totalising, permanent states. It was the American legal scholar and feminist theorist Catharine MacKinnon who coined the 'fish in water' term for her theory that this total objectification of women shapes all human activity and experience.

There are plenty of examples of how this long-armed idea can play out. For instance, in 2021, Britain was shaken by a school sex scandal, which reinforced the widespread assertion that we live in 'rape culture'. Over 15,000 allegations were made against boys at schools across the country on an anonymous online forum. The allegations included non-consensual sharing of nude photos and instances of assault: all disgusting and requiring punishment. Soma Sara, the founder of the Everyone's Invited website – the forum in which many of the allegations were made – took a clear lesson from these incidents: The website, she wrote, is documenting a 'universal problem – it's everywhere, in all schools, all universities and all of society.'[16]

'All of society' gives a flavour of the kind of lazy political thinking that is holding girls and women back. Clearly there have been severe and disturbing problems at schools and on campuses. Indeed Netflix's *Adolescence*, about a very online teenage boy suspected of the murder of a female classmate, was revered, even in Parliament, as the social document for our times. There were heated discussions around whether to show it in schools as an educational piece.

Flashpoints like these have caused my friends and I to reflect on our own experiences of school. And they feel as if they belong to a completely different universe. In the late 1990s, for the last two years of school, I was at an independent, mostly-boarding school in

Hampshire. I spoke to old classmates about that time. We remember hankering after, and sometimes dating or hooking up with, boys. But being sexually harassed or made afraid of them? Not a single one of us remembers anything like that. If anything, the boys were scared of us.

Not only have I searched my memory, I've also been re-reading my diaries from back then, and they're packed with a kind of boy-related anger and misery that must seem strange and possibly offensive to the likes of Soma Sara. I was angry not because I was receiving unwanted sexual attention, but because I was getting none at all. Is it possible my friends and I are in denial about what we experienced? I don't think so, though memory is selective. It's not that boys in the 1990s were kinder and gentler; I'm sure you could go back and dig up plenty of things that would be deemed truly unacceptable by today's standards that were hushed up then.

Of course there's social media now, which renders gender dynamics in brutal, harsh technicolour. But the major difference between now and then, I think, is only partly the presence of social media and influencers like Andrew Tate. The bigger thing is that thresholds for fear have changed, and with them the sense of what is manageable and unmanageable, what counts as the cut and thrust of life versus what is the rankly 'not ok'. What's changed is a fevered awareness, drummed into children now through sex education and other resources, of danger lurking in all sexual advances, especially the unexpected or unwanted.

What of the universal access to extreme porn? The extent to which this leads to real-life objectification is unclear. Time and again research is inconclusive on the correlation between porn and sexual violence. In 2020, a major American study, published in the journal *Trauma, Violence and Abuse*, concluded that policymakers should look for 'other' causes of sexual violence, since research collected since the 1970s suggests there is no correlation at all for non-violent pornography and only 'weak' correlation, unverifiable, with the consumption of violent pornography, which might reflect the already-violent predilections of the watchers.[17]

## *Objectification Theory*

Catherine MacKinnon's arguments in the 1980s about sexual objectification being in the drinking water, made along with fellow anti-porn warrior Andrea Dworkin, were important and powerful. They arose during a decade in which the feminist 'porn wars' had exploded alongside the bulletin board messaging services of the early internet, which opened vast new horizons for pornography makers and consumers. Generally, the 1980s were far more inflected with both rank and respectable forms of misogyny, and far closer to the long epoch in which such brazen sexism underlay the very rule of law and religion.

To MacKinnon and Dworkin, men's consumption of pornography consolidated an entire system in which men, as a group, are objectifiers and women the objectified, despite some individual exceptions.[18]

Objectification had been theorised by Immanuel Kant in the 1790s as a degrading consequence of non-marital sex, in which 'the loved person [is made] an Object of appetite; as soon as that appetite has been stilled, the person is cast aside as one casts away a lemon which has been sucked dry.'[19] Two centuries later, feminists including MacKinnon, Dworkin, as well as Susan Bordo and Sandra Bartky drew on Kant's theory, but widened it into a totalising phenomenon, inseparable from patriarchy rather than being a byword for unromantic intercourse.

Some tried to contain this sprawling term. In 1995, feminist philosopher Martha Nussbaum offered an influential seven-point definition of objectification: the treatment of a person as a tool or means to an end; denial of a person's autonomy; the assumption of inertness as if the person were lacking in agency; the treatment of a person as interchangeable with other objects; the treatment of a person as lacking in boundary-integrity; treating someone as if they can be owned, bought or sold; and finally, the denial of objectivity, as if a person's experiences and feelings (if any) need not be taken into account.

As for what the demon of objectification entailed outside Nussbaum's neat list, it remains a snagging mess of the forces at play in making a world in which some women feel they have no choice but to work for their own destruction as porn actresses, and in which women evolve their own need to be seen as objects for validation ('self-objectification theory'). Simone de Beauvoir described this process as narcissism – becoming a woman 'consists in the setting up of the ego as a double "stranger"' . . . The adolescent girl 'becomes an object and she sees herself as an object'.[20]

The implication that women are forced into complicity with a system that always looks at them as sex objects is complex. Here art theorist John Berger's thoughtful elucidation of the male gaze and how it is felt and courted by women is helpful in showing how objectification isn't some obvious crude evil, but rather baked into many forms of interpersonal assessment. In *Ways of Seeing*, he argues that the woman constantly imagines and surveys herself, splitting herself between the surveyor and the surveyed. Her self-value is therefore measured through the way she appears: how she is portrayed in her own eyes, in others' eyes and more specifically in men's eyes. In Berger's estimation, men survey women before they relate to them in order to determine their proper relation to them. And since women know this, their actions and appearance are indications of the manner in which they would like to be treated.

This is why so many women recognise the weird sense of feeling obliged to have sex with someone they are not attracted to or don't want to sleep with simply because the man wants and expects it, and it's more effort to swim against this than with it.

What's interesting is the way this having sex out of 'politeness' or simply the desire to know you are wanted, is, in the progressive interpretation, a sure sign of patriarchy. It must be objectification, exploitation, subtle coercion. Except sometimes it's just . . . bad sex, sex for validation or sex for any number of other 'unhealthy' reasons. I've done it out of politeness sometimes, sometimes out of grim curiosity and many times to make sure I was still able to attract someone. This made it mediocre, but not dangerous, traumatic or exploitative.

Of course the line between bad sex and coercive or abusive sex can be very unclear, whatever your lens. MeToo was, in part, about redressing the wrongs against those women told that the sometimes very bad things they experienced were nothing. The timing, therefore, of the viral *New Yorker* essay 'Cat Person' was knife-edged: December 2017, three months after the MeToo dam broke. It was a delicious, fascinating, gripping read about something so banal and yet so utterly familiar for women. It tells the story of Margot, a second-year undergraduate who is chatted up by Robert, a thirty-four-year-old man, at the movie theatre where she works. After he asks for her number, they strike up a text relationship full of wit and chemistry. A real-life date eventually follows, which proves a different kettle of fish: lacklustre, awkward, culminating in sex Margot really does not want by now, but which she decides to have because to craft a refusal would involve too much energy and be even more awkward. She then essentially ghosts him, eventually sending a breakup text written by her friend, later runs into him at a party, avoids him and then, by the end of the night, ends up on the receiving end of ever-more jealous messages from him culminating in the word: 'whore'.

Roupenian's descriptions of the sexual encounter with Robert are lusciously spot-on; they were an anthem for the age. 'He kissed her then, on the lips, for real; he came for her in a kind of lunging motion and practically poured his tongue down her throat. It was a terrible kiss, shockingly bad; Margot had trouble believing that a grown man could possibly be so bad at kissing.'

Straddling him later in the car, she 'could feel the small log of his erection straining against his pants. Whenever it rolled beneath her weight, he let out these fluttery, high-pitched moans that she couldn't help feeling were a little melodramatic.' Such moments lay the groundwork for the big one, the one that launched this essay all around the world, for years to come. It was in these lines that what appears to be very definitely bad sex, done for the wrong but relatable reasons, got taken up as a precise anatomisation of how the sexual exploitation of women takes place in consensual everyday situations due to society's failing to have a nuanced language of consent, and 'by revealing the lengths women go to in order to manage men's feelings, and the shaming they often suffer nonetheless,' as Olga Khazan wrote in the *Atlantic*.

I'm going to repeat the lines here partly as they are still so delightfully on-message, nearly ten years later. But also as they perfectly encapsulate the register in which most non-optimum sex takes place. Robert has just taken down his trousers but forgotten about his shoes, a sight which makes Margot 'recoil'. But

> the thought of what it would take to stop what she had set in motion was overwhelming; it would require an amount of tact and gentleness that she felt was impossible to summon. It wasn't that she was scared he would try to force her to do something against her will but that insisting that they stop now, after everything she'd done to push this forward, would make her seem spoiled and capricious, as if she'd ordered something at a restaurant and then, once the food arrived, had changed her mind and sent it back.

The desire not to seem 'spoiled and capricious' is so well observed, and could end there as a relatable point, about one of the categories of crap sex women participate in. But 'Cat Person' got swept into MeToo's cascade of material about the experience of objectification, as so many ordinary experiences have since been swept into an overarching cultural politics that puts as much as possible in the grammar of trauma. This tsunami raised awareness of what had for too long been seen as just the way things are (or not seen at all) – and it also expanded and made more vivid the domain of terror in which women as a group have historically been treated on streets, in sheets and in workplaces.

I did not doubt what women were saying; far from it. Much of it horrified me. The scale of the problem was grotesque. All the same, I found quite a bit of the discourse that emerged irritating, almost showy. When young, beautiful women working in elite jobs in government, law and consultancy began to go public about this or that powerful man who couldn't help but send smutty texts, or touch a knee, make gross jokes or ask for dates, with the result that oops, these women were forced to speak up and nearly bring down the government or corporation, I thought: huh, there are quite a few women who might either shrug that stuff off while barely noticing it, or enjoy, yes, enjoy, it as proof of being attractive.

## *'Longing for the Male Gaze'*

It became laborious and exposing to say, after MeToo, that a lot of women want two things at the same time: one, not to feel menaced or insulted, and two, that we also enjoy looking attractive, usually though not always for men. And that when that feedback loop works, it involves things like unexpected advances and flirtatious behaviour.

So yes; there is a tension here. Most of us would rather look hot and risk the bad objectification to get the good kind. I'm going to go a bit further with the obvious but gauche observation that women and men, but particularly women, have much to gain from being hot. The sociologist Catherine Hakim is an unusual-seeming lady when you meet her. But her book *Money Honey* captured something taboo but true.[21] Hot women earn more in all fields.

Hakim's argument overall was regarded as rather peculiar, because it seemed both feminist and anti-feminist in an awkward, unexplored way. But she was right about the way that sex appeal is used by a great number of people who can lay their hands on it. 'Today, the financial returns of attractiveness equal the returns of qualifications,' she wrote. 'Many young women now think beauty is just as important as education. . . These people smile at the world and find that the world smiles back and remembers them.'[22] Creepy, maybe, but not entirely off the mark – both men and women earn on average 26 per cent more if they're good looking, and there appears to be an 'attractiveness premium' for women, almost entirely achievable by vigorous grooming.[23]

A year after Nottinghamshire became the first police force to criminalise wolf-whistling under banner of street harassment, a 2017 YouGov poll showed that women and men held almost equal views about wolf-whistling – about 56 per cent of both thought it was harmless fun – and the older the women, the keener on it they were. The poll had followed an interview with Eve Pollard, ex-*Mirror* editor (and mother of BBC presenter Claudia Winkelman), who, at seventy-one, bemoaned the fact that she would never be gawped at 'with a hint of lust again [because] of course, like most women over 50 I know, I am invisible.'[24] And that is not something they enjoy being. Confronted with story after story about yet another encounter, exchange, or meeting ending in inappropriate attention or a sexual proposition, these less sexually visible women can feel downtrodden by the current dominance of a vaunted parade of endless, unwanted lewdness.

Women who are plain, overweight, older, disabled, or endowed with some other attribute that many men consider undesirable may struggle to find sexual attention at all. And yet, women's libidos are, as in-depth studies have shown, omnivorous and female sexual frustration is real. The nagging misery of women who struggle to find suitable men to date or have sex with is therefore also real.

There was a moving piece in *The New York Times* in 2016 titled 'Longing for the Male Gaze' by Jennifer Bartlett, who has cerebral palsy with some impairment to her gait and speech. Bartlett wrote that being looked at in a sexual way was alien to her. She had never been harassed in college or at work. And on the street and in bars, having attracted pity, anxiety or avoidance, she would much prefer to be stared at with desire: 'Am I blessed to be sexually invisible and given a reprieve from something that has troubled women for centuries? It certainly does not *feel* that way . . . I *like* it when men look at me,' she concluded. 'It feels empowering. Frankly, it makes me feel like I'm not being excluded.'

To women like Barlett, the 'boohoo, everywhere I go men can't help but lust after me' genre must be excruciating. Consider *Sex Object: A Memoir,* by Jessica Valenti, a New York-based journalist and, according to the *Guardian*, 'one of the country's best-known feminists'. Valenti is a very attractive, prosperous woman with a lot of confidence and the kind of career a lot of women (and men) would kill for. She has also, she says, garnered incessant unwanted male attention on the streets of New York and wrote a memoir about it, and its effect on her, along with the usual call for change (MeToo, which exploded a year later, would answer that call).[25]

Valenti's introduction encapsulates what is going wrong for women in progressive orthodoxy. The moral of a recollection from high school is that women and girls don't have much agency or independence of mind or sense of self. Once she experiences objectification, suggests Valenti, a girl will likely go on to conclude that she is indeed no better than an object, which then reduces her sense of worth and potential. But this is so depressing. Does the 'narrative' really determine all?

Mary Wollstonecraft understood that it need not. She forcefully urged women (and men) to think outside limiting gender narratives. She raged at Jean-Jacques Rousseau for his indulgence in 'stories' about feminine traits and predilections, berating him for not seeing how self-perpetuating such narratives are. 'I will venture to affirm, that a girl, whose spirits have not been damped by inactivity, or innocence tainted by false shame, will always be a romp, and the doll will never excite attention unless confinement allows her no alternative,' she says to his circular conviction that because girls play with dolls they are born to play with dolls.[26]

In the face of our self-obsessed treatises about how terrible everything is, how predatory and scary the streets are, Wollstonecraft would probably say: take action, and don't be defined by the narrative of being a sitting duck.

Talk about those narratives. One reviewer of Valenti's book was Andi Zeisler, founder of Bitch Media, a now-shuttered non-profit feminist organisation based in Portland, who startled me by appealing to what she assumed was a universal experience, except I didn't recognise it. Being almost summertime it was 'time once again for many women and girls, particularly in big cities, to craft their journeys to work or school into tactical missions, planning out routes and schedules in order to avoid the hisses, grunts and catcalls that seem to multiply exponentially whenever women and girls dare to walk down the street in sundresses, shorts and halter tops ... There is an ocean of difference between being admired and being objectified,' Zeisler continues primly, 'but western culture has been unparalleled in conflating the two for fun and profit.'[27] Zeisler is a slim, attractive brunette; her experiences may be unpleasant to her, but many women who are overweight, older, handicapped or otherwise deemed sexually invisible would find their patience wearing thin at the idea that their 'sundresses' drove men wild.

The thing is, the insatiable, savage and ubiquitous liberty-taking, insulting and sexual intimidation of women on city streets was completely the way things were, in the lifeblood of any city, and par for the course right into the 1980s. I have read accounts in magazines in the 1970s and 1980s that tell, in a matter-of-fact way, of a genuine endless nightmare of predation, menace, misogyny and insult. At home, wife-beating when drunk was entirely normalised into the 1970s, while disgusting treatment on streets was commonplace and made women think twice about their routes, the timing of it, and light sources.

But the welter of discourse thrown up by the MeToo period and its immediate predecessors made it seem like things have got worse. It's always hard to get the balance right between a legitimate movement of complaint and fight-back and acknowledgement of improvement and gains. Nobody much tries, understandably, as taking stock or perspective can seem like giving ground or minimising. But damage is done when the movement story – that objectification and predation are ubiquitous and a source of righteous outrage constantly – inhibits rather than bolsters confidence, colouring the world in darker hues than is necessary. When they ossify into stereotypes about 'men' and 'women', it becomes even harder to escape. Indeed, it is a matter of methodological doctrine in the social and psychological sciences that stereotypes profoundly influence what people do.[28] In that, Valenti makes a good point. Narratives are powerful. But they're not that strong when you experiment with moving out of them and trying something else. As Wollstonecraft said, just because people say girls are born to play with dolls does not mean they actually are.

## *Cyborg Emancipation*

### *Women gaze back*

Social media as all things terrible is old hat. Now there's growing interest in how objectification of women is encoded in AI and algorithms. Microsoft, Google and Amazon are quick to class images of women as far more racy than those of men in equivalent positions, while pregnant bellies sound the alarm at Google and Microsoft as 'very likely to contain racy content'. Even images released by the US National Cancer Institute showing how to do a breast examination triggered 'explicitly sexual in nature' and 'explicit nudity' warnings.[29]

It's not all bad though. On the contrary. Still, while researching the 'commodification' of women through online dating (just before Tinder emerged), I found that it was common for women to describe their experience of dates on a spectrum from cheap (signifying being taken advantage of) to valued (worthy of commitment). They were distinctly aware of the adage: Why buy the cow when you can get the milk for free?, which means why would a man 'invest' in a relationship with a woman when he can have sex with her without any additional tax on his freedom?

The assumption among most people is that male desire – not women's – is to blame for making the internet more of a one-sided perv fest than it technically should be. Even so, for the first time in sexual history, norms are not governed by the rule men-can-be-free and women-must-be-chaste, and where men only want sex and women only want commitment. Remnants of these dynamics still exist on dating sites, but the social stigma attached to women's promiscuity is hampered by the sites' anonymity. You can do whatever you want via Tinder or Feeld and one man will never know about the next, even if they've both been in your bed on the same day. This agency, under cover of privacy, is particularly a boon for women getting out of close-knit communities and into the world at large. They may encounter norms that tend towards violence, coercion and stigma in their real-life, family communities, but on the apps, it's about their searching style and impulses.

Actually, the internet – AI, social media, the apps, whatever – carries the potential for distinctly female-associated forms of empowerment, one of which is consumption. Browsing, choosing, rejecting or buying stuff is one exercise of private fantasy, offering a feeling of mental freedom, the ability to range freely away from the oppressive watchfulness of certain gender regimes.

Then, of course, there is agency in choosing who to date or to whom to sell one's wares. Whether Tinder or LinkedIn, women browse just as, if not more, powerfully than men: our gaze is all-important, both in sexual and non-sexual marketplaces. And while there are conflicting scholarly discourses about this, you can easily argue that in dating and sexual domains, women have far more choice and power than men. Throw in identity tourism, the ability to try out different sexual practices, sexualities and personas and you have a space in which women (as well as men) can be sexual but anonymous. This opens up a lot of freeing possibilities.

Freedoms such as these were anticipated by the queen of technological feminism Donna Haraway. In her iconic essay, 'A Cyborg Manifesto', Haraway declares: 'the cyborg is a creature in a post-gender world,' the result of a coupling between machine and live woman, 'of both imagination and material reality'. Picture here the woman pouring a glass of wine while thumbing insouciantly at her iPhone, checking messages and browsing fresh options. Any future can roll out in front of her, and she can stay in her room, smoothly moving between her glass of wine and her screen, her mind on an isolated, unjudged journey, at liberty to veer off into other runnels – perhaps a chess game in which an opponent has just made a vexing move, or a TikTok showing a massive fridge being restocked. It is with such an image in mind that one might see how the cybernetic coupling envisioned by

Haraway, replete with 'an intimacy and with a power that was not generated in the history of sexuality', resonates here.[30] By uncoupling women from the snare of organic reproduction, and organic life full stop, the internet frees as much as it objectifies.

But hyper-vigilance of objectification and conspiratorial thinking about capitalist exploitation has resulted in a paranoid interpretation of dating apps as themselves forces of patriarchal violence speaking through the market. None of this stops the sexual left from congregating on apps like Feeld and Hinge, but still, the consensus is that the apps do terrible things 'to' women because they give apparent free reign to men to use them as 'a free sex service'. American journalist Nancy Jo Sales has boldly and tenaciously uncovered far worse than callous, unsatisfying and transactional sex, unearthing stories and statistics about how some men use dating apps in order to carry out sexual assaults against women.[31] Sexual assault via dating app is obviously a very serious issue. But luckily the majority of women, even heavy users, are not sexually assaulted by dates.

Once again, the point is not that bad things don't happen to women or should just be accepted. It's that once women latch on to the narrative that objectification suffuses all of their interactions with men, and leaches into all aspects of life, especially online life, we end up thinking like Rousseau: that we're born to experience such injustice and that it is inescapable. This is needlessly limiting.

Far better would be to let that idea go and assume that women can pursue what they please, how they please, without too much holding them back, even with sexist, limiting narratives swirling around. One of the norms that could follow from this courageous letting go would be a more productive sense of anger to the one currently in place. In the world I'd like to see, women would feel empowered to be angry in the moment, and then take any further action as necessary, including physical action, as outlined above.

This would replace the soul-sapping default of waiting, ruminating, then punishing the offender using mediators, whether official channels or social media, and then, worst of all, taking a forensic approach to grievance, trauma and the slow-burning resentment against the society and 'system' that so can naturally ensue.

# PART THREE

*Good Slut*

## Chapter Seven

## In Defence of Promiscuity

Promiscuity: having or involving many sexual partners; not restricted to one sexual partner or few sexual partners (modern usage)
Not restricted to one class, sort or person, indiscriminate (c.1500 onward)
Casual, irregular
Composed of all sorts of persons or things

Two buxom blondes aged twenty-three and twenty-five. A 'sex challenge feud' reported the world over. Bonnie Blue, real name Tia Billinger, and Lily Phillips, engaged in a sex record challenge, complete with angry one-upmanship, with Blue bedding more than 1000 men in one night in January 2025 to ensure she outgunned Phillips, who had at the time of writing topped out at only one hundred in a night. Grim? Unbelievably so. Sobbing, Lily told host Josh Pieters afterwards: 'Sometimes you just disassociate... it's not like normal sex at all.' No indeed. Phillips also tugged heartstrings and spawned many a shaking head when she confessed: 'I don't even know what self-respect means at this point.'[1] The internet world was immediately obsessed with Blue and Phillips. 'Is the Bonnie Blue effect ruining your lovelife?' asked the *Daily Mail*.[2] Because 'half of UK men's fascination with the porn star has made them less satisfied in a relationship.' Even the *Economist* got interested: 'Welcome to Bonnie Blue's Britain,' it opined. 'A place of sin, spin and soft power.'[3]

Blue interested me, even more than one would expect, because she seems entirely uninterested in the concept of normal anything and appears to be well endowed with self-respect; she is made of sterner, and madder, stuff than most. 'I say to them all the time – the dads, the husbands, the students – leave your mark on me. Bite me, make me yours for that amount of time.'[4] She continues to shock in all ways, having claimed after the 'stunt', visibly bruised on camera, that her parents are 'so proud' (her mum is her PA) and – most extreme of all – that she is 'aware' of the risk of catching HIV, 'the big one', and is undeterred.[5]

As I say, all this is shocking, utterly shocking, and obviously this is not a set of choices that will be at all good for most young women. But there are things to celebrate here. Blue, nee Billinger, was born in Nottinghamshire, and worked in recruitment. By entering porn, and doing so in a ruthlessly savvy way, she is now rich. She has a following online she can bank on for future earnings in other areas, should she choose. And she is showing that you can live at the outer limits of the allowed, admittedly with some inconveniences. 'I tried to go on a night out with my friend and my sister recently in Nottingham and it just ended up me taking photos for hours and hours, people coming up wanting to speak,' she told the *Daily Star*. As for regret, she is frank about the downsides of her kind of fame. 'It's definitely hard sometimes but not hard enough that it makes me think I regret this, I don't at all.'[6]

She shows what a truly robust liberal society looks like: we can squawk and condemn, shake our heads and troll her, but we can just about handle it, by which I mean, such women can be healthy (and, when they catch an STI, treated effectively) and rich. They can live and flourish and build a business empire. I know. I sound mad. But press pause on the indignation for a second. Just consider for a moment that it's ok for Bonnie Blue to exist and do what she does, and if you feel passionately and instinctively that it isn't, pause on why, list a few reasons. Despite fears that she is a role model of sorts for young women, it is nonetheless unlikely her activities will contaminate many or even any women, so why?

That the thousands of men, young and old, who Blue and Phillips have shagged have probably had the best time of their lives is perhaps less interesting than the fact that, when it comes to women, Bonnie Blue is the worst of times and the best of times rolled into one. And the ways in which it is the latter is more important than the ways in which it is the former.

I felt the same way in 2010 about Karen Owen, a Duke University senior whose 'fuck list', written up in the style of an academic thesis, in PowerPoint, went viral after one of the three friends she shared it with forwarded it on. Called 'An education beyond the classroom: excelling in the realm of horizontal academics', Owen ranked the numerous varsity athletes she'd bedded on various metrics: athleticism, creativity, entertainment, sexual aggressiveness, 'length and girth of the Subjects' hardware', and talent. Each encounter received a score, which was recorded on a bar chart. There were thoughtful and deeply concerned essays about the false consciousness of Owen, who, beneath the braggadocio, appeared to have internalised men's desire for violence; after all, she looked favourably on rough play and the resulting bruises. It's not that there isn't anything in that observation. On the contrary. But for me, just as important a point was captured by a Duke student newspaper, which called the fuck list a 'feminist victory' given that 'a seemingly innocent and fairly generic Duke girl' could now destroy 'a dozen varsity athletes'' reputations with a PowerPoint file, and be 'punished with nothing worse than a hint of a book deal'.[7]

But lest you think I am also completely mad, having praised Bonnie Blue, let me own up to having written a book in 2011, age twenty-eight, before I'd ever used online dating and before Tinder had been invented, called *The Man Diet*. I launched the whole book on an anecdote that captured, basically, how rubbish intimate activity with someone who doesn't care about you in the slightest can feel. I'd seduced this absolutely gorgeous man, whom I had met at a spa, where he was the best masseur I had ever experienced (not saying that much at age twenty-seven, but anyway). But when I got home, after the incredibly unlikely, thrilling encounter, instead of feeling jubilant, I lay on the bed and felt 'down. Rejected. Crap. Tired . . . What had I been hoping to gain?'[8]

I had chapters in the book called 'Refuse to Have No Strings Attached Sex', 'Dwell on Your Sense of Self' and 'Cut Down on the Booze'. I recommended reading *War and Peace*. This book came from a realisation I'd had at twenty-eight, after a decade in which my policy had been to grab as much 'action' as possible, partly in pursuit of the spangly plains of fun, excitement, self-realisation and friendship depicted in *Sex and the City*, and partly because I felt neurotically driven to do so – for reasons that are as interesting, or uninteresting, as the next neurotic person's reasons for pursuing unwholesome intimacy.

I also think that it's ok to experiment and see what happens – interactions with other people, including men, rarely follow entirely predicted paths. Extremity is also part of life; often part of a process in which someone pushes themselves to crisis, and on to recovery and enlightenment. And even if a young woman does wade through a swampy period of selling herself short to hop into bed, or be seduced into bed, by some hot young man, I am not convinced it's the worst thing in the world. Having been through hookup culture myself and been somewhat (metaphorically) buffeted and bruised by it, as well as genuinely diverted and entertained, I think it is a good thing. And the existence of the Bonnie Blues and Lily Phillipses, despite being out on the margins, pushing our society's tolerance, norms and laws to the limit, are part of that bundle.

The key thing about casual sex, and why we need to defend it fiercely, whether we personally like it or not, is fairly simple: having it as an accepted feature of society is profoundly better than all other alternatives. I'll go so far as to say that hookup culture is a representation of the very architecture of choice we should be proudly defending, not trashing and attacking.

Much of the outrage that Blue and Phillips have provoked centres on the idea that these girls are just two of many throwing everything good for human flourishing, and themselves, under the bus while shrieking: 'but it was a choice!'

I am not being facetious when I say I don't understand this. So many 'progressives' sneer at those who take 'choice' seriously and literally, like Bonnie Blue and, different but similar, Sheryl Sandberg, a folk devil accused of selling out herself and women more generally to get rich in a boys' world. It's as if the obvious explanation for their career paths – that they freely chose them – is the maddest of all.

### *Promiscuity's 'Moralist' Past*

Even though actual promiscuity is pretty normal among women, it's still amazingly contentious – seen as pitifully (or grotesquely) naive, or simply morally offensive – to celebrate it. The reason, of course, is a hard-to-shake, very long cultural memory of 'promiscuity' as something with exclusively bad connotations. 'Indiscriminate', 'all sorts of persons or things': as the meanings of promiscuity over the past half millennium reveal, the crime of a promiscuous person is not simply wanton sexuality, but the crime of indiscriminateness, lack of judgement, and is thus a moral flaw: lack of trustworthiness.

Promiscuity has always been seen, in most cultures, as a moral failing of particularly female quality, indistinguishable from unseemliness and redolent of the violation of the order of things. Whereas this sentiment is now generally spewed out by have-a-go moralists in the Magasphere and Manosphere, and on X and TikTok, it used to be articulated by proper ones, the actual 'moralists' of the late eighteenth century and early nineteenth. The period's first major tectonic shift in sexual mores was hotly debated.

Like today's trad wives, trad femmes, postliberals and right-wing populist men, the moralists were also reacting against a perceived sexual revolution, though in ideas rather than contraceptive technology. Some of the directions the arguments went in seem surprising. Influential philosophers and poets argued that women were just as entitled and prone to 'variety' as men. The poet James Lawrence, opining around 1800, wrote: 'Let every female live perfectly uncontrolled by any man, and enjoying every freedom which the males at present enjoy; let her be visited by as many lovers as she may please, and of whatever rank they may be.'[9]

This was a cruder version of a key plank in Mary Wollstonecraft's *A Vindication of the Rights of Women*, a treatise electrified by her insistence that the sexual mores ruling women's acculturation and view of the world were lethal for intellectual and, above all, moral development. Wollstonecraft 'produced many arguments' to 'prove' that:

> . . . the prevailing notion respecting a sexual character was subversive of morality . . . and that chastity will never be respected in the male world till the person of a woman is not, as it were, idolized, when little virtue or sense embellish it with the grand traces

of mental beauty, or the interesting simplicity of affection . . . Woman in particular, whose virtue is built on mutable prejudices, seldom attains to this greatness of mind; so that, becoming the slave of her own feelings, she is easily subjugated by those of others. Thus degraded, her reason, her misty reason! is employed rather to burnish than to snap her chains.

This whole quote is utter gold. Wollstonecraft is again stressing that the narratives, or 'prejudices' limiting women are 'mutable', e.g. not set in stone. And that the more women buy into the idea that they should be the slave of 'her own feelings', the more steadfast her chains.

But working hard against this new libertine grain was an ultimately more powerful ideology. The moralists reminded readers of the central importance, not just for women but for societal moral hygiene in general, of the fairer sex keeping its legs together. As the historian Fara Dabhoiwala writes in *The Origins of Sex*, the need for 'respectable women' was all the greater and more urgent since judicial punishment for sexual indiscretions had ebbed and men were busy enjoying greater freedoms. With propriety foundering the ability of women to marshal discipline was key to all sexual propriety. 'For a woman to fail in this duty, when her entire culture depended on it, was therefore unforgivable'.[10] Fallen women were corrupting influences, stealing men, and thus 'degenerated into repulsive, unfeminine harpies'. So for influential late eighteenth century moralist William Paley, since 'a woman collects her virtue into this point, the loss of her chastity is generally the destruction of her moral principle'; and, thought Paley, the pollutant of immodesty would be visible whether the 'criminal intercourse be discovered or not'.[11]

There are other parallels with our times. Then, as now, Britain found itself in the midst of demographic and cultural upheaval, losing wars of independence against American radicals, with an influx of migrants and growing evidence of urbanisation and sprawling poverty. The lax sexual morality of upper class libertines and prominent intellectuals like Wollstonecraft and Godwin was blamed for a wider social fall, with 'adultery and concubinage' seeping into the behaviour and customs of the lower classes. 'How can we expect a nation to flourish where the people are so abandoned!' shrieked the *Anti-Jacobin Review*.[12]

The politics and hysteria of the anti-promiscuity movement have proved malleable, stretching down the centuries. In fact, the first wave of feminist activism was inseparable from a drive for 'purity' in both men and women. Women like Josephine Butler and Laura Chant made eradicating prostitution their aim, though their first campaign concerned the (ultimately successful) repeal of the Contagious Diseases Act (1864), which put prostitutes in prison if they were caught with venereal disease. To these warriors for women, prostitutes reflected the worst habits in men, whose vile and uncontrolled appetites infected and destroyed susceptible female targets, namely the poor and desperate. The feminists thought their existence tarnished all of society, not least with rising rates of VD and illegitimate births. This was a striking direction for feminism to travel in. As the historian Lucy Bland puts it: 'A number of feminists, once apparently laissez-faire and anti-statist in matters of sexuality and morality, were now, in the 1880s and 1890s, adopting a more repressive stance and were taking to closing brothels, clearing the streets of prostitutes and attempting to cleanup indecent leisure pursuits, from literature to music halls. Why were these women acting in this way?'[13]

The answer once more shows how history rolls around. Then as now, there was an evolution from feminist aims – to overturn the asymmetry of the most repressive, inhumane laws privileging men and punishing women, particularly around prostitution – into a more wide-ranging social conservatism. As Bland points out, the 1880s was 'a period of low profit, high unemployment, severe cyclical depression and chronic housing shortage.' Such economic instability was combined with political volatility: the rise of socialism, trade unionism and an uptick in foreign immigration to London's East End of anarchists and socialists from abroad. This sense of a nation falling apart at the seams, tugged down by the roiling working classes, fed the conviction that lower class cultures required urgent yanking into a more middle class respectability (let us not forget the social class of Bonnie Blue). Social purity feminists came at this idea of respectability from a background of philanthropy and religiosity, which tilted all their activities back to anti-immorality sex activism. If the upper working classes were subject to persuasion, then the 'criminal classes' of the very poor were deemed to need a far rougher, more authoritarian and statist approach. Some of the solutions proposed by the National Vigilance Association, whose founding members in 1885 included purity feminists Josephine Butler and Elizabeth Blackwell, resulted in the outlawing of brothels, which meant women being thrown out onto streets, where they were often charged with vagrancy.

It was assumed that no sane woman would want such a job. But the funny thing about these moves to shut down prostitution and its businesses was the *failure* to persuade women to 'leave their sinful life', which they evidently rather liked, or at least preferred to the alternative they were being pressured to accept. When a fleet of brothels was shut down in Aldershot in 1888, William Coote, the NVA's secretary, undertook in court to take charge of and support the four hundred girls and women who had worked at the brothels if only they were 'anxious to make an effort to lead an honourable and honest life'. Only one took him up on the offer, and ninety of the rest marched – singing – through the streets in protest.[14]

Of course, most people calling themselves 'feminists' have abandoned any self-description that includes the word 'purity', but many nonetheless have the exact same concerns about women selling their bodies, whether for sex-related services or surrogacy ('the pimping of pregnancy' as veteran feminist and anti-sex abuse campaigner Julie Bindel has called it). It's seen as exploitation plain and simple. Casual sex is an overspill of male vice and so on.

However, among the increasingly influential internet coterie of those who openly despise feminism, the message is more direct. And it is coming from religious voices, particularly from within Islam.

## *The Return of Religion*

For Dilly Hussain, a Bedford-based editor of *5Pillars News*, a website and podcast covering Islam-related issues with nearly 200,000 X followers and nearly as many on Instagram, female promiscuity is so wide-ranging in its corrosion of personhood that it extends to what women eat for dinner. Hussain posted this scathing and horrible message to his many followers on X. 'The life of an average non-Muslim woman in the West: Double digit sexual partners before the age of 25. Not even pretence of modesty or chastity. Unmarried, no kids, with mummy and daddy issues. Living pay cheque to pay cheque. Microwave meals. Little to no extended family or faith community support. Fake friends for socialising and self-validation. A dog or a cat as company from the age of 40.'

For me, double digit sexual partners before twenty-five was actually the goal; sadly not achieved, but achieved not long after. Not having to offer 'the pretence' of chastity is one of the huge reliefs of living in a liberal society. There is enough fear and cognitive dissonance in life without having to try to hide one's body while also craving male attention. Being unmarried is also a lovely option, which I am grateful for. If being married to someone like Hussain is the other option, I'd happily choose a life of pure celibacy. But luckily I don't have to make such a choice!

What even does 'no kids' mean? If a woman has a child at forty with a sperm donor, does that count? I assume this is a further sign of degradation to Mr Hussain. And how does he know that women have 'fake' friends? Is he, in fact, all-knowing, like so many men before him have thought they are? It is also unclear to me what is wrong with either 'socialising' or 'self-validation', since last time I checked, both of these were vital for happiness. And there is nothing wrong with a dog or cat. Some married people with children also have pets. You get the idea.

Another man with a considerable following and political clout in the UK is Dr Tallha Abdulrazaq, a scholar at Exeter University's Strategy and Security Institute, winner of the Al Jazeera Young Researcher Award and 2024 candidate for Independent Councillor for Exeter. On December 7, 2023, as more in-depth reports surfaced of the mind-bending cruelty of Hamas's sexual violence towards Israeli women on 7 October, US Vice President Kamala Harris posted a standard condemnation, saying the attacks were 'reprehensible and must be condemned', adding: 'I've spent my career protecting women and girls from heinous crimes of sexual violence and will continue to do so.'

Under the post, Dr Abdulrazaq, who has Palestinian family, commented: 'F\*\*k off, you dirty toothy whore.' He refused to apologise, saying his recourse to such language was justified. It's a logic we are seeing more and more openly since 7 October, 2023: either to dispute the fact of the sexual violence Hamas visited on Israeli women, or to say that the Zionist whores deserved it, and anyone who disagrees is also a whore. Female immodesty is at the core of all sorts of spitting derisions and prejudices that have persisted for millennia. In the present day, ideas of whoredom still map onto whatever it is that the person is obsessed with hating. Western and

Jewish whoredom are fused. 'Zionist whore' is a common insult for women who dare to associate with or defend Israel. I get it quite a lot. What they don't realise is that it's actually a compliment. There's no better sort of person to be!

Christian revivalism is the interesting one, with its alt-right misogyny. These dudes want an authentically modest state of nature whose tagline is: 'be a lady in the streets, and a freak in the sheets'. They hate female promiscuity. It probably terrifies them or provokes envy. The sheer obsession of such men with what women do with their bodies is an electrifying force for their followers.[15]

Winston Marshall, the kind-hearted, softly spoken conservative commentator and former banjoist of the pop-folk band Mumford & Sons put things just as firmly, if more softly, of a picture of Madonna dancing suggestively: 'When they are young we celebrate pop stars for their promiscuity and excess. But in their old age we see how damaging that lifestyle is to body and soul. Don't fall for it.' Incels feel the same, though unlike Marshall, who is a handsome former pop star and something of a babe magnet (manosphere leader Carl Benjamin, aka Sargon of Akkad, has a wife and children), they fume at home, sexless and full of rage at women for preferring to 'ride the cock carousel' in their twenties (with other men) and corroding their stock as the ideal, pure wives later . . . that they'll never meet for obvious reasons.

Women's motives for protecting and advancing the cause of their own modesty were strong up until the midway point of the twentieth century. Yet despite the intervening period of liberalisation, 'promiscuity' has refocused itself as a pejorative term that applies mainly to women. Perhaps this is no surprise, given how prevalent are societies that still punish and fear open female sexuality. In fact, only 15 per cent of the world's population follows Western liberal values – everywhere else punishes female immodesty with various degrees of harshness, and often sanctions violence amounting to death. It is almost universally true that in societies or milieux that police modesty through real apparatuses of power and punishment, not just scattered cultural discourse, there is an instability that tends towards authoritarian and chaotic political outcomes.

### *The Right to Promiscuity = The Right to a Decent Life*

On the specific and material level, the ability of women of all ages to sleep with multiple people outside a committed relationship is a great cultural convenience. News flash: quite a few heterosexual women have the kind of desire that is not so ladylike and passive that it can only be satisfied in the embrace of loving commitment – and we saw in Part One how very commonly 'nature' has seen to it that it is not. It is also handy for those women who, however much they would like a love affair with a wonderful man, can't find such a person, but are still horny. Sometimes that means making 'unhealthy' choices. But they're nowhere near as unhealthy as having to maintain some kind of delusion of modesty, perhaps wrapped in orthodox religion. Or a society emboldened to punish women for letting skin show, and in which murder is all too commonly considered the just response to alleged infidelity. Which is, of course, the ultimate promiscuity.

The takeaway of this whole discussion about promiscuity is this. It's not all good. We all know it's not all good. But it's so important to defend equal treatment, justice and protection to women who act at the outermost legal limits of female desire, for whatever reason, because the counter-arguments for 'letting' them do so are so dark and twisted. That goes for Bonnie Blue; my overly keen, *Sex and the City*-influenced younger self; and anyone else swimming through a tsunami of transactional sex.

As recently as the 1970s and 1980s, those counter-arguments were simply standard. I always like to refer to *Singles*, a magazine dedicated to the talking points, experiences, injustices and gripes of Britain's single population between the 1970s and 1990s. It's a unique source that offers a true snapshot of ordinary opinion about the vaulting forward of women's status. There were dozens of letters from readers lambasting women, and 'women's lib' for perverting femininity and the very essence of civilisation. The main crime? The medical and social changes that had made it possible for women to have casual sex. One typical response from a male reader went: 'Who'd want to marry, or even live with, the new breed of female predators?' The 'new breed of female predators' were those guilty of operating outside marriage and motherhood. They were blamed not only for promiscuity, which usually entailed 'gold-digging' on top of having a career, but for ruining romance full-stop. In countless letters and first-person articles I read in the *Singles* treasure trove, such women, more often than not a figment of over-heated imaginations that had read of 'women's libbers', were accused of overturning the delicate balance of gender complementarity. They had done nothing short of creating conditions in which it was impossible for men to be loved or to love.

The people ruining romance were the same people getting newly safe and legal abortions. It's odd to have spell this out (again), but since it's one of the cornerstones of the derided sexual revolution, it seems one has to. Lack of access to safe and respectful abortion poses risks, in the words of the WHO, to 'women's physical and mental wellbeing throughout the life-course' and can violate the very 'right to life' of women and girls, 'the right to benefit from scientific progress and its realization', 'the right to decide freely and responsibly on the number, spacing and timing of children' and 'the right to be free from torture, cruel, inhuman and degrading treatment and punishment.'[16]

Given that these are all still risks associated with unwanted pregnancies, the pill – which all but guaranteed painless contraception for the first time ever – seems a very good invention indeed. Yet post-liberal feminists rue that the pill has made sex, in not risking pregnancy, less hot.[17] This is odd, given that non-reproductive sex can be very steamy, to judge by gay sexuality. Even if we keep it to heterosexuals, for two-thirds of any given menstrual cycle, pregnancy isn't an option anyway. Perhaps critics of the pill envision hot sex in the five days sperm can live prior to ovulation. This is sacrificing a lot on the altar of hotness. Others in the new conservative crew (not zealots in Texas but in the drawing rooms of London, where wine flows freely) also say they despise contraception. Not because it makes sex less hot, but because they feel it has cheapened it, and made it transactional, encouraging people to 'use' sex thoughtlessly, rather than as the sanctified blessing of family it is meant to be.

These arguments are playing with fire, as well as being rubbish. Do their proponents really want us to have a high chance of dying if saddled with an unwanted pregnancy? What kind of society would we get should we side with those who see in the sexual revolution all that has gone wrong? There are plenty of examples. Most of history provides them, as I have alluded to. Hardline Muslim countries in the present also show the price tag of being against women's freedom, Western-style.

In Iran, peacefully protesting for the right to wear hair freely, and against the discrimination encoded in sharia law, results in rape and torture by security and intelligence forces. Amnesty's report on the 2023 women's protests included testimony from forty-five survivors, including twenty-six men, twelve women and seven children, 'who were subjected to rape, gang rape and/or other forms of sexual violence by intelligence and security forces following their arbitrary arrest for challenging decades of oppression and entrenched gender-based discrimination.'[18] Tunisia, hailed as one of the more secular and modernised of the Muslim countries, only repealed its 'marry-your-rapist' law in 2017 – which had meant that all charges or punishment against a rapist would be dropped so long as he married his victim. This was seen as satisfactory in a society that prizes female virginity and modesty over basic physical rights and freedom – and its repeal is rarely enforced because of strong family backing for this 'private' solution to rape.[19]

Jordan, the most liberal country in the Middle East, believes very firmly in sexual modesty and prosecutes those who get caught romping outside marital strictures. Sleeping with any unmarried member of the opposite sex is considered adultery, which is a punishable crime that can result in three years in prison. Snogging in public – which admittedly is a bit gross – is seen as a crime there, due to public decency laws.

There is not a single country that insists on female chastity and modesty at the state level, or tribe or subculture that enforces it, where sexual promiscuity does not result in punishment, and where that punishment does not fall on women's heads hardest. In these same cultures, there are entrenched programmes of female inequality that come with a violent edge. Rape is used liberally as a weapon, or simply as a lark by male authorities, from husband to police officer.

### *Tinder Terror, Slut-Shaming and the Problem of Bad-Tinted Spectacles*

Like most things in Western culture, hookup culture remains opt-in. It may be a phase many young girls have to consider, but it is definitely possible, even normal, to opt out. Romance still has a very high status in our society – and so does its pursuit.

But it's no wonder that, given how loaded 'hookup culture' has become, young women live in constant terror of 'unhealthy' sex. They've been terrified out of their wits, told they are far too fragile to withstand one too many bad Tinder dates. 'I don't think there's any question that dating apps are rape culture,' writes Nancy Jo Sales, the author of the *Bling Ring* and the viral *Vanity Fair* piece about the 'Tinder apocalypse'. 'I would argue that women should delete their dating apps en masse in some Lysistrata-like move of self-preservation.'[20]

Except the apps are also indispensable. Crucially, they're the main outlet for those who want to maximise choice in pursuit of their own ends, from dating like a machine to shagging around, or both. Or take Feeld, the kink-friendly app, which works in exactly the same way as Tinder. This is the easiest way the Earth has ever known for people to 'explore' what used to be known as 'perversions' with others who share the commitment to their judgement-free pursuit. Are we to tell those people that their life should be made more difficult, that their sexual predilections should be hidden, that perhaps they ought to re-experience all that sexual shame we so recently dislodged? The chastity-belt crew may well think so, but progressives wouldn't.

Many happy experiences have been made possible by apps such as Feeld – especially for those men and women (yes, women) who just want sex. Accounts like this are familiar to those who follow such things. 'Last year I felt I needed to get back on the saddle as I'd had a bit of a drought, and I just wanted sex,' said Lisa, a forty-one-year-old, in an interview with *The i Paper*.

> I wanted to experience more in my mid-forties and not have any ties, or not want to get into any relationship. A friend recommended me some casual hookup apps for sex-positive people, where you can meet up and explore kinks. I'd always meet them for a pint beforehand to check they seemed ok, then usually go back to their house. As a woman I was quite protective about inviting anyone back to my house for the first time, but I felt safe with everyone I met. I had some of what was probably the best sex of my life.[21]

You'd never believe, reading the harangues of the Tinder terror-mongers, that women could rampage through apps and feel safe 'with everyone I met'. Tom, a man in his early forties, interviewed alongside Lisa, also couldn't help but note how gleefully women were taking advantage of the new landscape of app-enabled sexual freedom. 'I've met some fascinating women and had some crazy sex,' he said. 'I think it's so good that women are able to express themselves sexually in these spaces, after men have had it their way for so long. As long as everyone's on the same page and nobody's getting hurt, I think anyone who wants to should crack on.'[22] Indeed. And a politics in which people genuinely took women seriously as free agents would not be so quick to argue that women are coerced into bad sexual choices because of the 'system', whether that is tech bros or capitalism.

There's something else I don't like about Tinder terror. This discourse dehumanises encounters that are, in fact, human encounters with all the potential that goes with that.[23] Stranger danger is understandable and women must be prudent, but strangers are not all monsters intent on violent attack. That these encounters are potentially transactional or not, does not prevent them from also being an exchange between two consenting people having a nice time.

Focusing on the dangers of promiscuity blots out the good things that come from meeting new humans. And there is every chance the good things will trump the bad. In my case, no fewer than three of my favourite, quirkiest friendships today began as casual hookups: one on Tinder, one on Bumble, one in a bar. I took gambles on all three, engaging in behaviour that would be regarded as dangerously promiscuous by the fear mongers and chastity-belt evangelists. Romance did not last from that initial fiery spark, but a friendship emerged from the embers with all three. Indeed, there is a particular kind of friendship that comes from ex-lovers, found on the internet or otherwise. Both of you have had to make peace with the demise of the relationship, usually caused by one person tapping out. And there is intimacy in this. And then you get the bonus: the pleasure in knowing that the chemistry that drew you together wasn't just transactional or sordid or misconstrued and one-sided, but that it matured into a more substantial, if platonic, spark. This is enriching!

The mainstream feminist position is understandably wary about the 'full humanness' of unknown horny men. But this orthodox perspective is too stony, too hostile, and too wedded to the idea that all app-mediated and otherwise casual hookups are exercises of male power, and that the sexual encounters they entail all too often count as 'grey rape'. This is an ambiguous event somewhere between coerced and consensual sex, with disagreement over whether unenthusiastic or secretly unenthusiastic consent knocks it into the 'coerced' category.[24]

The resurgence of suspicion about the true status of the sex that happens in the course of casual relationships marks a return to the intra-feminist debates of the 1980s and 1990s about date rape. Heightened awareness of the ways women are tacitly coerced or harassed spread quickly into a discourse of universal male predatoriness, especially on college campuses. In 1994, shock jockette and NYU creative-writing professor Katie Roiphe argued something of great prescience: that feminism's new lens was fear and victimhood rather than the sense of courage, fierceness, opportunity and exploration Roiphe herself had discovered in the second-wave feminist movement. While we might be uncomfortable with her assertion that whatever happens on a date, the 'responsibility for our actions is still our own', the point is ultimately about women's agency and power, whether that's verbal power, physical power as outlined earlier, or the power of perspective: to embrace, reject, or frame situations independently of narrative.

I was lucky enough to have a long conversation with Dan Savage, the American sex advice columnist and podcaster who has millions of devoted, progressive listeners and readers. We discussed the increasingly heavy way in which casual sex is described and his perspective was, as usual, illuminating. 'Yes, there are rapists,' Savage said from his kitchen table in Seattle.

> There are people who are coercive. Men consciously, sometimes unconsciously, at other times, will exploit. A woman's fear of saying no in the moment to sex and then the man will walk away feeling like that was consensual and the woman will walk away feeling like they were violated. That happens. But . . . Bad sex is sometimes something two people do with each other. It's not always something that is done to you.

Savage identifies the irony of illiberal liberalism in the way fear and anger suffuse the discourse about women and sex. He detects a fending off of responsibility for certain types of regrettable sex and associates this with the silent victory of slut-shaming: the idea that you'd have to find an excuse for the kind of sex that didn't end in hearts and roses. 'And that's what unnerves me about all of this: the enormous impact of slut-shaming and our desire to always get ourselves off the hook for . . . sexual things. We talk, we feel compromised when we have sex. It makes us vulnerable. We feel weak. We feel implicated and if we can create a narrative that shifts all responsibility for everything that happened off our shoulders, say it was the culture, it was misogyny. It was patriarchy. It was them. They were a bad actor.'

Examples of what Savage is talking about spring to mind in Christine Emba's book, like a young woman who thinks: 'I don't want to have sex with you, but I'm doing it because, like, I have to be' – she laughs dryly – "polite".' This is then held up as an example of women being used terribly by society/ patriarchy etc.[25]

Savage has been giving advice to people with sex and relationship 'quandaries' for more than thirty years. Conversations about slut-shaming ballooned about fifteen years ago and then vanished, he says.

> We talked about slut-shaming constantly and then along came, you know, different conversations about sex. And we just kind of memory-holed the slut-shaming conversation. Slut-shaming is not just something that men do to women. It's something that women do to women. It's a cultural force that I think has an enormous psychological impact. We want to exonerate ourselves from anything we might have done sexually, because that would mean we're a slut if we like had desire and agency and made choices and did things that were slutty. So we want to reframe it as like these things were done to me, I was just borne along by the storm and in the hands of some manipulative mastermind who was a seventeen-year-old boy. And what could I do?

## Chapter Eight

# Choice: Free and Miserable vs . . . Unfree and Miserable

As the conversation between me and Dan Savage rolled on, Savage pinned his analysis of casual sexual culture into a wider frame of change. In the second half of the twentieth century, women began to have choices – real choices – about how to spend our lives. We were no longer 'playing the game of musical chairs anymore' where we had to 'pick a seat eventually or not exist. Socially, financially, politically, we changed what it meant to be male and female. Seventy-five years ago, eighty years ago.'

Yet 'choice' is a word that quite often invites rolled eyes. So naive! It's true that where there is 'choice' there is not necessarily feminism. There's a scene in *Sex and the City* where Charlotte garners disapproval from her friends after quitting her job to focus on being a wife: 'I choose my choice!' she yells. 'I choose my choice!' It's a poignant scene, illustrating why choice alone is not commensurate with the specific goals enshrined in the two main waves of feminism. And, personally, I am surprised and disappointed when women 'choose' to drop out of the workforce entirely to pursue motherhood full-time, permanently. From my point of view, it's not motherhood that's demonised, it's the pro-career perspective; sound too much like Sheryl Sandberg and you're going to invite some serious side eye. Not all choice fits with the quest for autonomy: sacking off work for full-time eternal domesticity often works against it.

But the truth of women's 'choice' now is that while not all of it falls within the framework of feminism, the concept of women's choice, and the infrastructure that sustains it, is extremely real. The idea of consequence-free sex for women in the post-Pill, post-universal abortion, divorce-prone West is not a liberal lie and does not proffer false choice. It's real choice, and it's a prerequisite for the kind of decent life for women that Mary Wollstonecraft imagined. Among others, it's choice about how to approach sex howsoever one chooses, including to shun it altogether or keep it to a marriage relationship; to have loads of sex, then settle down and be a mother, to never be a mother, or to be one once and never again, or to be one late and multiple times. It is most certainly not a liberal lie that women today in the West can pursue single motherhood through sex casual or more serious or through a sperm donor, or use assisted reproduction technology, or shun the whole caboodle and just work, or travel, or drink, or smoke.

Safe abortion on demand, and an end to punishment for sex. These hallmarks of the 'sexual revolution' did two things: they bequeathed choice, and they also flattened choice – so that there is no truly awful option now. Isn't that great? Why would you want to dismantle rather than build on that?

Promiscuity IS a choice, and it is right that it is so – even if it is an 'unhealthy' or even a dangerous choice in some instances. I do not minimise the horror and injustice of violent harm against women. And it's true that there is no personal autonomy without risk. But it is way, way better to be free and miserable than unfree and miserable – which, when it comes to women and sexuality, history suggests is the only other option.

# CHOICE: FREE AND MISERABLE VS... UNFREE AND MISERABLE

## *'What People Wanted was to Live a Little'*

Dan Savage has learned through thousands of letters that those who:

> ... did it the way Louise Perry et al think people should do it, who married relatively young, had one sexual partner ... write to me twenty years in, miserable and desperate for variety, for different experiences. What was possible for them erotically now seems impossible for them. Not because at thirty-five, they've aged out, but because they boxed themselves into a corner with the expectations of a monogamous marriage and a partner. And they didn't live up to expectations. I frequently mention that when I was growing up, there was this kind of vast literature and cinema of the midlife crisis. And it kind of disappeared. Because straight people began having lives before they settled down, before they got married, before they had kids. My parents married and had kids at twenty and had four kids by twenty-five, and that was it. They were locked in and then they had a kind of midlife-crisis divorce. Because of course they did.

Savage is one of the most famous gay voices in the world and has chronicled the political and cultural dynamics between gay and straight communities in the US for decades. One of the defining features of this evolution is the biggest sexual switcheroo of the twentieth century: gay men seeking out the bourgeois, monogamous norms of heterosexuals (marriage, children, sometimes even monogamy) and straight people adopting (albeit to a lesser extent) the promiscuous sexual customs of gay men. I think he's so smart, so experienced, and so sensible that I am going to quote him here at some length. He's a star.

Right-wingers, Savage says to me, expressed terror that

> ... our hedonistic lifestyles would be adopted by straight people, but that's kind of what happened. Like straight people saw gay people moving into city centres, having an apartment and having multiple partners and then straight people started doing all of that too. We called them fuck-buddies. You called them friends with benefits. We called it tricking, you called it hooking up. We were accused of hedonism. You guys began to call that serial monogamy. Everything we did, straight people began to do ... and then settling down at thirty. And, of course, gay people pushed for marriage and the ability to have children or adopt and what everybody proved was there was nothing gay about the gay lifestyle or straight about the straight lifestyle. You see in the way people behaved once they were sort of free, gay people included, from that trap. What people wanted was to live a little. Before they made that final choice, before they sat down on that final chair. And people who do live a little, fuck around a little. And have some different kinds of experiences, have different kinds of relationships [so that] when they do marry or decide to have children with someone, it seems like a conscious and informed choice and one that is more stable and lasting. There are people who are going to draw the very short straw having sex with people that you don't know. We know there are no guarantees and everybody can trot out their own worst-case scenarios and disastrous individual results. But I think what I see in the mail are people who did it the way Louise Perry wants everyone to do it and they're unhappy. But Louise Perry sees people doing it the way I think people should do it, who are complaining to her that they are unhappy. I mean, there's a lot of unhappy people out there.

### *The Learning Curve*

Sure, riding the 'cock carousel' can induce depression about the state of men and the world. But nothing else is quite like it either when it comes to combining up-close-and-personal encounters with the cute and creative potential of human interaction. Learning about sex and what you want from sexual relationships doesn't have to be a school of hard knocks. Nor does the overall effect of a culture that supports and occasionally cheerleads female sexual promiscuity.

Take it from me. I'm not an armchair commentator here, like many scholars of intimacy. Casual sex culture shaped large swathes of my adult life. It's been the on- and off-ramp for serious relationships, a way of letting off steam, a source of mini-heartbreaks, frustration, tension, triumph, misery, self-loathing, pride, extreme disappointment and sometimes elation. And for all the discomfort of uncertainty and change, the backdrop felt strangely solid because I felt free, not trapped, safe in the knowledge I could jump on a plane to pursue interesting work or simply to escape without having to explain myself.

Unlike a period of druggy hedonism, my years of casual sex were not just some trippy set of episodes, leaving nothing but a mess in their wake. They were excellent for gaining self-knowledge, learning the ins and outs of expectations and how to manage emotions in ways that have been useful in all sorts of social domains.

Have I made 'unhealthy' choices? I have. Do I wish I'd been hastened to the altar by a prince, a high price set on my virginity? Or that I'd aimed at serious committed coupledom my whole life? No, no and no.

Every now and then – though more rarely as the cultural climate has become more victim-obsessed – a jolly story about a young woman's encounter with dating apps is released in a respectable broadsheet and reminds me of how I used to see things, even when I was in the thick of it. I was truly disturbed by a harrowing account by Kitty Ruskin in *The Times* of ghastly encounters with dates, including rape, so I was relieved, soon after, to read a little diary piece of the sort I used to write, by one bikini-clad, festival-going twenty-seven-year old called Hannah Skelley, who, 'when real-life encounters had failed', tried six apps in a week, with ratings. Tinder got 1/10 for the app ('chronic') but 8/10 for the 'date rating' ('surprisingly brilliant'). All six men she met seemed chivalrous and keen; checking she got back ok, asking to take her out again. None of what Skelley writes in a week of immersion in app-land fits the paradigm either of assault-adjacent behaviour or self-eroding performativity. It was . . . fun.

I heard the same story of fun and 'personal development', as they put it, thrown into the bargain from three sylph-like women sunbathing on the meadow of the Hampstead Heath ladies pond. They were having an extended discussion about how they had enjoyed recent phases of meeting men 'in the club'. One said how she would get dressed up, arrive, immediately select the man she wanted to have sex with and do it with him, there or at home. The others listened attentively, nodding along. Another told the story of how someone she met this way became her partner and the love of her life. All three spoke fondly and with amusement of these eras. None of them sounded even remotely regretful, or as if they had low self-esteem. Their favourite part was narrating these 'crazy stories' to their girlfriends, a legendary source of pleasure and release for young women. One remarked that it was strange that she'd never thought twice before bringing a man from the club home with her, and that, if anything, she felt more uneasy going on stilted dates with strangers than having a one-night stand with someone she'd barely spoken to. What was most interesting was that at the time of my eavesdropping, they were either in or looking for serious relationships. They were aged between twenty-seven and thirty-two. It was

## CHOICE: FREE AND MISERABLE VS... UNFREE AND MISERABLE

satisfying hearing them talk so positively about hookup culture. I'm glad they had evidently and unapologetically – and without anxiety – enjoyed such lifestyles. Recent history shows there is a lot to be gained by taking the foot off the judgement and moralism pedal where promiscuous female sex is concerned, e.g. sex that falls short of the gold standard of commitment and monogamy.

Compare the zestful analysis of bad sexual experiences and the acutely trauma-aware retrospectivism of today to the responses of the young women of the 1960s (who evolved into the feminists of the 1970s). As the sociologist Massimo Perinelli notes, 'there exists a myth about the sexual revolution being a tool of domination for men against women's struggle for independence and self-determination'.[1] This is from a quiet chapter of his that attempts to rescue the sexual revolution from the pervasive idea that it was just an advantage-taking exercise, 'that if ever it was acknowledged as pleasure, then it was only by the former at the expense of the latter. As a consequence of this myth,' says Perinelli, 'women as an integral part of the sexual liberation movements of the 1960s were concealed in historical studies on the subject.'[2]

A similar thing is happening now, with women's pleasure in, or gains from, casual sex often being overshadowed and mocked by the politics of disapproval. But those women who experienced callous or bad behaviour during the 'sexual revolution' also had amazing and interesting, galvanising experiences of politicisation and intellectual growth.

As ever, the beating heart of the 1960s and 1970s – when there wasn't the well-established language of repudiation of disrespectful or abusive male behaviour – provides insight. As noted by Marcus Collins, the historian and author of the excellent book *Modern Love: An Intimate History of Men and Women in Twentieth-Century Britain*, the 'wild idealism' of the sexual revolution 'encouraged women to stop accepting their lot as being "how things happen". Its giddy curiosity made novelist Angela Carter ask questions about nothing less than "the nature of reality" that inexorably led to her "questioning the nature of her reality as a woman".' Collins, who combed vast amounts of archival material, writes that women's expanded 'sense of the possible made their hurt all the rawer, their questions, their feelings of injustice the greater and their willingness to tolerate unsatisfactory personal relationships far less pronounced. The gap between hope and experience formed the grounds for revolt.'[3]

In the absence of normalised talk about feeling 'unsafe' or 'triggered', I can't help but notice how briskly women converted their experiences in the sex bonanza to thought, and then action; 'grounds for revolution', 'questioning the nature of her reality as a woman', 'hope and experience'. It was ok not to enjoy one's sex life, or parts of it. It was ok to even feel treated badly by it and admit to this. It wasn't necessarily the end of the world.

I like this testimony from a Miss E, describing her first experience of sex as a thirteen-year-old teenager in the early eighties. To the contemporary eye it looks almost madly callous and game-like – the double take is that it's the girls creating that impression. What is striking about the whole thing is how self-aware Miss E is, and how spacious her sense of what sex might be as something that can grow or shrink in meaning and pleasure depending on familiarity or circumstances. From her vantage point, given that its fruits have yet to be revealed, she might as well get a perfunctory amusing experience out of it. The casual liberty of calling out to her friend as if it's a mildly amusing competition or a task so boring it requires reading a book to get through it! I just love the whole tone of this account. It deserves to be quoted at some length.

> There was me and my friend, and her boyfriend and my boyfriend. It was sort of very basic, man on top of woman. She

was in the other room, and we suddenly started calling out how many times we'd done it – 'Oh, I've done it three times,' or 'I've only done it two', you know? I think she beat me, though. I was expecting to feel pain and blood gushing everywhere, or something like bells, cos of these adverts and movies where it seems to be so romantic or sexy. It wasn't earth-shattering, put it that way. It was just basically something to do at the end of a party, I think. I'd seen things like porno magazines and thought, 'They all look like they're enjoying that,' so I knew there must be something else to it. One bloke I went out with, I used to sing while he did it to me and wave to people, read a book. I think somebody did it to me in the end properly. Obviously, as you grow older you realize there's much more to it, and there's more entangled with it, and it gets a bit more complicated then.[4]

As for the prospect of sex leading to maternity: 'The thought of pregnancy put a shiver up my spine'.[5] This was not a controversial statement and has been echoed many times over by young women in word and deed for time immemorial, and, luckily, since the late 1960s, it was something that was achievable alongside a sex life.

### What's Wrong with OnlyFans?

'It was a platform where I could fully be all of me and was cherished, praised – and paid for it.' She pulled in up to twelve times her previous earnings.[6] 'I love it,' the hyper-woke Lebanese-American former porn actress and OnlyFans's biggest star, Mia Khalifa, confessed to the *New York Times* in late 2024. And there's Bonnie Blue, rolling in cash, thanks to OnlyFans, and tough as nails (OnlyFans turned prudish and banned Blue from the site after her 1,000 men, but Blue does not seem particularly stymied by this).

Trafficking, crime, violence, depression, long-term trauma are certainly to be found everywhere people sell sex, but exponentially more of this occurs when these encounters take place in real life. Despite its comparative safety and autonomy, selling sex – or indeed buying a sexual-romantic fantasy – on a digital platform gets a terrible rap from conservatives and an important cadre of feminists, as if it is the most dangerous of all arenas to sell sex. Part of this is a response to the equally dubious claims by many progressives that sex work not only has the dignity of work, but is especially empowering and wonderful. This may or may not be true. For a woman like Khalifa who has talked about her OnlyFans work as a 'reclamation' of her 'brand' (and therefore herself) and become fantastically rich doing so, it seems true enough. In the imagination of some male authors, all the way back to Jon Cleland, author of *Fanny Hill: Memoirs of a Woman of Pleasure* (1748), it is certainly true. For many, it may not be especially empowering, but simply the most efficient way of making money for a decent quality of life for the woman and her child or children. Really, sex work shouldn't really be parsed and judged through the binary of empowering or not; why try to force it through that feminist needle?

Because of history, mainly. The question of whether sex work is legitimate work and should be regulated, not banned or its providers punished, has preoccupied feminists for over a century.

The first 'purity' feminists and campaigners argued over who should be punished for the use of prostitutes. Those campaigning for the repeal of the prostitute-punishing Contagious Diseases Act believed it ought to be men and that this would more effectively lead to the outlawing of the whole trade which, they were convinced, brought down all of society in its embrace of vice.[7]

Later, the women's liberation movement would also experience enormous rifts over sex work that developed into what became known as the 'sex wars' of the 1980s and which were electrified by the rise of mass pornography. Echoing their early twentieth century foremothers, one front of feminism, led by Andrea Dworkin and Catherine MacKinnon, demanded an end to porn, insisting it was pure exploitation of women by men, and entirely synonymous with rape.[8] But the 'sex positive' feminists wanted a reinvention of female sexual experience away from this narrative of victimhood and false consciousness; some argued that sex work, including prostitution and porn, could be a dignified profession as well as offering the possibility of self-empowerment, while others argued that the problem wasn't the sex work, but the endless stigmatisation of it. Lose the stigma and you could clean up and make safer the industry through regulation, with sex workers and porn stars laughing all the way to the bank, unharmed.

Some women have investigated sex work after participating in it, taking it seriously, and examining their own experiences and motivations.[9] These are nuanced depictions of a very mixed bag. But to observers like *The New Yorker* essayist Ariel Levy, by the early 2000s, sex-positivity had led to a self-harming 'raunch culture', leading her to opine with shrewdness that: 'Because we have determined that all empowered women must be overtly and publicly sexual, and because the only sign of sexuality we seem to be able to recognise is a direct allusion to red-light entertainment, we have laced the sleazy energy and aesthetic of a topless club of a Penthouse shoot throughout our entire culture.'[10]

Levy was smart, and mostly, I think, bang-on. She was responding to a very offline moment of apparent exhibitionism and stripping and nudey pole dancing, dubbed girl-time or exercise. But there are pragmatic, choice-driven ways in which new technological environments – from the Chat GPT-5 hologram wives of

Japan to OnlyFans, JustforFans, Cameo, Replika and their ilk – are used by people for economic and psychological reasons, or simply for reasons too complicated to fit past condemnations. And they are better than their older alternatives. Way better: aka safer. Selling nudes online may be distasteful to some, but people are entitled to choose their own solutions to how to pay their mortgages or go on holiday.

Old-school prostitution, on streets and in brothels, occupies a different terrain. Let's not pretend for a moment it's rosy. The anti-prostitution campaigner and former prostitute Rachel Moran has the kind of first-hand knowledge that demands attention. In her memoir, *Paid For: My Journey Through Prostitution*, this kind of sex work is 'neither sex nor work'. Moran writes that 'in prostitution, the cash is the coercive force, the evidence of the coercion, and the great silencer all at the same time. What right to complaint is a woman seen to have when she's been compensated for her own violation?'[11]

Does it have to be 'violation'? Others argue, including those who work as prostitutes, that the kind of sex they have should be seen mainly as part of a financial transaction that is chosen and then agreed to in full knowledge, *compos mentis*, by an adult. And while paid sex may feel naturally like 'violation' to many or even most women, it does not have to, as a rule of law or nature, feel like that for all. We know it does not.

Still, compared to the genuinely mean streets, full of violent and hideous men and their body parts and bodily fluids, OnlyFans and the digital universe provides relief, release and even a degree of smugness and satisfaction. Rather than feeling played by the system, some feel that they are beneficiaries of it – playing it at its own game, with enjoyable results. Remember Mia Khalifa's unqualified: 'I love it.' Are we supposed to assume she's lying and doesn't even know it?

'I'm a good feminist because I'm a bad woman,' writes the

feminist Melissa Kerman in an analysis of OnlyFans, where she has an account. 'Vexing misogynists gives me wings, and OnlyFans merely adds to my 'deviant' womanhood. For years I've flaunted my body on social media and received catcalls from strangers on the street. Now I'm able to monetise it.'[12]

Is it really the 'the system' (patriarchy, capitalism, neoliberalism, colonialism) that makes Kerman and Khalifa and Aiella, the 'intellectual's porn star', 'choose' all this? We all get it. Critics of sex work would never choose it for themselves and do not 'have' to.

## *People Need Money*

But the truth is that private life and intimate connections have always been inseparable from money, even in the most wholesome of family spheres. 'We like to think of money and intimacy as separate domains and worry that money turns our personal life into a calculating market,' says Princeton professor of sociology Viviana Zelizer, when in fact we all 'use money and more generally, economic activity to create, maintain, and renegotiate important intimate ties without necessarily damaging them. Far from corrupting intimacy, people regularly sustain their intimate ties with economic transactions.'[13]

Digital sex work is not a line of work I would go down the way things currently stand, but given that nearly half a million people per year in England alone say they consider suicide because of financial stress, which for many (especially in countries that offered less of a cushion) became more acute in the pandemic, a DIY subscription model for explicit material offers considerable financial relief that could potentially be literally life-saving.[14] The testimonies of the lucky fraction who have been successful on OnlyFans and its ilk do not suggest pitiful false consciousness, exploitation by 'the system' or patriarchy, or miserable labouring under the inhumane harness of neoliberalism. They suggest a rational and savvy response to economic realities combined with professional and personal taste.

'I set up an OnlyFans page early in the pandemic to rebuild the income I had suddenly lost as the coronavirus descended on the world,' recounted *Slate* sex columnist and pornographic actress Jessica Stoya.

> The first weekend in March 2020, I had flown to Minneapolis to perform in a burlesque act; a week later, I could barely leave my apartment in New York. As a performer and pornographer, I couldn't work on sets, and I couldn't do events. OnlyFans helped stave off that loss, and it kept my professional photographer roommate and I busy. Followers I had built over years, also now isolated, came with me and had fresh content, too. Crucially, they also had someone to talk to. My DMs are always full.[15]

Stoya says the 'tens of thousands of others who also turned to OnlyFans in the pandemic, many without my base and in far more acute financial distress' are what helped the platform 'explode.'

This wasn't just desperation – it was fun, even delirious fun. One thinks of Courtney Tillia, a former special education teacher in Arizona who felt depressed by financial worry and underappreciated at work until her husband encouraged her to pursue her passion. She was promptly earning twelve times more than she did as a teacher. 'It was a platform where I could fully be all of me, and was cherished, praised –and paid for it.'[16] Selling sex doesn't seem to have been a showcase of self-hate and self-degradation. It can clearly also help some women to find liberation, self-respect, belonging, security, and the earnings are a big part of that.

Tillia's testimony is fascinating for her initial attraction to the pursuit itself, with the money a bonus. 'I fell in love with being

## CHOICE: FREE AND MISERABLE VS... UNFREE AND MISERABLE

liberated and being able to share myself in different ways. I started this for my own expression. I had no idea there was so much money to be made in it as there is.' Tillia sees her work as also 'help[ing] to bring [fantasies] alive in some way – and [I] get paid well to do it ... It's a win for everyone, except those who are committed to reasons to be mad.'[17] The money has paid for her to help support her children, for her house and to travel widely.

It's the financial transaction that worries people. But if one listens to the people selling their sexual services online, in the new portfolio of subscriber sites where the site is the only middleman (OnlyFans takes a 20 per cent cut), it's hard to find much hatred of 'neoliberalism'. On the contrary: 'neoliberalism' is what is letting them laugh all the way to the bank, relieving them of terrible financial stress, allowing them to explore new bits of themselves (literally and figuratively) and allowing them to improve the whole business, making it safer and fairer. There is even a belief that 'tech and finance' are not the obstacle to achieving these goals, but are, in fact, necessary for them.

According to Cindy Gallop, the founder of user-created explicit site MakeLoveNotPorn: 'The answer to everything that worries people about porn and sex is not to clamp down, block, repress, but instead, to open up. When the tech and finance industries do what they've done for every other sector – welcome, support, fund, and facilitate disruption and innovation – we will see a dramatic transformation of what is deemed 'adult'. The only thing that stops a bad guy with a business is a good guy with a better business – and infinitely better financial returns.'[18] Now, Cindy is a true liberal.

And the results of excluding consensual sex workers from that bogeyman known as mainstream banking? Only that the 'lives of sex workers [are made] more precarious and ... workers [are opened] up further to predation by entities ranging from check-cashing services to exploitative managers.' As for the particular medium of DIY platforms: 'When people get this autonomy to showcase themselves the way that they want, to monetize themselves the way that they want, that is huge.'[19]

Let's assume that for many sex workers, the remuneration is the lure. But for a sizeable segment, not just individual cases like those of Courtney Tillia, it's the work itself. As Dan Savage knows from thousands of letters and calls (more Dan Savage! I know; bear with me), for a segment of society, it's not fake empowerment masking a deep sense of violation, or desperation for money masquerading as pleasure. It actually is pleasure. He sees OnlyFans and other such sites as a scrappy market response to that desire to exhibit. After all, you can't have a business without supply as well as demand.

> People want to be affirmed as objects and as erotically desirable, and so there are people who are exhibitionists, or have moments of exhibitionism, even if they aren't an exhibitionist, and OnlyFans created a platform where you didn't have to show up in Times Square and go up to some studio on the tenth floor of a rotting office building and sit with some skeezy photographer. What we saw when people had agency, control and a modicum of safety was there are a lot more people out there – a lot more women out there – who are willing and interested in [creating this content] than anybody could have predicted or would have predicted based on what we're all supposed to pretend to believe is true about all women everywhere.

As for the progressive critique of sex work, Savage has a well-developed view. 'There [are],' he acknowledges, 'a certain number of people who are doing it under economic duress, and this comes up whenever you talk about decriminalising. [Some] people are going to do this because they have no other options. That is true. People flip burgers for the same reason, [and] nobody gives a shit about those people. If you don't want people doing shit or being surrogate mothers out of economic duress: universal basic income, housing, healthcare, education.'

\*

All of these things – twenty-somethings shagging around courtesy of Tinder, ensnared in hookup culture, sometimes regretting it, sometimes not; the thousands of women (and men) doing rude things on the camera in exchange for money – are forms of promiscuity. They exhibit, to their critics, lack of discrimination or proper 'boundaries'. But they are neither objectively morally terrible or objectively morally great and, in a sense, it doesn't matter. I have tried to argue in this chapter that female promiscuity, from loads of one-night stands to selling tricks on OnlyFans, whether good or bad, should not just be tolerated and allowed, but defended as essential to the true values of liberal democracies like ours. This society, worth defending, knows that respect for lawful individual freedom is vital to a healthy collective. It knows that the distasteful, the unhealthy, the exhibitionist, and the improper must be just as acceptable for women as they are for men. If women find them damaging and unpleasant, hopefully they can find a way to stop. But if they can't or don't, and are made miserable by a promiscuous life, then that is *still* far better than the alternative.

When it comes to female sexuality, we could gain much by curbing the impulses to punish and interfere when we could observe and be curious; to enforce when we should persuade, and to proscribe when we should support and allow. Failure to be at political and moral peace with women's right to promiscuity – whether one personally likes or approves of it or not – can only degrade a society.

In much of the West today, that promiscuity is defended properly; deplored by many in all sorts of settings, from TikTok to megachurches to mosques to pro-natalist Instagram accounts, but defended and protected, nonetheless. But the gathering storm of a rising generation's mistaken ideas about 'neoliberalism' and 'the system' and their relationships to women's sexual freedom, an increasingly widespread and vocal religious Islam, and a voguish upsurge in a TikTok and Instagram-friendly pro-natalist Christianity means this is the most important moment in generations to double down on women's right to be slatternly shag-queens. In insisting, without shame, on this aspect of our society, we will be supporting, not degrading, the core Enlightenment values that still just about make the West the West – and the end of the rainbow for people, and especially women, the world over.

## Chapter Nine

# The Tenacity of the Romantic Ideal

'Stop hedging, start marrying', writes Mary Harrington in the New Social Covenant Unit set up by Danny Kruger MP and former MP Miriam Cates in 2021. 'Once I did make that commitment to life in common,' Harrington, a vocal former gender-queer practitioner of polyamorous relationships continues, 'all the things that were missing from my life suddenly became possible, as if by magic. A permanent home; more stable employment; children; even, imperceptibly, something I thought I was psychologically incapable of: a sense of belonging to a place.' Harrington's apparently seismic decision to get married is set out in contrast to the state of 'atomised individualism' that engulfs those resisting or unable to find someone to say 'I do' to, and 'the crashing birth rate, housing crisis, and epidemic of loneliness.'[1]

For the marriage evangelists of the feminist right; the trad wife influencers, and the rationalist pro-natalists who want their breeding projects to take place on a conjugal ticket, the purported death of marriage is a key sign of cultural decay and a grave existential threat. Depending on who is prophesying it within this motley crew, doom is envisioned as a world without children, depopulated and amoral, reduced to rubble by a victorious environment lobby; a world in which the problem is not too few children but swarms of them born to feckless single parents, unanchored by the traditional form of hearth and home; a world, as Harrington fears, sickened by armies of atomised lonely and morally sick young people slowly wasting their reproductive potential on the altar of selfishness and a false idea of freedom, sowing the seeds of a lifetime of grief and emptiness as they drink down their oat milk cortados in an endless parade of airport terminals bound for the next heavily Instagramable destination and the next casual tussle in bed with a stranger. But that is nothing like the reality. It is spin.

## *Is Marriage Really Dead?*

Before considering the truth about the marital edifice, it's worth addressing whether doing so is even worth the energy. As our conservative friends would have us believe, 'marriage, as it once was, is now more or less dead'.[2]

But is it? The short answer is no. There are changes in trends where details are concerned, such as civil partnership being recognised alongside legal marriage, including of same-sex couples, plus the rise of cohabitation and other forms of commitment. But the committed couple, whether straight or same-sex, remains the bedrock of what is considered normal. This is the finding of sociologist Sacha Roseneil, the Vice Chancellor of Sussex University, in her book *The Tenacity of the Couple-Norm*, a study of the meaning, experience of and resistance to coupledom in the UK, Bulgaria, Norway and Portugal. Roseneil and her co-authors are highly attuned to 'normative' expressions of sexuality – namely the broad models of intimacy that structure the way people try to organise themselves – and her findings are important. They show that poking through all the change – the non-monogamy, singleness, same-sex marriage, hookup culture that has enraged and flustered the new reactionaries – are the old sharp outlines of traditional notions of coupledom. These are so powerful that, in Roseneil's view, committed coupledom still constitutes a social 'basis of citizenship'. She finds that the idea of the couple isn't just fodder for romcoms, but actually still shapes 'the intimate life choices and trajectories, the subjectivities, deepest longings and desires, of those who seem to be living aslant to the conventional heterosexual cohabiting couple-form.'[3] Including, of course, all those women bonking their way miserably, or merrily, through the years of their education and beyond, phone glued to their hand.

Broad statistical trends obviously show that fewer people get married now than they did in the 1970s. This does not mean that weddings are rare. Nearly every friend of mine in a serious relationship is married. My younger cousins, in their late twenties, are constantly at weddings. We hear a lot about the reluctance or inability of Gen-Z to venture outside to meet people at all, let alone strike up intimate relationships – yet a growing body of surveys suggests that they may be keener than the previous three generations on marriage and commitment. According to a survey by Her Campus Media, a marketing firm that studies the preferences of university-aged women, 90 per cent of American twenty-somethings say they want to get married one day. 'Older generations may have felt drawn to marriage out of necessity or obligated based on societal pressures, which also led to high divorce rates, but Gen Z sees things differently,' observed Stephanie Kaplan Lewis, a founder of Her Campus Media to *Newsweek*. 'For them, there is renewed hope in committing to a partner and having a built in support system.'[4]

Because heterosexual marriage is the end-point of a powerful idea that still scripts intimacy narratives, hopes, desires and actions. Marriage rates are actually up and divorce rates have been in gradual decline since the turn of the millennium, less than a decade after the peak in the early 1990s.[5] In the very short term, the pandemic precipitated a spike in people tying the knot, with rates up in 2022 compared to 2019.[6] This was partly because of rescheduled weddings and partly because circumstances conspired to throw people into more committed clinches, which they chose to consecrate with marriage. As for the decline in divorce, sociologists and psychologists spell out the obvious: gender roles are more flexible, people are better at communicating respectfully what they want, and they are bringing a more sophisticated set of criteria to the decision to marry in the first place, choosing companionship from the outset, as well as, or even more than fireworks.[7]

Meanwhile, the fantasy of 'the perfect day' went stratospheric after marriage ceased to be socially compulsory.[8] British sociologists Julia Carter and Simon Duncan interviewed heterosexual couples tying the knot in contemporary Britain about why they were taking such pains, in a society of sexual liberality, to present a lavish day with the trappings of tradition. Their respondents suggested that there was more to it than social displays of success or manipulation by a powerful wedding industry. Weddings actually took on new meaning by sacralising the hard work that went into the 'project of the couple', the enduring desire to be 'normal' but beautifully so, combined with new and irresistible forms of 'romanticised consumption'. Being beautifully normal in the way you display romantic success is very expensive, but seems to be a price many are willing to pay. Weddings reached an average cost of £16,000–£17,000 in the UK in 2005 – considerably more expensive than decades before. By 2023, the average amount spent on getting hitched was £20,000 (and $30,000 in the US). It's rising by the year with inflation.

Of course, those worrying about the decline of marriage don't just want people to get hitched, they want them to do it within tight frameworks, especially theological ones, so that it's fruitful and forever and duty-bound. At least on the surface. But perhaps they can take comfort in the equally tight framework of 'romanticised consumption' that drives people to the altar. Remember how Eva Illouz wrote in *Consuming the Romantic Utopia* that when people fall in love they do so through the meals, the cigarettes, the cocktails and the holidays that advertisers have made an essential part of making magic?[9] Well, fine. Even if the romance of holidays and wine-tastings, and the prospect of a big white dress and plush 'wedding dinner' at a stately home plays as big a role in marriage as propriety once did, then once married, perhaps the difference is more minor than it appears. After all, marriage is the jumping off point for financial entwinement, if only through property. And, as Princeton sociologist Viviana Zelizer argues in *The Purchase of Intimacy*, her influential analysis of the ties that bind, the flow of money and assets between couples becomes its own powerful system of meaning.

For a society allegedly on the brink of torching all vestiges of commitment and responsibility, of family formation and love, we sure have a healthy interest in and reverence for weddings. This obsession intensified as marriage rates sunk then stabilised. As feminist scholars Jackie Stacey and Lynne Pearce concluded after organising a conference on romance in 1993, in light of the media frenzy surrounding Princess Diana's relationships, the 'combined fascination and anxiety with romantic love' emerged precisely because it was 'against all the odds (social, political, intellectual)'.[10] Marriage and romantic love have not been discredited. Far from it. Nor has the apparatus around it; there are tax breaks for married couples, and divorce, while easy to obtain, is still legally nightmarish when it comes to sorting out custody and assets. Marriage is not something most people take lightly.

Marriage in popular culture is interesting to consider. It has gone hypersonic. We are obsessed. *Say Yes to the Dress* is an entire series, aired on TLC, about brides-to-be shopping for the perfect dress at a New York bridal shop. *Marriage or Mortgage?* pits dreams against each other, as does the phenomenon *90 Day Fiancée* – which follows pairs becoming engaged for US immigration purposes, for which they must demonstrate intimate knowledge of each other. In *Ultimatum: Marry or Move On*, couples must decide whether to marry, ditch or couple up with an attractive alternative; just carrying on together as before is not an option in this show's universe. Meanwhile, in programmes like *Married at First Sight* and *Love Is Blind*, lavish (filmed, non-legally-binding) weddings between relative or complete strangers are the start of the relationship. As such, they do relatively little to answer the programmes' animating question: can they get along under the eye of their fake-real wedding rings and the cameras? It's a global conundrum, as *Jewish Matchmaking*, and India's *The Big Day* and *Indian Matchmaking* (all on Netflix) make clear.

## *Divorce 'Epidemic'?*

Every generation of grown-ups has condemned technological progress. Radio would kill reading! Video killed the radio star! The same pattern is true for social progress; women's suffrage, or the admittance of women to law or medical school, for instance, would destroy everything! And now, society has gone to the dogs because of too much freedom!

The conviction, and associated fear, that marriage is dead, killed off by the forces of modernisation – individualism, selfishness and secularism – has been aired for as long as divorce reform has been a matter of public debate, beginning in the 1940s and escalating in 1951 with the establishment of the royal commission on the matter.[11] Long before any 'sexual revolution', there was Dr Edward Griffith, a popular sex-education author and founding member of the National Marriage Guidance Council, speaking in August 1948 at the International Congress on Mental Health, lamenting the demise of British reverence for marriage and family life – one in four British brides became pregnant before marriage, he pointed out, while abortions (still illegal and therefore dangerous), illegitimacy and sexually transmitted diseases were all 'on the increase'. Most distressing, he argued in tones that sound awfully familiar to followers of the new reactionaries, was the 'divorce epidemic . . . In this country in 1900 there were 500 divorce and separation cases; this year there will be at least 50,000.'[12]

Headlines from the period of divorce reform debate in the late 1960s offer a snapshot of hot takes. The *Daily Sketch* had 'Divorce – English style – where the man always comes off best'. The *Catholic Herald*: 'Polygamy on the State'; the *Sunday Telegraph*: 'Will girls give up marrying?'. The *Spectator*: 'Towards a bigamy bill?' And the *Sunday Express*: 'Who decided we wanted easy divorce?'

In the following decades, anxieties about selfishness bloomed. 'We are concerned that . . . individualism may have grown cancerous,' wrote sociologist Robert Bellah and colleagues in *Habits of the Heart: Individualism and Commitment in American Life*, published in 1985, which set out the argument that the contractual style of commercial and bureaucratic life had infiltrated the private domain.

From the late 1970s onwards, academics and commentators connected Margaret Thatcher's ascendance with a 'hyper-individualism' that reduced morality to nothing more than a matter of individual choice and preference'.[13] It wasn't just morality: the 'interior self has no structure'.[14] Moderns were being diagnosed by sociologists and anthropologists as being unable to make meaningful attachments; family itself was beyond such people.[15]

Like those perpetually suspicious of 'neoliberalism' today, the political theorists and anthropologists worrying about excessive individualism and its effects on family life and social bonds saw at root a problem of 'consumerist ideology'. The consumerism of late capitalism and its architects and handmaidens fragmented the self and made people act out scripts that suited capitalism, not themselves, or the community, opening up 'a frightening picture of a world in which there is no vision of the common good and in which rampant individualism is in the process of destroying the very foundations – the family and the community – on which . . . modern liberal democracies depend.'[16]

But the links between the introduction of no-fault divorce in 1971 and rocketing rates of divorce in the following decades were always far more obscure and intricate than the family values tub-thumpers allow. We know two things. One is that the pro-marriage vanguard tends to misinterpret the results of the Divorce Reform Act. They decry the apparent explosion of divorce that followed it, to the surprise, it is suggested, of its architects. In fact, the historical consensus is – as was widely acknowledged at the time – that the dam burst because there was an intolerable build up, not because the legislation suddenly made married people behave with selfish cruelty.

And two: there is no way of knowing what came first: the shift in norms, values and desires away from marriage-for-life or a liberalising law that made divorce easier. But it is generally thought that law follows, or messily tries to move in tandem with, social change. In her discussion of responses to rising divorce rates in the late twentieth century, sociologist Jane Lewis, notes that those most convinced of a plague of atomisation, individualism and selfishness are making assumptions from the dramatic changes made in the statistics recording family change. But, she says, 'these studies do not in the main investigate what is actually going on inside personal relationships'. She adds that the relationship is far from 'direct' between what is going on inside the family and what is going on in, for example, the labour market or family law.[17]

There is another familiar dynamic at play in the revived family values movement: backlash. When women appear to be making gains in earnings and sexual freedom, new voices emerge carrying old messages: stop them. In *Backlash*, Susan Faludi pinpointed a heightened discourse on the benefits of coupledom and marriage in the 1980s and 1990s that particularly targeted single women.[18] Others have chronicled the resurgence of a pro-marriage, family-values movement at the end of the twentieth century as a response to and sometimes exploitation of the trauma of AIDS.[19]

All in all, then, it seems unlikely that Louise Perry's lament that 'the institution of marriage, as it once was, is now more or less dead', can be true, in any sense. Many if not most things 'as they once were' are 'more or less dead', whether by dramatic changes or through a slow process of modifications, as in the case of the framework surrounding marriage. But not marriage itself.

Central to the family values caucus is the idea that, with their newfangled throwaway attitude to everything, people began simply waltzing into divorce. Also not true. Divorce remains agonising, and always will be, because it means dividing up money, assets and time with children. It used to be even worse because of the stigma attached to it. If one looks at accounts from marriage counsellors and social workers, divorce at its peak in the 1970s and 1980s was an unimaginably raw, painful and grisly affair experienced as 'worse than bereavement' – indicating that those who trod that path did so at great personal cost and must therefore have been deeply motivated by terrible emotional strain in moribund marriages. 'All divorces are hard-won,' writes Lyons, and 'the finality of loss, the ability to hope for the return of the lost person, and the apparent temporary nature of the "bereavement" all make it in some senses harder than losing someone to death' – an event which, she argues, at least has a more thorough, less isolating emotional support structure.[20]

Her account, untouched before I ordered it up from a grey desk in an empty room at the Wellcome library, makes for fascinating reading about gender and emotion. 'Repeatedly we come across shell-shocked, depressed men who seem dazed by their feelings,' Lyons reports.

> Our women seem much more resilient, often ruthlessly determined to pursue the divorce. This difference may in part be related to the different extent of the concrete losses faced but also seems linked with different experiences and expectations of intimacy. The women on the whole have become dissatisfied with what their husbands have offered at a much earlier stage in the life of the family – often with the arrival of children – and this process of disillusionment has remained and increased, whereas the men if they have thought at all about the state of their marriages, either have believed the degree of intimacy to be all right, or have believed that any problems can be overcome or ignored. This pattern is very clear and very compelling.[21]

## *The Real Housewives of the 1950s and the State-Sanctioned Duty of Women*

One could even argue that marriage (and thus divorce) is more alive today than it would have otherwise been had the state not made a concerted and explicit effort to encourage it after World War Two. The historian Teri Chettiar, who spent years combing the archives of the Marriage Guidance Council between 1940 and 1980, has written in great detail about the 'psychopoliticisation' of the state: the decision to push marriage for political ends, not to shore up a conservative or progressive agenda, but rather the strength of the state, the nation and democracy itself. It was felt that miserable marriages and specifically miserable wives – already an archetype in the 1960s – were bad for the business of the state since they confused

# THE TENACITY OF THE ROMANTIC IDEAL

the labour market, threw the male breadwinner off his path and created psychological problems in children, which would become a health and productivity headache later. From a post-war nation-building perspective, the urgency of keeping people married was profound, and the agenda was ambitious: nothing less than a major plank in the enactment of William Beveridge's welfare state plan to end 'want, disease, ignorance, squalor, and idleness'.

A strategy of outreach and encouragement ensued, aiming to sell marriage, and staying in it, with couples encouraged to explore emotions and pushed towards a briskly expanding menu of free marriage therapy. A network of marriage welfare services, argues Chettiar, 'was integral to the wider welfare-state project of eliminating class divisions . . . by [affirming] the universal importance of emotional relationships as the central determining fact of citizens' lives . . . marriage services were embedded within key discussions about Britain's future, in exchanges between pioneering marriage therapists as well as in debates within the halls of Parliament.'[22] But this was all based on bolstering a traditionalist's idea of marriage, which made the male-breadwinning, female-homemaking nuclear family a cornerstone of the plans for the welfare state. For women who were already feeling listless and stuck in the thickly protected domestic sphere, this offered little encouragement.

The historian Claire Langhamer, now the director of London's Institute of Historical Research and my PhD supervisor at Sussex, has spent more than twenty years studying twentieth century intimate life in Britain. Again and again her work returns to two contradictory threads. The first is the traditionalist state promotion of marriage, through discourse subtle and less subtle, which is also what Teri Chettiar found going through the records with a fine-toothed comb. In the late 1940s, women were as good as told, thank you very much for your help during the war while the men were away, but now your national duty is to be a good wife and take good emotional (and domestic) care of your husband. 'A happy home is the bulwark of the nation' was the view of wartime respondents to the Mass Observation survey; no prizes for guessing on whose shoulders fell the labour of making the home happy. The state agreed. 'In particular,' as Langhamer reminds us in her study of women's work in the 1950s, 'the mother-child relationship was heralded as the bedrock upon which the health of the nation was to be built; a fetishisation of emotional security stemming directly from the experience of war. Relationships between spouses were also deemed crucial to the process of national reconstruction. The feelings of returning servicemen needed particularly careful management and this was a task for which their wives were to be primarily responsible.'[23]

But the second thread woven through Langhamer's work is that by the 1970s when, shaped by cultural rather than top-down conservative forces, marriage became explicitly about love and 'compatibility'. Not just love, but a magical synergy of soulmates – bonded by sexual passion, deep friendship and the alloy of deep and abiding romantic love. Married under the pressure of such expectations, many of these relationships were doomed to buckle. Immense pressure to get it right in all ways had been built into marriages from the 1950s, a time when, as Langhamer puts it, 'love and marriage became the bearer of post-war hopes for a rationally planned, efficient and hopeful future'.[24] Curiously, that rational view of a well-ordered future was bound up with new expectations to, in the words of the mid-century social researchers Eliot Slater and Moya Woodside, indulge in 'the cult of the "personality" . . . [the demand for] temperamental compatibility' and the sexual felicities this entailed.[25]

In both of these versions of marriage, the same thing is true: its modern problems come from being overburdened, not underburdened, with meaning and importance.

## *Damage Limitation*

The common view among the new pro-marriage conservative vanguard of intellectuals is that we have lost all the good things and gained only the bad. When it comes to marriage, I am inclined to flip this: we have lost most of the bad things – like conjugal entrapment felt and real; decades of misery whose escape is curtailed by the Church – and kept the good things, like the public vow of commitment, the joyful and excitingly lavish celebration of love, and the fact that for many people, engagement and marriage provide an attainable goal that makes them feel rooted, offers a compass in their journey through life and soothes their fears of being all alone.

It is argued by the new pro-family feminists that 'fidelity, forbearance, duty' have been chucked out in favour of easy and frictionless musical chairs, and a selfish the-kids-be-damned attitude. But the reality, as most divorced people know, is much different. Divorce, though further simplified in 2023, is still not a walk in the park as long as children are involved, which they often are; finances are also a nightmare. As for the kids, the story isn't as clear-cut as marriage evangelists suggest. Divorce can be grisly and truly disrupt children's lives. In that sense, it is a sorrowful and regretful event. We saw before how shocking it all felt in the 1970s to people raised on mid-century ideas about family and propriety.

But is divorce still the eternal toxic waste-trail and trauma factory that self-described reformed slut Bridget Phetasy insists it is, guaranteed to destroy children's lives forever? Of course it isn't: experiences like hers are the extreme, not the norm. Just as Perry stresses bell curves, perhaps so as to ward off accusations of blanket illiberalism ('most women aren't as horny as men', 'Marital satisfaction is [almost] normally distributed'),[26] so there is a bell curve of divorce – most do not appear to have lifelong catastrophic effects on the children, and some are a relief for them, improving their lives and their psychological functioning dramatically.

When I was researching the effects of divorce reform on the emotional fabric of British relational life, I read countless testimonies of social workers, mothers (and fathers) and children about the effects of family breakdown. The picture was varied and complicated, entirely dependent on the quality of the parents' relationship and each individual parent's ability to make life feel secure for the child, and limit stress and acrimony of the divorce and also in relation to subsequent marriages and children. I read the words of Helen, a -sixteen-year-old, who was quoted in the *Daily Mail*'s 'Junior Letters', of all places. In October 1979, she wrote to say that her mother, father and step-mother were happy. 'I am surprised when my friends, most of whom know of my parents' divorce, say they feel sorry for me. I resent the way they are taught to believe that divorce is necessarily a sad ending to a marriage. Sometimes it is a happy beginning to a better life'. Simon, another child of divorce, wrote in 1979: 'suffering? It's all in adults minds'.

## Chapter Ten

# In Praise of Single Motherhood

Marriage is no absolute good because, like all human relationships, it's only good if it's good, and it helps if the people in them are good – a perspective that modern secularism and greater gender equality has allowed us to engage with full frontally. Jonathan Rothwell, head economist at Gallup and two decades into a career producing and scrutinising survey data relating to families, says this about marriage: 'I don't think we're ever going to get to a point in social science where we can say whether or not and with any precision whether marriage causes happiness.'

Indeed. So, would a world in which singleness, not coupledom or marriage, was the norm, really be so bad? One in which the two statuses switched and those who went it alone grew accustomed to peering pitifully at people who turned up at parties with partners?

No. In fact, it would probably be a much better world. But only for women.

First, the painfully raw facts. Intimate committed relationships – including marriage – remain key sites of murder, violence and abuse against women. In fact, entering a committed relationship with a man is the most lethal decision a woman can make.[1] So when we are told that casual sex demeans or threatens women, we should put these risks in the context of heterosexual activity more generally. According to Rape Crisis England and Wales, five out of six rapes against women are committed by men they know; one in two by a committed partner or husband.[2]

Crudely, on a broad scale, and this is something the new conservatives don't bother with: marriage is good for men and bad for women, and divorce is bad for men and good for women. When I researched accounts of divorce from professionals like social workers and marriage counsellors in the period of its greatest surge this is the trend I kept coming across.

As for the presumed causes of marital breakdown – perpetually repeated by conservatives for nearly a century – there is the contradictory insistence on a universal plague of post-Christian selfishness on one hand, and a plague of rapacious opportunistic men on the other of whom all sensible decent women are better off without. Both views rely on skimming off the cream from a wide body of pro-family research. But this research tends to leave human agency and experience out of the picture and both blames women and absconds them from responsibility, often failing to account for the actual motivations of women who initiate divorce.

Zawn Villines is a happily married American activist from the Deep South who believes 'birth doesn't have to be traumatic, motherhood doesn't have to be exhausting and demoralizing, and marriage shouldn't mean giving up your dreams or yourself.' Unfortunately, insists Villines, it very often does. She produces statistics from proper sources (IPUMS, the global census data service, *ScienceDaily* and academic articles) to support her assertion that, statistically, marriage is bad for women in every possible way. It will 'shorten women's life expectancy, lower women's earning power, erode their mental health, make them less happy over the long-term, weaken women's relationships with family and friends, erode women's libido, reduce the quality of a woman's sex life, immediately increase household labor, increase risk of and exposure to abuse and violence, and elevate risk of depression, anxiety, and trauma'. In this light, longitudinal data showing that single women (as opposed to single men) lead lives of far greater pleasure and health than married women is not surprising.[3]

Despite obvious improvements not emphasised in Villines's vituperative posts, marriage's badness for women has driven more women into choosing single motherhood, or just singleness, ever since divorce came more easily within their reach. In her PhD thesis on women's experience of single motherhood between 1945 and 1990, Bristol University historian April Gallwey found that rising numbers of women in the 1970s choosing to raise their children away from the father were not sad victims or dupes, but 'driven by their rejection of an untenable social and economic division of labour in marriage.' This is academic parlance for 'women were fed up with being domestic drudges in male-run, sometimes physically dangerous households and so they got out.'[4]

Nonetheless, single motherhood has always fit all the tropes of sexual moral panic. In the late twentieth century, its apparent social and cultural evil was enumerated in former Conservative Party MP Keith Joseph's much-publicised 1974 speech at the Grand Hotel in Edgbaston. He sounded the alarm about the

> high and rising proportion of children . . . being born to mothers least fitted to bring children into the world and bring them up . . . who were first pregnant in adolescence in social classes 4 and 5. Many of these girls are unmarried, many are deserted or divorced or soon will be. Some are of low intelligence, most of low educational attainment. They are producing problem children, the future unmarried mothers, delinquents, denizens of our

borstals, sub-normal educational establishments, prisons, hostels for drifters.[5]

Such ideas persisted. At the Conservative Party conference in 1992, Peter Lilley, the Trade and Industry Secretary, said he: '. . . had a little list of benefit offenders who I'll soon be rooting out . . . young ladies who get pregnant just to jump the waiting list. And dads who won't support the kids of ladies they have kissed.' With rhetoric like that, it could be hard to distinguish between reality and discourse – and especially the reality, for those with their ear to the ground, resulting in surging divorce rates, and leading to more fatherless households.

Naturally, there is plenty of evidence pointing to the negative effects that unplanned or unanticipated fatherlessness can have on children, with poverty emerging consistently across the twentieth century as a key cause of discontent in families headed by a struggling single mother.[6] Certainly for many women and children, single motherhood puts intense pressure on the family. But the social poison that allegedly wafts off the fatherless household – both in terms of the old idea of 'illegitimacy' and the ongoing worry that the single mothers are 'sexually promiscuous, lazy, and/or pathetic victims of predatory men' – is simply not a reflection of an inherently complex, multifarious reality, replete with countless arrangements, scenarios and emotional responses.

British studies of single motherhood following divorce tend to rely on testimony of social workers and state marriage counsellors, and therefore pay particular attention to working-class testimonies since this demographic is more dependent on state assistance. American writer Ashton Applewhite, however, is an expert in a more middle-class (American) set of motivations, experiences and outcomes, although her exhaustive prescriptions are intended to apply to women from all backgrounds. The theme that runs through her analysis of the problem (too often, marriage crushes women and serves men) is the persistence of old gender systems that dragoon women into taking a medicine designed to serve men and the Church but that metaphorically (and all too often literally) kills them. In her book *Cutting Loose: Why Women Who End Their Marriages Do So Well*, she tells the story of her own divorce, a million miles away from the squashed, dangerous strain of desperation, hunger, rape and fear gone through by married women throughout recorded history. And yet the tropes are there – only the crushing, the strain, the squashing are thankfully metaphorical.

> I had the luxury of spending as much time with [my babies] as I wanted to, and for a long time was busy with babies and books. I was the breadwinner, the mom, and a more productive and ambitious person than my ex-husband. Unfortunately, he was both deeply insecure and extremely competitive. To compensate I tried in any number of ways to 'make myself small', as I came to think of it – not because he demanded it but because it conformed to some inarticulate notion of mine of how wives should behave. It took years to acknowledge the depths of my anger and resentment and depression.[7]

Just like the stats chosen by Louise Perry to help her link sex and marriage in *The Case Against the Sexual Revolution*, Applewhite has also read 'well-publicised figures [showing] a divorced man's income soaring while his ex-wife's took a nosedive.' She wondered:

> If that was indeed what lay ahead, how come wives have always sought divorce in greater numbers than their spouses, two to one at the turn of the [twentieth] century, almost three out of four (71 per cent) in 1928, and 75 per cent in the 1990s? Had my predecessors, like me, believed this grim prognosis but decided to

take their chances anyway? Could it be that the consequences weren't actually all that dire? I resolved to find out . . . If I'd been willing to haggle longer or go to court, I probably could have gotten a better financial deal, but I'd do it again tomorrow.[8]

This is not a triumphalist sentiment, but realist, mature. 'I know something precious has been lost, but also that much of what I mourn was illusory.'

Applewhite's children were soon 'thriving' – because their parents were. And although her expenses increased, no longer having to make herself small allowed her to pursue more professional opportunities more adventurously and vigorously. 'I'm deeply involved with a wonderful man who delights in my competence and understands why remarriage holds little appeal. Best of all, I feel great: in full possession of myself, responsible, sexy, independent and powerful. Society doesn't look kindly on this sort of transition,' she adds.[9]

But society is riveted by divorce, and willing to spend a lot of money reading about it, as suggested by the lucrative new genre of memoirs of marital breakdown. Brooklyn essayist Leslie Jamison's recent book *Splinters*, about the dissolution of her marriage after her daughter was born, was an 'instant *New York Times* bestseller', heralded by Oprah's Book Club, and praised as 'stitching together the intellectual and the emotional with the finesse of a crackerjack surgeon' (NPR). 'This memoir is a masterclass,' raved Maggie Smith in the *New York Times*. 'An astonishing achievement,' stated Esmé Weijun Wang, also in the *New York Times*, explaining: 'This is a memoir of emotional depth that reminds us of how love, in its fullness, is as much a construction of jagged and flinty edges as it is an ideal of cloudless skies.'

That 'construction of jagged and flinty edges' and 'the terrors and triumphs of becoming whole' may sound appalling to right-wingers, but this splintering is what people want to read about. It speaks to the real and difficult cost-benefit analysis of marriage in the freest society for women ever.

## *Causes of Conjugal Decline*

Here we find more evidence for positivity about declining (though still strong) marriage rates. For if we look at the reasons for the decline, they are broadly positive, more to do with major, necessary social changes – chiefly the accession of women to full humanhood – than the rise of lovelessness and selfishness.

Feminists of the nineteenth and late twentieth century wanted marriage gone because they saw it – along with constructs of romantic love, full stop – as a lose-lose for women, a trick to ensnare them and make them offer their bodies and their household labour for free, with nothing in return but more subjugation and dependency. First-wave feminists, riffing on Mary Wollstonecraft, saw that until women could earn good money for themselves they would be unable to freely enter a marriage. Second-wave feminists focused on the way marriage depended on entrenching gender roles that were injurious to women, with Shulamith Firestone articulating the most powerful critique of all, that love itself 'is the pivot of women's oppression today'.[10] Women's liberationists therefore sought alternative structures for love and child-raising in communal living with other women, sometimes choosing lesbianism as a political act. Such ideas never entirely fizzled, and today there is renewed interest in cooperative living projects providing women-only and mixed living for those who want to live closer to the land and in a communal fashion. Some of these projects are urban-based and don't have the land aspect.[11]

In a sense, then, reactionaries are right to accuse feminists of wanting to destroy the social order, and particularly marriage, but they are wrong to think feminists were the ones who did it. Rather, a slower process of economic social change, buttressed by the legislative work of centrist liberal governments in Britain, the US and parts of Europe, eroded the male-breadwinner model and boosted women's participation in the economy, and thus their independence.[12]

Greater fluidity in approach to relationships and marriage has coincided with the weakening of the male-breadwinner model, showing how heavily old notions about the proper family roles for men and women leaned on ideas that, by the mid-twentieth century, many women were desperate to break free of. The old ideas increasingly failed to match the late twentieth century and twenty-first century educational landscape, economy and job market given that, as the US Bureau of Labor Statistics puts it helpfully, and in a way that applies to Britain almost equally: 'women in the labor force increased their numbers at an extremely rapid pace in the past 50 years'.[13]

One of the dubious things about the 'male-breadwinner model' is that it was mostly just that: a model, anchored so firmly in atavistic ideas of women's proper role that even when the reality had or has nothing to do with it, the model didn't – and doesn't – budge, tyrannically foreshortening women's horizons for a fantasy of male ability and dignity. From Amanda Vickery's iconic study of the 'separate spheres' idea in Victorian Britain, to Joanna Bourke's study of working-class cultures in Britain in the twentieth century, historians have repeatedly shown that the reality actually has always included substantial work outside the home for most women as well as inside it, often translating into a huge burden of extra labour. I used the example in Chapter One of poor women toiling to earn their bread, to show how money – far from being something trendy progressives should scoff at – was and is literally make or break for them. But even they laboured under the male-breadwinner model's iron grip on marriage and were obstructed and discredited even while they went out to work, had babies and held the house together.

By the 1980s, when marriages were really falling apart fast in Britain, the US and Europe, women had become much more economically active, not just in the low-income, part-time work that coincided with marital change in the 1970s, but (still to a disproportionately stunted degree) in traditionally masculine professional jobs. In the UK, the 1980s was the period of the most-ever accelerated growth in female labour market participation, helping ratchet up the numbers from 57 per cent in 1975 to 78 per cent forty years later.[14] In the US, the number of female lawyers, and those in management and finance leapt in the decade.[15]

But as wives' earnings rose with work outside the home, husbands' domestic activities did not. But by this point, in part thanks to the discourse and ideas unleashed by the women's liberation movement, women were better able to articulate what was going on and the intense, actionable dissatisfaction that went with it. The sociologist Arlie Hochschild coined the term the 'double shift' to denote women's enormous dissatisfaction with the way the dual-earner model hadn't erased the male privilege (to laze about at home being served after 'a day at work') of the male-breadwinner model. In addition to a workable solution that saw fed-up women supporting themselves and children, at a pinch, divorce also became a function of the *confidence* to articulate and act on dissatisfaction with the double shift.

The other major cause of the decline in marriage fits with the notion I discussed earlier (and which forms the backbone of most studies of the global sex trade): that regulation and punishment can coerce people into broad structures and norms but doesn't change their actual desires nor necessarily their behaviour.

## *Morality From Within*

Thus, as we have hurtled past the clenched post-war period into the late twentieth and twenty-first centuries, norms and values were no longer imposed from on high and became a domain regarded as more appropriately governed personally. Indeed, a hallmark of late twentieth century social theory is that Western societies experienced a shift towards the belief that 'morality should come from within'.[16] Naturally, there were problems and hiccups in this transition. There was exhaustion and misery and clashing and acrimony and alienation as each couple, composed now of two individuals seeking self-realisation within the traditional confines of romantic commitment, had to re-draw from scratch what had for centuries been decreed and inherited from on high. This process prompted the sociologist duo Ulrich Beck and Elisabeth Beck-Gernsheim to write their classic *The Normal Chaos of Love*, whose central thesis is that because family and romantic life has become increasingly rigged around the contradictory demands of the market – to be flexible and available in order to suit the job market, while also maintaining a secure home – this creates extreme strain. Even so, they saw the potential for a new way of organising intimate life so that it honours women's integrity and rights to equal freedoms, which would ultimately be good for everyone.

We must not forget either, amid the cries of chaos and atomisation and individualism brought about by fracturing families and sex willy-nilly, that in Britain and the US, the 1970s were the first decade – the very first – in which neither church nor state controlled sexual activity, policed 'vice' or banned explicit content. Even then it wasn't a complete leaf-turning: as late as the early 1970s, there were instances of police arresting gay men for 'indecency' in the UK and attempts to shut down elements of the countercultural press, with the longest-ever running obscenity trial for an advert printed in *Oz Magazine* in 1970. And in the US, despite some states throwing out anti-sodomy laws in 1963, many kept them till the early 2000s, with a number reintroducing them in the early 2020s as the deranged new right grew in legislative power and influence.

So we really haven't had all that much time in which to adjust to the freer, kinder, and more fragmentary landscape of intimate bonds. It is laughably hasty then, and still far too soon, to conclude the whole liberatory project was all a big fat failure. This seismic shift in the norms and structures governing sexuality is so rich with potential that we are still only beginning to reap the benefits –in terms of the expanded personal liberties, innovation, adventure, excitement and new kinds and configurations of love and care for and between men and women. That there are still problems is not a surprise.

But should the unpleasant side effects of these changes dominate *entirely* the treatises and polemics of the indignant young chastity-belt right – and the exploitation-obsessed left – the way they do? Of course not: the attitude that the sexual revolution only destroyed things, and that the breakdown in marriage must be a sign of the breakdown of all proper values, is as wilfully blind as it is harmful.

### *Less is More*

In elucidations of the better world that was, some go so far as to mourn the end of the 'shotgun wedding' – and the fact that men no longer have to fear it, just as others writing amid the first spoils of the sexual revolution wrote nostalgically of curfews for women and strict no-drinking regulations.[17] But this seems a strange way of looking at it. Isn't it better that when people marry it's because they really, really want to, whether the woman is pregnant or not? The results of this freer choice to marry have clearly been better for relationships as well as happiness: divorce rates are actually going down now because people report more happiness in marriage.[18] This is not out of a sense of coercion and duty, but because of the political overhaul in gender that took place in the second half of the twentieth century and sped up towards its end. Even if they happen too often still in marriage, drudgery and abuse are no longer the Western woman's lot, and when they are discovered or explained or publicised, they are not simply mocked, ignored or downplayed like they once were.

The less people feel they have to marry, the less they will divorce. As for the association between declining marriage rates and people (by which is really meant women) marrying later, the latter is a superb trend. It translates into more maturity and a better ability to deploy emotional intelligence: marriages between people, and especially women, getting hitched at a later age do better and myriad recent studies show that the children of older mothers also tend to be happier and healthier.[19] A large 2012 study published in the British Medical Journal showed children up to age five with older mums not only had fewer accidental injuries but also better language and emotional skills than their peers with young mums. A Danish study found the obvious: that older mothers had less anxiety during pregnancy, were less likely to lose their tempers with their children, were better at setting boundaries and had better relationships.[20]

And thanks to the burgeoning, if still frustratingly slow rise of alternative forms of family composition and living arrangements, such as women-only developments and kibbutz-style housing developments, the traditional marriage will face still more competition – just as it did in the 1970s with the rise of cohabitation. And there's nothing like competition for driving up standards. Marriage may remain the gold standard of harmonious and erotic human self-arrangement, or it may not.

## Chapter Eleven

# Motherhood Unshackled and the Fertility 'Crisis'

We are hearing a lot about a fertility crisis. Hundreds of panicky headlines blend into a background hum of unease that seems very much not borne out by observable evidence of pram-packed streets and oversubscribed nursery places.

Still. Let my eyes not deceive me. 'The global fertility crisis is worse than you think' ran the headline on a 2024 article in the *Spectator* by economics professor Jesus Fernandez-Villaverde. 'Why Gen-Z doesn't want kids: we are living out a fantasy of eternal youth' by Poppy Sowerby in *UnHerd* also in 2024. Also in *UnHerd*: 'Can liberals save themselves from extinction?'. 'Declining birth rates and the case for kids' is the subject of a YouTube video with Louise Perry and John Anderson. 'No amount of tech is going to fix the fertility crisis because the crisis itself is downstream of tech,' tweeted Mary Harrington. Elon Musk leads a growing crew of libertarian/right-wing men who are very worried about the birth rate and personally want to help.

But this is not just a right-wing hang-up. Much institutional economic effort has gone into the crisis, culminating in another

2024 report from the OECD. 'The fertility crisis is here and it will permanently alter the economy', summarised CNN of the actually quite unspectacular findings. Neuroscientists have also weighed in on the crisis: Michael Platt and Peter Sterling published an earnest hand-wringer on the 'depths of despair' caused by the now-familiar usual suspects of 'increasing inequality, economic uncertainty, and social fragmentation' – which are, they say, causing young people to stop having children.[1] (One man's despair is another one's freedom, though – after all, in countries with poor access to family planning services, and a brutal authoritarianism reigns supreme, from North Korea to Yemen, there is plenty of despair and plenty of fertility).

If not weighed down by despair, we are hearing that young people think having babies sounds awful, too hard, an imposition, bad for the climate and inimical to the 'me time' that is thought to define the generation. For the chastity-belt feminists, the population crisis is intermeshed with the undesirability of marriage and the 'atomised' belief in sex as nothing to do with reproduction.[2]

This view has spilled further into the mainstream as political allegiances have been recalibrated. 'Why aren't British women having babies anymore?' asked an article by the archly reasonable and very excellent Janice Turner of *The Times*, who allows that she doesn't want women 'to lie back and breed' like Miriam Cates does, but worries that 'motherhood, if it is spoken of at all now, gets a horrendous rap'. On one hand, I know what she means; as we have seen, the popularity of 'warts 'n' all' complaining about motherhood among the literati is a definitive and lucrative trend. But back in the real world, it seems that for most women above the age of about twenty-five, all you hear about is fertility, motherhood, pregnancy, hoped-for or not, egg freezing or not – whether from on-high (advertising; social media; media; worried government ministers) or from friends. It was partly because I was so sick of hearing about motherhood, and also of peering over the fence at the Motherland inhabited by my friends (almost every single one) that I eventually buckled and decided to give it a whirl myself at forty-one.

I am no climate-change denier; likewise I am not a denier of demographics that show clearly that fertility rates among dominant groups in rich nations are falling to below replacement level. I do, however, deny the necessity of interpreting these data in the most politically expedient and unthinking way. Some people are having fewer babies for a variety of reasons, including more personal autonomy. But why is this a fertility 'crisis', even if rates have dipped below 'replacement level'? Plus, we can't have it all ways. If there is a fertility crisis it would be hard to argue that 'we' are killing the planet with all our babies and complain about overcrowded schools and nurseries and maternity units bursting at the seams.[3]

Now: to unpick that 'crisis' number – Britain's population has grown by 34 per cent since 1953, from 50.4 million to 67 million, so that's a lot more women averaging 1.57 kids. The fear is that under 2.1 children on average per woman won't meet replacement level, causing labour shortages and fatal economic shrinkage. But falling birthrates are a long-term trend and only part of the picture. More than 1.5 million adults of working age in the UK are economically inactive, 85 per cent of them are women saddled with care of family – so policies to encourage, or demand, more people to work would help mitigate this problem without needing to lurch to conservative, panicky politicking over the choices people make in their intimate and private lives.[4]

In fact, the 2.1 child per woman average hasn't existed since 1971,[5] and there was always a sizeable proportion of women who refused to have babies, which they did by staying single. As Amy Froide reminds us, in the early modern period (sixteenth and seventeenth centuries) a surprising percentage of women remained single and, in general, non-reproductive. 'We can say with confidence,' she writes, 'that at least one-third of urban women were single in the early modern era.'[6] Froide elucidates the difficulties of being a single mother which, one would assume, would be a powerful disincentive. Some support could be garnered from the parish of, say, seventeenth century Southampton, for the transition to motherhood (shelter for the birth, money for the baby's first clothes), but admittance to the poor house with her child was the best such a woman could then hope for. With life hard enough as a 'single-woman', there was a strong incentive to stay away from men.

Fertility rates have ebbed and flowed quite dramatically over British history, and so has the age at which women have babies. Now it is later than it used to be, so some demographers will conclude that a woman is childless if they ask her at thirty-nine, when, in fact, many women will still go on to have a child. The fertility rate for women in their forties is greater than for those under twenty in the US and UK.[7]

The point of this isn't to wade into deep demography about fertility rates but to posit that panic about falling birthrates being part and parcel of weakening social and romantic bonds and values – and thus the decline of society in general – is overwrought. If individual women are having fewer than 2.1 babies on average, then this signals a degree of individuality of choice. Those who want to or can have two or three, those who are more tentative may have one, and much later than they'd have done before, or none. Greater respect for women as human beings, not just mothers, has radically remade the calculus determining fertility rates, and this is a good thing. When things are going well, women have fewer babies.

## *'Found Family'*

The new voices exploring the reasoning and circumstances of women who choose to never have children insist as much. Theirs is an intelligent new language that pinpoints unfair old assumptions and double-binds and articulates the thoughtful freedoms and pleasures of new, non-reproductive pastures. Amy Key, a poet, writes creatively in *Arrangements in Blue* about the ways she finds solace, meaning and love in a long-term single life. Swimming in the sea is described as an act of intimacy, the water able to hold and restore her, whatever she brings to it. Ruby Warrington, author of *Women Without Kids*, has also tackled the subject, though hers is another related form of female mould-breaking: the choice not to have children. 'When I decided at age nine that I was ready to be a woman, what I really wanted was the freedom to be *me*. The way I saw it, adulthood would bring the freedom to live how I wanted, and to prioritise my own needs without feeling guilty about it . . . But by the time I was in my thirties, my non-mom status meant I often felt an outgrown version of that same awkward teenager.' Podcaster Elizabeth Day is another one who has made a career out of saying that there is amazing freedom and happiness in accepting you might never have children.[8]

Warrington notes perfectly sensibly that there is much value in those 'seeking a sense of purpose outside of the tidy perimeters of what is deemed socially acceptable'. She wonders if you 'can blame us for holding out for something better, even if this means forgoing parenthood . . . and focusing on our Found Family connections instead?'[9]

Found Family is a term perfectly crafted to send a shiver down the spines of the trad wives and Maga family-values conservatives. It's a regrettably woke-sounding term for something adaptable and positive: community, and especially a community of kin-like relationships through close friends and networks of care. This includes those found through doing good, by volunteering, helping old people, helping kids and so on. Or hobbies. A chess or cooking club might be an example of something with 'found family' potential.

Found Family, says Warrington, is something that women without kids can help pioneer. We are already seeing signs of it in those women-only housing developments and other kibbutz-like cooperatives, such as Women's Pioneer Housing, which owns 1,000 properties in eight boroughs in west and north-west London and is expressly for single women who can't afford private rents and may have been victims of abuse. New Ground Cohousing is a smart housing development in Chipping Barnet for older women only. Meanwhile, a critical mass of women exploring their choice not to have children, or their experience of bitter regret at not having children, is finally forming after decades of lone voices. There is Jody Day, founder of Gateway Women, a network for childless women; US psychologist Jeanne Safer, author of *Beyond Motherhood*; and numerous networks like Childless Collective, Fertility Network UK, the Non-Mum Network, the *Full Stop* podcast, Ageing Without Children (AWOC) and World Childless Week.

My only critique of Warrington's defence of the childless-by-choice woman is that she falls into the meta-trap of having to explain that she and her peers are not child-free because they are selfish, bad people or narcissistic partyers – her book is a long defence of her life choices. Reviewers fell into the same trap. 'Choosing to be child-free doesn't make women selfish, failures or freaks,' Marianne Power's *The Times* review opened. Kate Ng's review in the *Independent* ran under the headline: 'Society says I'm selfish for not wanting children.' And so on. But in insisting on this they're being cowed by the very things they put so much effort into dismantling: the idea that women's reproductive choices are tied up with their moral soul and worth, their normality. But the kind of society we ought to live in – and can with just a little mental discipline and creativity – is one where women can remain child-free for any reason, including selfishness, failure (whatever that means) . . . or being weird or a freak. This is a type of person that has, in our acceptance-and-inclusivity obsessed culture, been sadly and ironically chased to the sidelines as more and more highly atypical people demand to be accepted as a standard type instead of embracing being atypical.

'I'm changing the narrative around being single, because so far it's had pretty bad PR,' writes Shani Silver, host of a podcast called *A Single Serving* and the author of the book *A Single Revolution*. 'I'm not an advocate for singlehood. I'm an advocate for women *feeling good while single* – there's a difference.' Silver, who has lustrous brown hair and a low, sharp-cut fringe, is a Brooklynite living in New Orleans. She is hip, successful and smart. In the conversation we had for one of her podcast episodes in the early 2020s I was impressed by the focus and dedication she brought to exploring and boosting the experiences of single women climbing through their thirties and beyond. Indeed, as the author of an earlier book, *The Man Diet*, about how to be single as a young woman by sloughing off useless, time-wasting and unwholesome encounters with men (as a reset, like a juice cleanse, rather than long-term Gwyneth Paltrow), I had an above-average interest in her project.

And yet, it puzzled me that a woman with as much to offer as Silver must spend so much time on it that it became her full-time job to hoist middle-aged female singleness out of the weeds and rescue it from its questionable, slightly embarrassing status. What Silver and a number of 'single-by-choice' voices want is for single-ness to become equal to coupledom in status, when, in reality, remaining single is often vastly more fun and fulfilling for women than marriage. This is also very much true of women who want children and take that leap with the support of people other than a biological father.

## *Single Over Thirty-Five: the Science, and the Choice to Go It Alone*

There are two tracks around singleness: one concerns discourse, perception and negative socially-generated feelings. We know plenty about the former from people including Silver and other prominent single women.[10]

The other is reality. On the latter, the Office for National Statistics shows that never-married single women are rising in every age range under seventy; between 2002 and 2018, the figure for those aged forty to seventy rose by half a million, while the percentage of never-married singletons in their forties doubled.

But still. Being single and childless is a big deal for women over the age of thirty-five. It's still an identity that comes with a whole raft of associations: mockeries, fake and real envy. And yet being a single mother who uses reproductive technologies is expensive and unusual. But despite the vilification of single mothers discussed above, having a child as a solo project is a sensible idea. Women often find bringing up children with men extremely difficult, and data suggests mothers outside a marriage are not only happier but live longer. I find myself particularly interested in a 2018 *Lancet* study of Canadian single parents, which found, rather bluntly, that mortality in single fathers was three times higher than rates in single mothers and partnered fathers. In short: 'Single fathers had a significantly higher adjusted risk of dying than both single mothers and partnered fathers.'[11] In the long list of chains women stand to shake off, partnered parenthood is squarely up there. I am aware that this is a taboo suggestion, and that it is difficult to actually pull off comfortably, calling on more resources than your typical woman believes she has.

## MOTHERHOOD UNSHACKLED AND THE FERTILITY 'CRISIS'

### *First Comes the Baby in the Baby Carriage*

Outside the data are the decisions of every-day life, which are informed by feelings and perceptions. By this point in both my career and my life, I have had dozens and dozens of conversations with women my age and younger, including close, old friends, about whether or not it's a good idea to take the plunge and have a child, even if there is no partner on the scene, such as with a one-night stand or a sperm donor. I differentiate this type of planned single motherhood from the type involving a father who was with the mother when they had the child.[12]

Most of my interlocutors have said (unlike me) that they have always wanted children, but that so long as they are single it isn't going to happen. One dear friend, whom I have been close to since we were nine, is single and without children. Her story is a modern one on one hand, and an old one on the other: at twenty-two she enabled an acquaintance to have a daughter by producing eggs for him and his wife. The money she received for this enabled her to pay off her college debts. Twenty years later, she has an interesting, sometimes dangerous job in New York City, working as an investigator for a New York crime agency (she carries a weapon). In her spare time, she is a navy intelligence reservist. She is reserved in character, as well as athletic, adventurous, loyal and kind. Her athleticism gives her an enviably slender, healthy-looking figure and since we were children she has always been groomed to perfection. Her several serious relationships have ended with heartbreak, and, always self-supporting, she has never in adulthood lived anywhere besides a small flat in Manhattan or Brooklyn, paid for by a public-sector salary. For this reason, she has remained both single and childless, as opposed to just single, despite wanting a family.

In a recent text exchange sparked by a visit from her, in which she met my baby, she shared some of her thinking. 'I didn't have a desperate maternal yearning,' she wrote on WhatsApp, 'at least not to have [a baby] sans partner. I think I feel worse about lack of husband. Although I would much prefer to have a husband and kid. But I've never been in a financial or lifestyle position to do it on my own so never seriously even thought about it. But it certainly is vexing to miss out on this key part of life that everyone else participates in.' I wanted to tell her that the baby might be a key part of life but the husband can come along at any time and make your life miserable at any time too. Emotionally, it is different to lead and love (parenthood) than to tether yourself through the contractual equality of the formal romantic bond. The former is surely more reliably, richly and universally rewarding than the second one which, to judge by divorce statistics alone, is only transcendent, or even worth the effort, in a little over half of cases. I know my friend wants the man more than the child, and ideally she wants them all together. I shared my view with her that I do believe she will find the man at some point. And perhaps he'll come with a child.

I have always found conversations like these poignant as forty approaches and recedes. Something feels off to me – not just off, but sad – about women sacrificing the potential for the baby who becomes a whole world in themselves, who might become Einstein or just a kind person in the neighbourhood who has their own children one day, to the hopes of finding a Man. (Or Woman). Women have endured enough grief and misery over the years because of their reproductive characteristics. The major upside, harnessable now for the first time, is that we can create babies pretty straightforwardly with or without a live man to hand. To me, it has always been intuitive that the profundity of a child is in a different league to the riches of romantic partnership – but it isn't intuitive for many (yet).

Of course, it is hard, maybe impossibly hard in some cases, to have a baby outside a partnership. I am aware of the costs of babies, having had one myself, but I am also therefore aware of all the help available. In the UK, at least, statutory maternity pay of about £700 per month is not nothing. It's not enough for a mortgage plus food, but if you have a decent mortgage, you are probably in a job that offers some paid leave. And if you have to go back to work after a short period, then your earnings won't sag and your child will be socialised to enjoy more people. As a freelancer, I had no choice, and I was dependent on my parents and my baby's father to be able to keep working, albeit in an erratic fashion, right after I had her.

The cost of having a baby is overwhelmingly in the struggle of lost sleep and lost time, especially if it means you can't work for money. Indeed, the duress of single motherhood by choice is often less in scale and longevity than that brought about by forcing reproduction to fit within a traditional brace that doesn't feel good. After all, once a baby starts sleeping, life returns, and when a baby is nine months old a full-time mother can get thirty hours' free childcare per week.

Making it all work without fountains of cash can push new mothers to breaking point. But the alternative can be worse. Many women report feeling burdened by their partners when they have children; 'wanting to kill' them is a common way of describing it, backed up in studies that show, for instance, that 67 per cent of couples are less satisfied with each other post-natally, or that just 7 per cent of mothers reported feeling more satisfied with their marriage after their babies were born (compared to 15 per cent of fathers).[13]

Among mothers I came across in recent years, it is abundantly clear that the single mothers – one primary school teacher in her thirties who used a donor, one European financier in her forties who became pregnant from a one-night stand – are thriving, not despite but because of their circumstances. Like the others, they are enjoying their babies but because they get support from family and childcare workers they get to do so without having to bargain, compromise or fight. It is a true luxury.

For those women who go it alone, there will be challenges of a changing nature, some predictable, as the child gets older, but most of the literature finds that consistency and love solves many of them, so that psychologically there is no difference in children conceived with donors versus biological dads.[14] It's true that good fathers are more common, and certainly more helpful and patient, than once they were, leaving aside the ongoing imbalance in the division of household work.[15] These better, more helpful fathers forge closer relationships with their children. By contrast, not knowing your father, if he died before you were born, or your mother used a donor, could obviously create psychological discomfort and questing. But these are thought to be entirely different in character and severity to the problems created by insufficient, unreliable or angry fathers, whose upshot, especially for boys, is wide-ranging enough to include crime, reoffending, inability to forge or keep relationships, emotional regulation problems, and difficulty keeping a job. But a mother able to keep such a father at bay, or manage, somehow, to protect her child from the worst of his influence, can help her child avoid these problems (often this isn't within her power).

So my view is that if you want a baby, and you're single, and you think you can scrape by (and even if you can't), then try to have one. If you're successful and have a good salary, it's a no-brainer. If you do want to go it alone, this is a good time to do it, with more fellow travellers, and more support, than ever before. Traci Kodeck, a member of Single Mothers By Choice, a transnational group with 40,000 members, put her rationale simply, and it is one that more and more women are comfortable expressing (though still too few, given how many women want babies at some point).

'I was with my best friend, and I said, "I don't have a partner, I need to be a mom,"' Kodeck told CBS News. So at thirty-nine, she embarked on a three-year fiasco that was entirely worth it, producing a daughter. 'Then it was, "Oh my gosh, I'm taking home a human." And she was perfect.' Emma Ramos, another member of Single Mothers By Choice, always wanted a child, but never fantasied at the same time about a husband too. She described life with the son that she went on to have with a donor, and is raising solo, as 'beautiful chaos'.[16]

Swathes of the new (and old) reactionary movement find the use of sperm donation and assisted reproduction by women tired of waiting for the right man to come along, or desirous of calling all the shots, a revolting, frightening marker of moral inversion and social collapse.[17] In their vision of single-by-choice motherhood, the destructive hot mess and toxic whore-wastrel figure of the single mother and welfare scrounger of the 1970s and 1980s has merely been updated. In both cases, she's selfish and conniving; in the first for handouts and a flat, in the second, in depriving men of their proper role as fathers, providers, and arbiters of beauty and grooming standards, and being smug while they do it.

And if such go-it-aloners are smug, it is with good reason. The Washington-based psychotherapist Karen Lewis has spent decades trying to help single women take advantage of, not bemoan, their singleness – including by having a child if they want one. Here's a thought experiment she likes to offer female clients. 'Imagine you look into a crystal ball. You see that you'll find your dream partner, in, say, ten years ... What would you do with that intervening time, freed of the onus to look for love?' The answer, often, is: 'I'd finally be able to relax. I'd do all the things I've been waiting to do'.[18] Indeed. History moves forward in circles: this is nothing less than a recapitulation of what the feminist Josephine Butler was saying in the 1860s: 'I cannot believe it is every woman's duty to marry, in this age of the world. There is abundance of work to be done which needs men and women detached from domestic ties; our unmarried women will be the greatest blessing to the community when they cease to be soured by disappointment or driven by destitution to despair.'[19]

The spluttering disparagement directed at such women, including single mothers by choice, is ungenerous and blinkered, rooted in severe misunderstanding and a lack of creativity of thought. We have seen that deciding to turn attention away from the quest to find the male partner one had pictured all one's life and not sublimating but decisively hurling all that energy into other pursuits with real and decisive rewards makes choosing to go it alone in all ways a rationally superb decision. It is absurd that women who don't tether themselves to a husband, or who choose to do other things besides systematically date, are still (!) blamed for being overly demanding or delusional for not, in the infamous words of the American writer Lori Gottleib, seeing 'the case for settling for Mr Good Enough'. Susan Faludi chronicled this in *Backlash* in 1991, but more recently there is a whole online culture of men, including incels, that spits and crackles with insults for those who dare ride 'the cock carousel' when young instead of settling down and marrying (or just having sex with), one assumes, one of them.

In the world I am looking forward to, signs of which are growing stronger, there doesn't have to be a 'case' for 'settling' for any sort of man at all, good enough or not. The much-maligned market dynamics of dating, which is, after all, the terrain in which lasting love and commitment is found, can be turned to advantage here. Today's picky women don't want to settle down with today's men? And vice versa? Fine. In that case, they will find alternatives and substitutes, such as in friendships, work, projects or travel, partaking of casual (not necessarily meaningless or cold) sex, if wanted. They will have strongly-desired babies by their own devices, funded by those extra hours spent working and being promoted when there were no men to emerge from the dating pool that they wanted to give over their freedom for. All this by their early forties. Later, maybe, a man will appear. And if he does, she might well find it a difficult adjustment, and exhausting negotiating her new loss of freedom. Or she might find that, settled and fulfilled through her own making, she is in a prime position to truly enjoy a relationship – and to offer far more within it.

There is still another advantage to women saying 'no, thanks' to the men on offer, or more broadly to the gruelling efforts often required to find them. There are signs this is already happening. The advantage is that the smaller the pool of women available, put crudely, the better the men will have to be to attract them. Sooner or later, the competitive pressure on men will be too great, and the continued insistence on high standards by women (being subjective, they may vary) will incentivise men to radically improve (also a subjective process, but likely to have predictable key aspects).

For me, one of these improvements would be a new interest in different kinds of relationships with different kinds of women. Whereas now, there is still a fair bit of romantic interference run around women who are brashly well-educated and plainly professionally ambitious. When men are motivated to widen their approach, they may see opportunities in respecting, collaborating with, or perhaps simply serving and supporting such women. They may find themselves naturally loosening beauty standards that cause women such grief (some of which is self-inflicted) and, in doing so, countering the continuous problem of women with outstanding qualities of soul and brains, but lacking standard markers of hotness, being overlooked as romantic options.

The mass take-up, or at least the mass consideration, of single-by-choice motherhood using assisted reproduction would be a big step forward for women, their happiness, autonomy and for the dating market's gender dynamics in general. I'm also a big proponent of later motherhood. I discussed some of the evidence in its favour previously, based on the obvious connection between a calmer, more mature mother and a happier, calmer, healthier child. Another plus is that the older mother will not bubble with resentment that she can no longer rush across town, or an ocean, at a moment's notice to drink, carouse, work, see friends or whatever – because she's done all that, endlessly. The baby becomes the adventure and, combined with a decent career and childcare, can soon enough also be combined with travel and cocktails in foreign climes. Parenthood is a big and universal bonding experience and you will therefore never be entirely alone, short of people to talk to, or without assistance. The older you are, the more prepared you'll feel to enjoy that side of it.

The practicalities cannot be ignored and, with a bit of experience with those myself, allow me to add my two cents on the 'how' not just the 'what' and 'why'. At the best age for having a baby (forty-plus), your eggs will be dicey, and you'll probably need more rounds of IVF, which massively increases the cost, assuming it's about £6k per go, not including injectables. So if you're one of those people who isn't sure about their relational status in the decade preceding forty-odd, but 'always wanted to be a mum', then you have two options. One is fairly cheap if you're fertile enough to get away with it and want to walk the plank right away. This is IUI, a £1,000-ish procedure in which a catheter delivers a sperm sample straight into the uterus right before ovulation. You might need to try it a few times. And even then it's a roll of the dice, like sex.

If you want to defer, you'll need to go through egg retrieval, one round of which for younger women (under, say, thirty-eight) may be all that is needed to get loads of eggs (fifteen-plus). Since there is no way of knowing the quality of the eggs without fertilising them, I'd recommend doing so, even if that means choosing some donor sperm. Then you can get your fertilised eggs – namely embryos

– genetically tested (around £600 an embryo) and freeze the viable ones. It's extortionate but you'll know exactly what you have by way of future baby potential (in ruling out chromosomal abnormalities you save yourself horrendous 'rounds' of IVF later; 80 per cent of miscarriages are caused through basic chromosomal errors). Once you've got your healthy embryos stored, if you're motoring in your career and have the cash, you could always freeze another round of eggs and leave them in the hopes that, if you do find a partner one day, at least one egg will become a viable embryo with his sperm. All the better if you didn't hate IVF, and why should you? Some women react badly, but many don't.

My 'journey' with all this shows how zig-zagging it can be. I used the second lockdown to find a sperm donor, despite enormous fear and ambivalence about motherhood. After I miscarried a pregnancy achieved from IUI (aka, the clinical version of the turkey-baster method using this donor's sperm), I did three rounds of IVF in order to secure at least one healthy embryo using the donor sperm – and ended up with two. I was dating someone at the time, who was supportive due to his own reluctance to have a baby just then; he is quite a bit younger than me. A year after I froze the embryos, still racked with ambivalence, I fell pregnant with this person. I remain shocked at how much I enjoy and love my baby.

To me, the confidence of a woman of thirty-one, forty-one, even fifty-one to have a baby regardless of whether she has found a man to build a life with or not, and to enjoy motherhood and to love and care and provide for her baby brilliantly, opens a glorious wormhole into what the future might hold. This future is already poking out through a combination of desire, willpower, bravery and social progress, but to allow it to take flight, women will have to cast off their shackles and pruderies and shame about sex, money and power, and pursue all three with joy, and without shame.

# Outro

This book has attempted to peel back the layers of fear and doom-mongering that have come to cloud women's horizons – embodied, sexual, economic, political, professional and otherwise. I have argued for a fearless new paradigm of unapologetic ambition and confidence, the one that was promised to my generation but which has since evaporated and for no good reason. I have focused on women's opportunities in free societies as individual agents – essentially, how we navigate our time without reference to, or the rule of, committed relationships, and how, every day and every moment, we are leveraging the gains of the 'sexual revolution', even as it is being newly reconsidered and its legacies maligned.

Since beginning work on this book, indeed since conceiving of it, my life has had more ups and downs than I had hoped for or anticipated. Personally, there have been some big knocks, some of which have taken me into the maw of the stuff I have written about here: breadwinning, motherhood, the transition to single motherhood, relationship breakdown, and the emotional and physical challenges all this entails.

Much violence and strangeness has gone on in the world at the same time. I have been forced, by my own life circumstances and the hurricanes blowing in the outside world, to ask: am I still optimistic, even bullish, about women's status and horizons? Am I still hopeful about the prospects of Jewish women, no less, to say nothing of those women caught up in woman-hating theocratic dictatorships, or the patriarchal trappings of the growing number of religious households in Europe and the UK? Is the discourse of complaint, pain, objectification and victimhood actually appropriate after all, and is it silly – naive, arrogant, unfeeling, elitist, non-aware – to insist that the counterbalance set out in this book outweighs all the bad stuff?

The answer now, as it was when I began this book, is that this is complex terrain; it cannot be that, as a whole, everything is either rosy for women or everything is terrible for women. For individual women, times and circumstances may be dire and ribbed with sexist and misogynistic injustice. But I believe now, as I did when I set out to write this book, that those struggles should be set against a bigger frame, one that is exceedingly promising. Of course we face ongoing struggles as women, individually and collectively as a (fragmented) political bloc. But there is innovation and finally, greater understanding, of these struggles. As we saw in Chapter Five, there is, for example, the rip-roaring 'vagina business', to use Marina Gerner's phrase (see page 110), which is using 'fem tech' to take women's physical embodiment – and the market – by storm and showing how the market in many cases services women best.

And, slowly, there is evidence of an increasing understanding about the way male abuse of women can cause enormous damage to relationships, female selfhood, parenthood and children in ways both clearly outrageous and subtle. It's official! Women's pain, women's injustice, women's experience, is meant to be taken seriously now. This means, at the very least, a template exists, albeit still a sketchy one, hard to use and patchy, pointing the way to a proper exit strategy for the many women who are still experiencing male abuse and violence.

But we can and should vault beyond these negative triumphs. For all the threats to the democratic West and to freedom, including women's freedom, which is always the first to go, we can enjoy a new tech-fuelled dynamism that our ancestors would have given anything to taste. Women's pursuit of all those glories outside the home that were forever the preserve of men – status, money, power, sex on their own terms – still also belong to men, but women are now encouraged to pursue them . . . if we want to. The familiar rebuttals to this are that we should not aspire to anything men have enjoyed since that's all rotten, and that women suffer under the pressure to do as men have done, thereby betraying their maternal destiny. I hope this book has cleared up some of those misconceptions.

The problem is summed up neatly in the fact that 'women can have it all' has become one of the most gauche, embarrassingly nineties things you can say, guaranteed to provoke mocking across the board. But, thanks to the cosmic changes we've experienced in society, culture, law, science and technology over the past half-century, I believe we can have it all. Even if it's hard. We can all have it all, and best of all, and most important of all, we can decide exactly what 'all' is. We can choose how to fill our cup so that it looks way more than half full; full, even, to overflowing.

# Acknowledgements

I owe my comfort with writing naughty ideas down in public, and a pleasure in free-range thinking more generally, to many people, but especially to my parents, who are outside-the-box thinkers themselves; David Deutsch, with whom I have, over decades, developed my ideas about what freedom means (and much more besides) and, as ever, my old friend Tom Stammers, who has always encouraged me to raise my game intellectually. The redoubtable Sam McAlister, a Good Slut par excellence and one of the sharpest people I know, is to thank for the title of this book. It is also with Sam that I developed some of my early thinking about what a Good Slut could mean. Friends that have helped keep me sane in the challenging times that have accompanied the writing of this book include Joanna Elias, Olivia Boyd, Helen O'Malley, Elena Langer, Anna Tobert, Arabella Byrne, Hannah Rosenfelder, Ariel Isaacs, Marina Gerner, Liz Marcus and Daniel Lee.

I am very grateful indeed to my agent Matthew Hamilton for piloting this idea into reality, to the suave and charming Andreas Campomar at Little, Brown, who saw the point of this book right away and believed in me, and to my insightful, lovely editor Holly Blood.

# Endnotes

## Introduction

1 The educational gap in the Anglosphere has been reported for decades: https://www.pewresearch.org/short-reads/2023/12/18/fewer-young-men-are-in-college-especially-at-4-year-schools/; https://committees.parliament.uk/committee/203/education-committee/news/200976/why-do-boys-lag-behind-girls-at-all-ages-of-education-mps-to-investigate/; https://www.mind.org.uk/news-campaigns/news/the-evidence-is-clear-the-nations-mental-health-is-getting-worse-mind/
2 https://media.samaritans.org/documents/ResearchBriefingGenderSuicide_2021_v7.pdf
3 https://commonslibrary.parliament.uk/research-briefings/cbp-9195/
4 'All the Single Ladies', *The Atlantic*, November 2011.
5 Michl L.C., McLaughlin K.A., Shepherd K., Nolen-Hoeksema S., 'Rumination as a mechanism linking stressful life events to symptoms of depression and anxiety: longitudinal evidence in early adolescents and adults', *Journal of Abnormal Psychology*, 2013 May, 122(2), 339–52.
6 See, for example, Jaipreet Virdi's series about her own experience of pain at the Wellcome: *Painful Realities*, Wellcome Collection https://wellcomecollection.org/series/painful-realities
7 Shrier, A., *Bad Therapy: Why the Kids Aren't Growing Up*, London: Swift, 2024.

8  For those who demand evidence for the obvious, there is plenty of that. Girls outperform boys in school and outnumber and outperform them in higher education. 'Women are much more likely to go to university than men and have been for many years. They are also more likely to complete their studies and gain a first or upper second-class degree,' according to a 2024 research document for the House of Commons Library. And even though salaries after graduation tend to be higher among men, this is because the men who do pursue higher education and graduate successfully tend to be more motivated, and men are still more likely to enter higher-paying fields requiring coding or maths. Rather than being mocked or discouraged, with fake obstacles thrown in their path every step of the way as was the case just 30 years ago, girls with an inclination towards careers requiring maths, engineering, computing and so on can now expect a red carpet of schemes, funding and mentorship to inspire, help and protect them (see, for example, support from groups like Women in Banking and Finance; Young Women into Finance; His Majesty's Women in Finance Charter; Investing in Women Code; the list goes on). The figures for 'professional occupations' betray amazing improvements: 28 per cent of women in employment worked in 'professional occupations' (such as engineers, doctors and nurses, teachers, accountants and lawyers) from October 2022 to September 2023, compared with around 27 per cent of men. House of Commons Library, https://researchbriefings.files.parliament.uk/documents/SN06838/SN06838.pdf. Teenage pregnancies are down as girls have the confidence, and resources, to control what happens to them sexually. There were more abortions in England and Wales among women over 35 than teenagers in 2017 (figures from the Department of Health). Slowly and with many betrayals, policing and the law are understanding that rape and sexual harassment and abuse are unacceptable, and, with the help of new vocabularies that have percolated down from therapy, safeguarding and charity cultures, girls and women are emboldened to demand respect for their sexual boundaries. Sexual violence is far more likely to be reported and prosecuted in part because of 'improvements in police reporting practices', https://www.ons.gov.uk/peoplepopulationandcommunity/crimeandjustice/bulletins/crimeinenglandandwales/yearendingjune2024

9  Cook, H., *The Long Sexual Revolution: English Women, Sex, and Contraception 1800-1975*, London: Oxford University Press, 2005.

10  Weeks, J., 'Wolfenden and Beyond: The Remaking of Homosexual History', *History and Policy*, pp.327-47.

11  Perry, L., 'I'm 30. The Sexual Revolution Shackled My Generation', *The Free Press*, 20 August 2022.

# ENDNOTES

## Chapter 1 Bonfire of the Actual Liberals

1 *The Telegraph*, *Chopper* podcast, May 2023, https://www.telegraph.co.uk/politics/2023/05/12/jeremy-hunt-miriam-cates-stay-at-home-mums-taxes-tory-party/
2 https://theotherhalf.uk/what-do-mums-want-report
3 https://www.arcforum.com/research-papers/the-subsidiary-hierarchy. There is a rising tide of books giving methodological weight to these ideas, such as Catherine Pakaluk's *Hannah's Children: The Women Quietly Defying the Birth Dearth*, Regnery Gateway, 2024, a series of interviews with educated women having more than five children; David Goodhart's *The Care Dilemma: Caring Enough in the Age of Sex Equality*, Forum, 2024 and Louise Perry's forthcoming book advancing the case for the family and having babies.
4 Illouz, E., *Consuming the Romantic Utopia: Love and the Cultural Contradictions of Capitalism*, California: University of California Press, 1998.
5 https://x.com/elonmusk/status/1880668164037685479
6 https://www.nytimes.com/2025/06/23/style/trump-maga-women.html; https://www.washingtonpost.com/style/power/2025/06/18/young-maga-women/
7 French, M., *The War Against Women*, London: Penguin, 1992, p. 36.
8 'People on all levels of income are better off than they were in 1979. The hon. Gentleman is saying that he would rather that the poor were poorer, provided that the rich were less rich.' *Confidence in Her Majesty's Government (1990)*. Parliamentary Debates (Hansard). House of Commons. 22 November 1990.
9 Mill, J.S., *On Liberty*, p. 115, in Himmelfarb, p. 59.
10 Fox-Genovese, E., *Feminism Without Illusions: A Critique of Individualism*, Carolina: University of North Carolina Press, 1991, in Roiphe, p. 63.
11 Warshaw, R., *I Never Called It Rape: The Ms. Report on Recognizing, Fighting, and Surviving Date and Acquaintance Rape*, New York: Harper Perennial, 1994, p. 62.
12 Ibid., p. 63.
13 Taylor Mill, H., *Enfranchisement of Women*, 1851, https://utilitarianism.net/books/enfranchisement-of-women-harriet-taylor-mill/
14 The term, widely used to epitomise a Victorian ideal, comes from the poem by Coventry Patmore: 'The Angel in the House', 1854.
15 Valenze, D., *The First Industrial Woman*, New York: Oxford University Press, 1995, p. 3.
16 Union, no. 2, 1 May 1842. Appendix to 7th Report on Public Petitions,

1842. Appendix 195, p. 90, in Gail Lewis (ed), *Forming Nation, Framing Welfare*, Routledge, 1998.

## *Chapter 2 Let's be Careerist, Bitches!*

1 Goodhart, D. *The Care Dilemma, Freedom, Family and Fertility*, London: Forum, 2024, p. 12.
2 Harper, J., *Your Fertile Years*, London: Sheldon Press, 2021.
3 These figures apply to the US: https://www.brookings.edu/articles/prime-age-women-labor-market-recovery/, https://www.bls.gov/opub/ted/2023/labor-force-participation-rate-for-people-ages-25-to-54-in-may-2023-highest-since-january-2007.htm
4 https://www.womenaloud.co.uk/mum-returning-to-work/
5 The classic researched-based argument that women are fundamentally different is Carol Gilligan, *In A Different Voice: Psychological Theory and Women's Development*, 1982; see also the women's anti-nuclear encampment at Greenham Common, parts of which equated feminism with pacifism: https://blog.history.ac.uk/2019/05/women-and-peace-pat-arrowsmith-and-greenham-common/
6 Slimani, L., *Sex and Lies: True Stories of Women's Intimate Lives in Morocco*, New York: Penguin, 2020, p. xii.
7 Ibid., p. 58.
8 Eaves, E., *Wanderlust: A Love Affair With Five Continents*, New York: Seal Press, 2011.
9 Royal Commission on Divorce and Matrimonial Causes, Westminster, P.S. King & Son, 1912.
10 https://www.theguardian.com/world/2024/apr/06/extreme-us-anti-abortion-group-ramps-up-lobbying-in-westminster
11 https://pmc.ncbi.nlm.nih.gov/articles/PMC2582082/
12 Ellison J.E., Brown-Podgorski B.L., Morgan J.R. 'Changes in Permanent Contraception Procedures Among Young Adults Following the Dobbs Decision', *JAMA Health Forum*, 2024, 5(4), e240424. doi:10.1001/jamahealthforum.2024.0424, p. 37.
13 https://www.newyorker.com/magazine/2024/01/15/abortion-high-risk-pregnancy-yeni-glick
14 https://www.bbc.co.uk/news/av/world-us-canada-64897629
15 https://www.newyorker.com/magazine/2024/01/15/abortion-high-risk-pregnancy-yeni-glick

# ENDNOTES

16 https://time.com/6320172/poland-abortion-laws-maternal-health-care/; https://news.un.org/en/story/2024/08/1153591
17 https://www.theguardian.com/global-development/2022/jan/23/death-threats-and-phone-calls-the-women-answering-cries-for-help-one-year-on-from-polands-abortion-ban
18 Owalade, T., *This is Not America: Why Black Lives in Britain Matter*, London: Atlantic, 2023.
19 https://theguardian.com/world/2023/apr/02/us-anti-abortion-groups-uk-far-righthttps://righttolife.org.uk/; https://www.amazon.co.uk/Anti-Abortion-Activism-Ultra-sacrificial-Reproductive-Reproduction/dp/1839093994. For global picture, see https://www.hrw.org/news/2021/07/14/ecuador-criminalizing-abortion-affects-rights-health
20 Coface Europe, Union of Equality: Gender equality strategy 2020-2025, https://coface-eu.org/mind-the-gap-the-eu-care-strategy-must-promote-gender-equality/
21 https://www.hungarianconservative.com/articles/culture_society/tusvanyos_mcc-feszt_tranzit_conservative-festivals_hungary/
22 Interview, https://stream.org/did-the-pill-and-the-digital-world-fuel-transgenderism/
23 https://www.rcpsych.ac.uk/mental-health/treatments-and-wellbeing/mother-and-baby-units-(mbus)
24 Nelson, C. and Sumner Holmes, A. eds., *Maternal Instincts: Visions of Motherhood and Sexuality in Britain, 1875-1925*. New York: St. Martin's Press, 1997. See especially, 'bachelor motherhood'.
25 Warhman, D., *The Making of the Modern Self: Self. Identity and Culture in Eighteenth-Century England*, Yale University Press, 2007.
26 Himmelfarb, G., *On Liberty and Liberalism. The Case of John Stuart Mill*, New York: Knopf, 1974, p. 100.
27 Sandbrook, D., *White Heat*, Abacus, 2006, p. 478–79. Jeffrey Weeks argues that the 1960s were still rather conservative and that the changes were actually slower than is assumed by 'revolution'. Weeks, *Sex, Politics and Society: The Regulation of Sexuality Since 1800*, London: Routledge, 2007, (ch 13). Ross McKibbin highlights evidence of rapidly decreasing rates of virginity in single women from the start of the twentieth century.
28 Cook, H., *The Long Sexual Revolution: English Women, Sex, and Contraception 1800-1975*, London: Oxford University Press, 2005. On single women having more sex before the pill: Brown, C., 'Sex, Religion, and the Single Woman c.1950–75: The Importance of a 'Short' Sexual Revolution to the English Religious Crisis of the Sixties', *Twentieth Century British History*, Volume 22, Issue 2, 1 June 2011, pp. 189–215.

29 Cook, H., *The Long Sexual Revolution*, Oxford: Oxford University Press, 2004, p. 1.
30 Ibid., p. 2.
31 Harrington, interviewed by Beverly Hallberg, *She Thinks* podcast, 22 April 2023, https://www.independentwomen.com/2023/04/21/mary-harrington-modern-feminism/
32 Hall, R., *Dear Dr. Stopes*, London: Andre Deutsch Limited, 1978.
33 French, M., *The War Against Women*, New York: Ballantine Books, 1992, p. 87.
34 https://srh.bmj.com/content/48/3/193

## Chapter 3 'But the Science Says!'

1 Marks, J., 'Nulture', *Popanth*, 10 November 2013. Retrieved from http://popanth.com/article/nulture/ on 21 July 2014.
2 https://www.theaustralian.com.au/nation/nation/lauren-southern-protesters-out-to-disrupt-right-wing-commentators-event/news-story/
3 https://www.firstthings.com/article/2023/01/anatomy-of-a-cancellation
4 Hoagland, S. L., 'Androcentric Rhetoric in Sociobiology', in *Radical Voices: A Decade of Feminist Resistance*, New York: Pergamon Press, 1989, cited in French, p. 12.
5 Fee, E., 'A Feminist Critique of Scientific Objectivity', *Science for the People*, 14 (July/August), 1982; Fausto-Sterling, A., 'Women and Science', *Women's Studies International Quarterly*, 4, 1981, 41–50.
6 Marland, H., *Dangerous Motherhood: Insanity and Childbirth in Victorian Britain*, London: Palgrave Macmillan, 2004; Faludi, S., *Backlash: The Undeclared War Against Women*, London: Vintage, 1993.
7 Ritchie, S., https://www.theatlantic.com/ideas/archive/2023/06/reactionary-feminism-differences-between-sexes/674447/
8 Perry, L., *The Case Against the Sexual Revolution*, London: Polity, 2022, p. 21.
9 Coyne, J., 'The Men Can't Help It', *Guardian*, 25 January, 2000, https://www.theguardian.com/books/2000/jan/25/society
10 Gandy, K., https://www.theguardian.com/books/2000/jan/25/society
11 King, M. A., 'The History of Sexual Selection Research Provides Insights as to Why Females are Still Understudied', *Nature*, 15 November 2022, https://www.nature.com/articles/s41467-022-34770-z
12 Ibid.
13 Bolhuis et al, 'Darwin in mind: new opportunities for evolutionary psychology',

*PLoS Biol*, July 2011;9(7): e1001109. doi: 10.1371/journal.pbio.1001109. Epub 19 July 2021.
14. Dupré, J., '14 Against Maladaptationism: Or, What's Wrong with Evolutionary Psychology', *Processes of Life: Essays in the Philosophy of Biology*, Oxford, 2012; online edn, Oxford Academic, 24 May 2012, p. 5, https://doi.org/10.1093/acprof:oso/9780199691982.003.0015
15. Panksepp, J. and Panksepp, B., 'The Seven Sins of Evolutionary Psychology', *Evolution and Cognition*, 2000, Vol. 6, No. 2.
16. Ibid., p. 127.
17. Fine, C., *Testosterone Rex: Myths of Sex, Science, and Society*, New York: Norton, 2017, p. 32.
18. Ibid., p. 39.
19. Ibid., p. 60.
20. Harrington, M., *Feminism Against Progress*, London: Forum, 2023, p. 49.
21. Dupré, J., 'Against Maladaptationism: or What's Wrong with Evolutionary Psychology?', *Knowledge as Social Order*, London: Routledge, 2016, p. 4.
22. Wolfinger, N. H. and Perry, S. L., 'Does a longer sexual resume affect marriage rates?', *Journal of Social Science*, 113, 2003, https://doi.org/10.1016/j.ssresearch.2022.102800
23. Jordan-Young, R., *Brain Storm: The Flaws in the Science of Sex Differences*, New York: Harvard University Press, 2011.

## *Chapter 4 Trad Femmes and the Menstrual Left*

1. https://www.salon.com/2021/02/21/tracy-clark-flory-our-culture-is-totally-ignorant-around-the-realm-of-sexual-fantasy/
2. https://www.opendemocracy.net/en/oureconomy/economics-millennials-interview-grace-blakeley/
3. https://www.latimes.com/entertainment-arts/books/story/2021-02-16/tracy-clark-flory-want-me-memoir
4. Taylor Mill, H., *Enfranchisement of Women*, 1851.
5. Ibid.
6. Vickery, A., 'Golden Age to Separate Spheres? A Review of the Categories and Chronology of English Women's History', *The Historical Journal*, Vol. 36, No. 2, 1993, pp. 383–414.
7. Ibid., p. 402.
8. Blythell, D. T*he Handloom Weavers, A Study in the English Cotton Industry During the Industrial Revolution*, Cambridge: Cambridge University Press, 1969, p.28.

9 Goose, N. (ed.), *Women's Work in Industrial England: Regional and Local Perspectives*, Hatfield: Local Population Studies, 2007, p. 11.
10 Blythell, D. *The Handloom Weavers, A Study in the English Cotton Industry During the Industrial Revolution*, Cambridge: Cambridge University Press, 1969, p.28.
11 ONS, Gender Pay Gap in the UK, 2022, https://www.ons.gov.uk/employmentandlabourmarket/peopleinwork/earningsandworkinghours/bulletins/genderpaygapintheuk/2022
12 Walby, S., *Patriarchy at Work*, London: Polity, 1986, p. 51.
13 Bennett, J., *History Matters: Patriarchy and the Challenge of Feminism*, Philadelphia: University of Pennsylvania Press, 2006.
14 For some classic modern analyses of women internalising anti-progress ideas, see Ariel Levy's *Female Chauvinist Pigs*, Natasha Walter's *Living Doll* and Naomi Wolf's *The Beauty Myth*.
15 For more on this topic, see Lucy Bland's *Banishing the Beast: English Feminism and Sexual Morality 1885-1914*, London: Penguin, 1995; and Beatrix Campbell and Anna Coote's *Sweet Freedom: Struggle for Women's Liberation*, London: Picador: 1992.
16 https://newleftreview.org/issues/i148/articles/angela-weir-elizabeth-wilson-the-british-women-s-movement.pdf
17 https://plato.stanford.edu/entries/neoliberalism/
18 https://www.theguardian.com/news/2017/aug/18/neoliberalism-the-idea-that-changed-the-world
19 Ibid.
20 Hochschild, A., *The Commercial Spirit of Intimate Life: Notes from Home and Work*, Berkeley: University of California Press, 1994, p. 13.

## *Chapter 5 Why Money and Capitalism are Good for Women*

1 Jones, G. S. 'Religion and the origins of socialism', Katznelson, I. & Stedman Jones G, S. (eds), *Religion and the Political Imagination*, Cambridge: Cambridge University Press, 2010, p. 181.
2 McLeod, H., *The Religious Crisis of the 1960s*, Oxford: Oxford University Press, 2007.
3 https://newleftreview.org/issues/ii56/articles/nancy-fraser-feminism-capitalism-and-the-cunning-of-history; see other elaborations of the incompatibility of capitalism with 'democratic' processes that would free women in Ellen Wood, e.g. *Democracy Against Capitalism*, 1995.

## ENDNOTES

4 The widely-circulated polemic, a shout of frustration, in this is Miroiu, M. 'Communism was a State Patriarchy, not State Feminism', *Aspasia*, 1, 2007, 197–201.
5 Dijana, J., Karkov, N. and Petrović, T. 'Editorial: Gender Relations and Women's Struggles in Socialist Southeast Europe', *Wagadu: A Journal of Transnational Women's and Gender Studies*, Fall 2020, p. 1.
6 *Spare Rib*, July 1977, p. 39; Spare Rib July 1980, p. 10.
7 *Spare Rib*, July 1989, p. 5.
8 *Spare Rib*, July 1979, p. 6.
9 https://jacobin.com/2019/09/capitalism-socialist-feminism-inequality-sexism
10 This is more explicit in the hard left. E.g., see: https://communist.red/british-capitalism-s-demise-and-the-tasks-confronting-us/
11 https://fee.org/articles/why-socialism-causes-pollution/
12 https://iea.org.uk/media/67-per-cent-of-young-brits-want-a-socialist-economic-system-finds-new-poll/ in the US this European style of thinking has also made big inroads https://www.thefp.com/p/progressives-against-progress
13 Arshad, M., *Harvard Political Review*, https://harvardpolitics.com/girlboss-gaslight-gatekeep/
14 Ibid.
15 Cudd, A. E. and Holmstrom, N., *Capitalism, For and Against: A Feminist Debate*, New York: Rutgers University Press, 2011, p. 4.
16 Ibid., p. 9.
17 Ibid., p. 90.
18 Ibid., p. 93.
19 There is a rich history of concern here: objections to labour markets that included women were articulated zealously in the nineteenth and early twentieth century with the strongest objections to the 'exploitation' of women in paid labour coming from conservatives who deemed it biologically wrong for women to work in factories or otherwise 'dangerous trades'. The cacophonous debate included doctors, politicians, working men and a range of feminist organisations. The government responded with dangerous-trades regulations, specifically to protect women and their unborn children from the white lead and pottery trades. While lead poisoning, and other workplace chemical hazards were harmful to men as well as women, the medical, political and legislative focus was on the specific interplay of lead and women's bodies. This important legalisation would go on to entrench gendered ideas of dangerous work that are still visible (Carolyn Malone, *Women's Bodies and Dangerous Trades in England, 1880–1914*, Royal Historical Society Studies in History New Series, 2003. Thus while toxic fumes and backbreaking work were

eventually recognised as bad for men too, there are still very few women in traditionally masculine – because physical, dirty – trades like waste disposal, building or plumbing. And the division according to gendered ideas of work persists in other, non-physical domains: banking, engineering, architecture, certain areas of medicine. All these have traditionally been seen as not the proper sphere of little ladies – and the little ladies have internalised this message.

## *Chapter 6 The Politics of Pain*

1  Haire, N., 'Birth-Control Methods', quoted in Cook, H., *The Long Sexual Revolution*, p. 146.
2  Ibid.
3  Ibid., p. 149.
4  MacKeith, N., *The New Women's Health Handbook*, London: Virago, 1978, p. 5.
5  Davis, K., *The Making of Our Bodies, Ourselves: How Feminism Travels Across Borders*, Raleigh: Duke University Press, 2007, p. 2.
6  Greer, G., *The Female Eunuch*, London: MacGibbon & Kee, 1970, p. 160.
7  Further reading on vaginas and frank sex chat in art: https://artuk.org/discover/stories/art-matters-podcast-the-vagina-museum-and-vulvas-in-art; https://www.backstage.com/uk/magazine/article/why-sex-and-sexuality-are-taking-over-london-theatre-68178/
8  https://www.thebookseller.com/rights/icon-snags-journalist-marina-gerners-the-vagina-business
9  Wendy Kline's recent book, *Exposed: The Story of the Pelvic Exam* London: Polity, 2024, is a rigorous work of history that zooms in on the terrible abuses of women's dignity, comfort, health and personhood through the development of this central procedure.
10  Jamison, L., *Splinters*, London: Granta, 2024.
11  Even in its heyday of the 1990s and 2000s, the demon of sluttiness masquerading as empowerment was blown somewhat out of proportion. Some of the more intelligent analysts of the phenomenon worried that the women who mistook pole dancing, stripping and sleeping around for empowerment and equality with men were actually internalising terrible ideas that did them more harm than good (see Levy, A., *Female Chauvinist Pigs: Women and the Rise of Raunch Culture*, London: Free Press, 2005, p. 26; Walter, N., *Living Dolls: The Return of Sexism*, London: Virago, 2009; and Cocker, R., 'Love Island lips', the Telegraph, 2019). While this did indeed seem the case among

the women that they studied, the extent to which the pole-dancing-as-empowerment mentality had overtaken the female feels small next to the warped, needle-reliant beauty standards that have since seeped off social media and reality TV.

12 Perry, L. *The Case Against the Sexual Revolution*, p. 14.
13 Ibid., p. 15.
14 White, P., 'Democratic Confederalism and the PKK's Feminist Transformation', in *The PKK: Coming Down from the Mountains*, London: Zed Books, 2015, pp. 126–49.
15 https://www.kravmagaexperts.com/women-stand-chance-men-real-fight/
16 https://committees.parliament.uk/oralevidence/10517/pdf
17 https://journals.sagepub.com/doi/full/10.1177/1524838020942754
18 MacKinnon, C., *Feminism Unmodified: Discourses on Life and Law*, Harvard: Harvard University Press, p. 50; MacKinnon, C., *Towards a Feminist Theory of the State*, Harvard: Hardvard University Press, 1989, p. 128; Haslanger, S., 'On Being Objective and Being Objectified', in Antony, L. & Witt, C. (eds.), *A Mind of One's Own: Feminist Essays on Reason and Objectivity*, Colorado: Westview Press, 1993, pp. 209–53.
19 Kant, E., *Lectures on Ethics*, Cambridge: Cambridge University Press, 2017, p. 163.
20 De Beauvoir, S., *The Second Sex*, translated by Parshley, H. M., London: Jonathan Cape, 1961, p 375.
21 Hakim, C., *Money Honey: The Power of Erotic Capital*, London: Allen Lane, 2011.
22 https://www.standard.co.uk/hp/front/attractive-wins-and-ugly-loses-in-todays-rat-race-6435454.html
23 https://www.sciencedirect.com/science/article/abs/pii/S0276562416300518
24 https://www.dailymail.co.uk/tvshowbiz/article-4575434/Eve-Pollard-m-sad-ll-never-wolf-whistled-again.html
25 Valenti's account dovetailed with objectification awareness-raising sites like Hollaback, Everyday Sexism, Project Unbreakable and hashtags like #YouOKSis and #YesAllWomen.
26 Wollestonecraft, M., *A Vindication of the Rights of Women*, ch3, London: Joseph Johnson, 1792.
27 https://www.theguardian.com/books/2016/jun/06/jessica-valenti-sex-object-book-review
28 Stone, J., Perry, Z. & Darley, J., '"White Men Can't Jump": Evidence for the Perceptual Confirmation of Racial Stereotypes Following a Basketball Game', *Basic and Applied Sociology*, Vol. 19, No. 3, pp. 291–306.

29 https://www.theguardian.com/technology/2023/feb/08/biased-ai-algorithms-racy-women-bodies
30 Haraway, D., 'A Cyborg Manifesto: Science, Technology, and Socialist-Feminism in the Late Twentieth Century', in Haraway, D., *Cyborgs and Women: The Reinvention of Nature*, Oxford: Routledge, 1990, p. 150.
31 Sales, N. J., *Nothing Personal: My Secret Life in the Dating App Inferno*, New York: Hachette, 2021.

## *Chapter 7 In Defence of Promiscuity*

1 Podcast interview with Shizzio, *The Shizzio Show*, January 2025, https://x.com/shizzio/status/1874493259315339407
2 *Daily Mail*, 13 March 2025, https://www.dailymail.co.uk/femail/article-14493971/Is-Bonnie-Blue-effect-ruining-love-life-Half-UK-mens-fascination-porn-star-satisfied-relationship-study-claims.html
3 https://www.economist.com/britain/2025/06/11/welcome-to-bonnie-blues-britain
4 https://www.mirror.co.uk/3am/celebrity-news/bonnie-blue-shares-horrifying-physical-34555618
5 https://www.dailymail.co.uk/femail/article-14322389/bonnie-blue-porn-sex-onlyfans-tia-billinger-hiv-interview.html
6 https://www.dailystar.co.uk/tv/bonnie-blue-rocks-up-tight-35620947
7 https://www.chronicle.duke.edu/article/karen-owen-shatters-glass-ceiling
8 Strimpel, Z., *The Man Diet: One Woman's Quest to End Bad Romance*, London: Avon, 2011, p. 1.
9 Lawrence, J., in Dabhoiwala, F., *The Origins of Sex: A History of the First Sexual Revolution*, London: Penguin, 2012, p. 126.
10 Paley, W., *The Principles of Moral and Political Philosophy*, 1985, in Dabhoiwala, F., *The Origins of Sex: A History of the First Sexual Revolution*, London: Penguin, 2012, p. 198.
11 Ibid, p. 198.
12 Ibid., p. 352.
13 https://www.tandfonline.com/doi/pdf/10.1080/09612029200200013
14 Bland, L., '"Purifying" the public world: feminist vigilantes in late Victorian England', *Women's History Review*, Vol. 1, No. 3, 1992, pp. 397–412.
15 Botto, M. and Gottzén, L., 'Swallowing and Spitting out the Red Pill': Young Men, Vulnerability, and Radicalization Pathways in the Manosphere', *Journal of Gender Studies* 33, no. 5 (3 July, 2024): pp. 596–608. Predictably, the

manosphere's obsession often distorts evolutionary biology, e.g. Bachaud, Louis and Johns, Sarah, 'The use and misuse of evolutionary psychology in online manosphere communities: The case of female mating strategies', *Evolutionary Human Sciences*, 5, e28 (30 Aug, 2023).

16 https://www.who.int/news-room/photo-story/detail/women-s-and-girls-health-throughout-the-life-course
17 Harrington, M., https://www.spectator.co.uk/article/make-sex-wild-again/
18 '"They violently raped me": Sexual violence weaponized to crush Iran's "Woman life freedom" uprising', *Amnesty International*, 6 December 2023, https://www.amnesty.org/en/documents/mde13/7480/2023/en/
19 https://www.sciencedirect.com/science/article/abs/pii/S0165032706004289?via%3Dihub
20 Sales, N. J., https://www.theguardian.com/commentisfree/2021/may/17/apps-tinder-dating-women
21 'The best sex of my life', 30 November 2022, https://inews.co.uk/inews-lifestyle/best-sex-life-mid-life-adventures-kink-apps-1999839?srsltid=AfmBOorxWnkHOrTO-1K42_x9ZQW9ZBDe-_Jl2xKHwwhnDC1NI5sOq_AM
22 Ibid.
23 Christine Emba insists that app sex and casual sex must dehumanise something inherently human and emotional.
24 Susuana Amoah founder of the I Heart Consent campaign, Rachel Thompson, and Kate Margolis.
25 Quoted in 'Why there's no such thing as casual sex', Time, https://time.com/6160096/rethinking-sex-christine-emba-review/

## *Chapter 8 Choice: Free and Miserable vs . . . Unfree and Miserable*

1 Perinelli, M., '"Sex Freedom Girls Speak Out". Women in Sexual Revolution', in *Sexual Revolutions*, London: Palgrave Macmillan, 2014, pp. 219–235.
2 Ibid., p. 219.
3 Collins, M., *Modern Love: An Intimate History of Men and Women in Twentieth-Century Britain*, London: Atlantic, 2007, p. 177.
4 Ferris, P., *Sex and the British: A Twentieth-century History*, London: Michael Joseph, 1993, p. 290.
5 Ibid., 294.
6 Stoya, J., https://slate.com/human-interest/2021/08/onlyfans-sex-banned-allowed-decision-history.html

7 For the arguments see, e.g. 'A few words to electors on a most serious subject / [by] the Scottish National Association for Repeal of the Contagious Diseases Acts' [1880s], Wellcome Library.
8 MacKinnon, C. A., 'Pornography: on morality and politics', in *Toward a Feminist Theory of the State*. Cambridge, Massachusetts: Harvard University Press, 1980.
9 See, for example, Eaves, E., *Bare: The Naked Truth About Stripping*, New York: Seal Press, 2004, a memoir of her time as a stripper in Seattle.
10 Levy, A., *Female Chauvinist Pigs: Women and the Rise of Raunch Culture*, London: Free Press, 2005, p. 26.
11 https://psyche.co/ideas/the-reality-of-prostitution-is-not-complex-it-is-simple
12 https://www.yourtango.com/2021340941/what-creating-onlyfans-account-taught-me-about-feminism
13 Quote from Zelizer's staff profile page: https://sociology.princeton.edu/people/viviana-zelizer
14 https://www.moneyandmentalhealth.org/financial-difficulties-suicide/
15 Stoya, J., https://slate.com/human-interest/2021/08/onlyfans-sex-banned-allowed-decision-history.html
16 Ibid.
17 *The Irish Sun*, https://www.thesun.ie/news/8835502/ex-teacher-only-fans-parents-colleagues-accuse-kids-temptation/
18 Stoya, J., https://slate.com/human-interest/2021/08/onlyfans-sex-banned-allowed-decision-history.html
19 Ibid.

## *Chapter 9 The Tenacity of the Romantic Ideal*

1 https://www.newsocialcovenant.co.uk/mary-harrington-blog-mhhbz/
2 Perry, L., *The Case Against the Sexual Revolution*, London: Polity, 2022, p. 164.
3 Roseneil, S., Crowhurst, I., Hellesund, T., Santos, A. C. and Stoilova, M., *The Tenacity of the Couple-Norm: Intimate citizenship regimes in a changing Europe*, UCL Press, 2020, p. 4.
4 https://www.newsweek.com/gen-z-could-change-marriage-rates-1869146
5 ONS in UK; National Center for Health Statistics in US.
6 https://www.ons.gov.uk/peoplepopulationandcommunity/birthsdeathsandmarriages/marriagecohabitationandcivilpartnerships/bulletins/marriagesinenglandandwalesprovisional/2021and2022

## ENDNOTES

7 Jonathan Kerner in https://edition.cnn.com/2024/03/17/health/marriage-divorce-rates-wellness/index.html
8 Carter, J., & Duncan, S., 'Wedding paradoxes: individualised conformity and the "perfect day"', *The Sociological Review*, 65(1), 2017, pp. 3–20. https://doi.org/10.1111/1467-954X.12366; Boden, S., *Consumerism, Romance, and the Wedding Experience*, Basingstoke: Palgrave MacMillan, 2003.
9 Illouz, E., *Consuming the Romantic Utopia, Love and the Cultural Contradictions of Capitalism*, 1997.
10 Pearce, L. & Stacey, J., (eds), *Romance Revisited*, London: Lawrence & Wishart, 1995.
11 Lewis, J., *The End of Marriage? Individualism and Intimate Relations*, London: Edward Elgar, 2001, p. 10–14.
12 Chettiar, T., '"More than a Contract": The Emergence of a State-Supported Marriage Welfare Service and the Politics of Emotional Life in Post-1945 Britain', *Journal of British Studies*, No. 55, 2016, pp. 566–591.
13 Strathern, M., *After Nature: English Kinship in the Late Twentieth Century*, Cambridge: Cambridge University Press, 1992, p. 12; Lewis, J. *The End of Marriage? Individualism and Intimate Relations*, p. 13.
14 Strathern, M., *After Nature: English Kinship in the Late Twentieth Century*, p. 159.
15 Sandel, M., J., *Liberalism and the Limits of Justice*, New York: 1982, p. 179.
16 Lewis, J., *The End of Marriage? Individualism and Intimate Relations*, p. 14.
17 Ibid., p. 25.
18 Faludi, S., *Backlash: The Undeclared War Against Women*, London: Vintage, 1993, pp. 21–66.
19 Patton, C., 'On Me, Not in Me: Locating Affect in Nationalism After AIDS', in *Love and Eroticism*, Featherstone, M. (ed.), London: Sage Publishing, 1999, p. 369; Wiegman, R., *Object Lessons*, North Carolina: Duke, 2012, p. 340.
20 Lyons, A., *Paper for Social Continuation Group*, Tavistock Clinic, 6 June 1985, p. 1.
21 Ibid., p. 5.
22 Chettiar, T., '"More than a Contract": The Emergence of a State-Supported Marriage Welfare Service and the Politics of Emotional Life in Post-1945 Britain', p. 568.
23 Langhamer, C., 'Feelings, Women and Work in the Long 1950s', *Women's History Review*, 26:1, pp. 77–92, 78.
24 Langhamer, C., *The English in Love: The Intimate Story of An Emotional Revolution*, Oxford: Oxford University Press, 2013, p. 179.

25 Ibid., p.179.
26 Perry, L., *The Case Against the Sexual Revolution*, p. 162.

## Chapter 10 In Praise of Single Motherhood

1 The statistics relating to intimate partner violence against women are greater than against men, but are still considered to be significantly under-reported: https://www.womensaid.org.uk/information-support/what-is-domestic-abuse/domestic-abuse-is-a-gendered-crime/. For stats, see: https://www.womensaid.org.uk/information-support/what-is-domestic-abuse/how-common-is-domestic-abuse/. This uses ONS statistics from 2023, Office for National Statistics (ONS) (2023). *Domestic abuse in England and Wales overview: November 2023.*
2 https://rapecrisis.org.uk/get-informed/statistics-sexual-violence/
3 https://www.theguardian.com/lifeandstyle/2019/may/25/women-happier-without-children-or-a-spouse-happiness-expert
4 https://wrap.warwick.ac.uk/id/eprint/49986/1/WRAP_THESIS_Gallwey_2011.pdf
5 https://www.margaretthatcher.org/document/101830
6 See work on the National Council for the Unmarried Mother and her Child, later Gingerbread; Thane, P. & Evans, T., *Sinners? Scroungers? Saints? Unmarried Motherhood in Twentieth-Century England*, Oxford: Oxford University Press, 2012; 'Women's wages as a percentage of males, 1970-82' in Littler, C. R. and Salaman, G., *Class at Work: The Design, Allocation and Control of Jobs*, London: Batsford, 1984, p. 17.
7 Applewhite, A., *Cutting Loose: Why Women Who End Their Marriages Do So Well*, London: HarperCollins, 1998, p. xi–xii.
8 Ibid., xii.
9 Ibid., xiii.
10 Firestone, S., *Dialectic of Sex*, New York: William Morrow and Company, 1970, p113.
11 https://www.bbc.co.uk/programmes/m001w0yg
12 Zweiniger-Bargielowska, I., *Women in Twentieth Century History*, London: Routledge, 2001, p. 76.
13 https://www.bls.gov/opub/mlr/2002/05/art2full.pdf
14 https://ifs.org.uk/sites/default/files/output_url_files/BN234.pdf, p. 3.
15 https://www.nytimes.com/1984/12/09/magazine/women-vs-men-in-the-work-force.html

16 Lewis, J., *The End of Marriage? Individualism and Intimate Relations*, 2001, p. 25.
17 Perry, L., *The Case Against the Sexual Revolution*, p. 167; Warshaw, R., *I Never Called It Rape*, New York: Harper and Row, 1988; Fox-Genovese, E., *Feminism Without Illusions*, Carolina: University of North Carolina Press, 1991, in Roiphe, K., *The Morning After: Sex, Fear, and Feminism on Campus*, New York: Little Brown and Company, 1993, pp. 63–64.
18 https://www.ons.gov.uk/peoplepopulationandcommunity/birthsdeathsand-marriages/divorce/bulletins/divorcesinenglandandwales/2023
19 https://familyinequality.wordpress.com/2022/05/29/science-says-get-married-at-age-whatever-you-want-and-these-are-the-odds-of-divorce/
20 Trillingsgaard, T., & Sommer, D., 'Associations between older maternal age, use of sanctions, and children's socio-emotional development through 7, 11, and 15 years'. *European Journal of Developmental Psychology*, 15(2), 2016, 141–155. https://doi.org/10.1080/17405629.2016.1266248

## *Chapter 11 Motherhood Unshackled and the Fertility 'Crisis'*

1 https://penntoday.upenn.edu/news/world-fewer-children-addressing-despair-behind-declining-fertility
2 https://www.maryharrington.co.uk/p/sexual-thatcherism
3 https://www.cqc.org.uk/publications/maternity-services-2022-2024/estates
4 https://theconversation.com/fears-about-falling-birthrate-in-england-and-wales-are-misplaced-the-population-is-due-to-grow-for-years-to-come-218655
5 Ibid.
6 Froide, A., *Never Married: Singlewomen in Early Modern England*, Oxford: Oxford University Press, 2005, p. 3.
7 https://www.cdc.gov/nchs/data/vsrr/vsrr-007-508.pdf
8 https://www.thetimes.com/magazines/the-sunday-times-magazine/article/elizabeth-day-podcast-magpie-how-to-fail-interview-hspvzgjgd
9 Warrington, R., *Women Without Kids: The Revolutionary Rise of an Unsung Motherhood*, London: Orion, 2023, p. 77.
10 'One of the cruellest tricks spinsterhood can play is to leave you feeling like an outlier and a freak,' journalist Emma John has written, *Guardian*, 17 Jan 2021.
11 Chiu, M. et al. 'Mortality in single fathers compared with single mothers and partnered parents: a population-based cohort study', *The Lancet Public Health*, Volume 3, Issue 3, e115–e123.

12 https://www.theatlantic.com/magazine/archive/2025/09/marriage-institution-value-comeback/683564/
13 https://www.apa.org/monitor/2011/10/babies; Doss B.D., Rhoades G.K., Stanley S.M., Markman H.J., 'The effect of the transition to parenthood on relationship quality: an 8-year prospective study'. *Journal of Personality and Social Psychology*, 96(3), March 2009, 601–619, doi: 10.1037/a0013969. PMID: 19254107; PMCID: PMC2702669
14 https://sciencemediacentre.es/en/reactions-20-year-study-psychological-well-being-children-born-through-third-party
15 https://www.pewresearch.org/social-trends/2023/04/13/in-a-growing-share-of-u-s-marriages-husbands-and-wives-earn-about-the-same/
16 https://www.cbsnews.com/news/growing-trend-women-single-parents-by-choice/
17 https://www.newsweek.com/culture-war-conservatives-battle-sperm-donor-business-72369
18 https://www.theatlantic.com/family/archive/2024/08/single-quitting-dating-relationships/679460/
19 Butler, J. (ed.), *Woman's Work and Woman's Culture*, Cambridge:: Cambridge University Press, 1869, p. xxxv.